CUBA:
Socialism and Development

CUBA:
Socialism and Development

by René Dumont
translated by Helen R. Lane

GROVE PRESS, INC., NEW YORK

To the Algerians

Contents

CUBA:
Socialism and Development

Preface

When there is talk of "the violence" in Bogotá, society ladies quickly make the sign of the cross. But this Colombian peasant uprising, which in the beginning had elements of banditry, is purifying itself as it becomes more political. The number of assaults is multiplying in Venezuela, where revolutionaries are fighting both in Caracas and in the mountains. Ecuador, the Dominican Republic, Guatemala, and Honduras are joining the clan of dictators in Haiti and Paraguay.

In this seething Indo-America, wrongly called "Latin America," which is making greater and greater efforts to escape its "Yankee" masters, the example of the Cuban Revolution, especially in its "agrarian" form, has rapidly become a decisive influence. In Santiago, Chile, at the other end of the continent, there are people fighting for or against Castro. The future of this Revolution is dominated above all by the threat of the United States, which, in order not to lose its hegemony on the continent, seeks to put an end to it. This experiment in "the building of socialism" must be allowed to develop freely; it must be helped to reach the age of reason more quickly, with constructive criticism.

After political independence, the two parts of the American continent went through totally different processes of economic development. In New England, farmers (of Anglo-Saxon origin, Protestants, educated, organized, and highly developed) cultivated the soil with their hands, and therefore sought to lighten their burden, to modernize, to mechanize. From the beginning of the nineteenth century, following the example of their former mother country, they became industrialized, and sought to protect their young industry. This put them at odds with the planters south of the Potomac, who exported tobacco from Virginia and cotton from Georgia and who wanted to secure, at a cheap price, products manufactured in Europe. Tilling the soil with the aid of black slaves, their wealth was based on landed property; therefore they were opposed to the free distribution of lands on the prairies. The question of slavery was the ideological cause of the conflict.

The Spanish and Portuguese nobles arrived with their retainers, their feudal ideas.[1] Having kept to the plantation system up to the middle of the twentieth century, a system modified only slightly by the replacement of slavery by peonage (or, in Chile, by *inquilinaje,* paying rent on the land through work) or by paid labor, Indo-America is becoming industrialized more than a century after the north of the continent. And the unconcern of the large landowners, who do not even manage to feed a depopulated continent properly because they work only two per cent of its surface, each day widens the gap between the rich of the cities, budding capitalists, and peasants or peons who get poorer and poorer.

If the Cuban "model" is a decisive factor vis-à-vis this South American economic "impasse," its influence nonetheless goes beyond this continent. Ben Bella is speeding up the efforts at socialization in 1963, as Castro did in 1960; he proclaims himself a "Castroite minus the Marxism," since he remains a Moslem. Algeria thus causes its two neighbors to fear it, but is not averse to having Chou En Lai call it "the Cuba of Africa"; for all that, it is not necessary, however, for it to repeat all of Cuba's first fumbling efforts. *The young nations that are turning toward socialism must become better acquainted with the Cuban Revolution in its totality.* Not only with its political and cultural aspects, which are what is best about it and best-known,

---

[1] An ideology that was bourgeois on the one hand and aristocratic on the other: and the weight of ideas, of its superstructures, had a great influence on later development.

but also with its accomplishments and *the economic difficulties that it has come up against,* which are not as well-known, having been distorted by various sorts of propaganda. This latest attempt to implant socialism in a natural, historic, ethnic, and cultural milieu very different from its first Eurasian spheres of action and constantly threatened by a powerful neighbor is of the greatest interest. In May 1960, I came to study it and put myself at its service; Castro then asked me to return the following August. Not having been able, on the twenty-sixth of August, to make him give up his idea of "people's farms" that were too "bureaucratized" (Chapter 3) and that were, in my opinion, not appropriate to the situation, I did not have an opportunity to study Cuba again until I was called back there as an expert in September 1963.

At the time of this third visit, my only intention (outside of two mission reports to the president of the National Institute of Agrarian Reform) was to prepare the chapter on Cuba in a rather important work. My plan was to study *the many difficulties of socialist agriculture,* from the popular democracies and Yugoslavia to the U.S.S.R., China, and North Vietnam. It is not easy anywhere to make agriculture progress at a rapid pace: all the backward tropical countries are only too well aware of this. Socialist regimes, developing the industrial sector, have an even greater need than the others for a rapid increase in agricultural productivity. They have shown how difficult this is, especially since their social transformations have often come up against the peasant. Thus there were Chinese famines in 1960–1962, and massive purchases of grain by the Soviet Union in the autumn of 1963. It is necessary to seek out the principal causes of these developments so as to propose valid remedies.

What I saw in Cuba in 1963 went beyond what I had feared. After having powerfully shown up the principal defects of neo-colonial capitalism, Cuba is today giving us proof not only of a powerful social effort but of an attempt at development in a socialist regime that is accompanied by a series of difficulties and economic errors. *I had underestimated these difficulties in building socialism* when it must be carried out at the same time as the technical education of the population and the economic education of idealistic guerrillas[2] who have not always had the time to really understand the conditions of application of the Leninism–Marxism on which they are basing their efforts.

Marx predicted that socialism would succeed capitalism, in an *already industrialized* society. In a country that is not at all industrialized, or industrialized to only a very small degree, *an original path of development* must be sought from now on; this accounts for the errors that have been made.[3] We shall therefore try to see (after having outlined the economic history of Cuba from 1959 to 1964) the conditions *other than political* (educational, technical, organizational, economic, moral) which will enable a planned socialist economy in such conditions to *succeed* (and not just inaugurate a system). Constructive criticism is something of a bother; it is easier than revolutionary practice; it's the most useful role for old professors—who are always annoying—from old Europe. As I had already begun to do after my visits in 1960,[4] I am going to try, therefore, to tell my friends, Cubans and others, *all* my thoughts about this attractive socialist "experiment," and above all what I think will help it to flourish. This in the spirit of free inquiry, that of an uncommitted friend, not forgetting that "to criticize is to orient." The Cuban satirical paper also points out that in order to criticize, one must *already* be well oriented. The problem then is to know whether the old heretic that I am is well oriented!

In order to do this, this study, focused on the search for better economic structures and organizations, finds itself obliged to emphasize above all the weaknesses of the Cuban experiment. We have therefore presented a very incomplete, unbalanced picture, in which its undeniable positive aspects do not have the

---

[2] "The leaders of the Revolution were only a group of combatants who had lofty ideas, but who were not sufficiently prepared," Che Guevara admits in *Revolución*, October 1963.

[3] The relative underdevelopment also explains a great many of the Russo–Chinese difficulties.

[4] *Esprit*, April 1961.

share that they deserve. The reader who limits himself to this one book will be left feeling hungry. We therefore advise him to read first of all *La Fête Cubaine* of Ania Francos,[5] who will show him the joyous political atmosphere of this young revolution. In it he will find the other face of the very complex Cuban phenomenon, one which is not at all contradictory, but rather, complementary to our own brief outline.[6]

[5] Editions Julliard, 1962. See the bibliography also.

[6] Charles Bettelheim (who has come on a mission to Cuba every year since 1960), Michel Gutelman, a Belgian agronomist and sociologist, Marc Balin, a Haitian economist, and a great number of Cuban friends have helped us a great deal in this work, which has also been read over by M. Mazoyer and N. Giron. The studies of Jacques Chonchol, Juan Noyola, Mestre, Alonso Olive, and others have also been very useful. Obviously these persons do not necessarily share all the opinions expressed in this book. The first draft of this work was more severe with Cuba: out of "Eurocentrism" I had underestimated certain difficulties arising from underdevelopment; and I somewhat wrongly extended to Cuba the solid reservations that I still have toward totalitarian communist regimes.

1 A Fertile Milieu, An Economy Long "Dependent"

1. An Archipelago[1] quite richly endowed by the gods

I recently emphasized the general severity of the Soviet natural milieu, its often mediocre potentialities for food production, by contrast to its wealth in oil, minerals, and sources of energy. This important cause of Russia's lag where agriculture is concerned does not suffice, however, to explain why Soviet productivity on farms is only 12 to 14% that of the United States.[2] Cuba, which is far less richly endowed than the U.S.S.R. in industrial raw materials, on the other hand enjoys natural conditions that are much more favorable to its agricultural development. The richness of the land is extremely variable; but the proportion of alluvial soils and lateritic clays, the most fertile types of which are the "Matanzas," the "La Havane," and the "Hatuey," is very important. There are very few that are more productive—among these few the basalt "red lands" soils of Cambodia and the *terra rossa legítima* of the north of Paraná in Brazil.

In this latter region, I have explained[3] that frost often attacks coffee plantations that are climatically marginal; and fire has just ravaged them. But in Cuba it is exceptional for the ther-

---

[1] The Cubans do not like people to talk of the island of Cuba, especially since their possession of the second largest island (Los Pinos) was long disputed by the United States, and because there exist a multitude of tiny islands, the "Cayos."

[2] As against 45 to 50% in industrial productivity.

[3] *Terres vivantes,* Chapter 4.

1

mometer to drop below forty-six degrees Fahrenheit, except at altitude. We have here a "marginal tropical" climate, mitigated by the proximity of the sea, and with a fairly regular rainfall: one of the most advantageous in the world, for vegetation persists almost all year round. Drouths as severe as that of 1961 are rare. Certain very limited zones, especially along the southern coast of Oriente province, are semi-arid however. And three mountain massifs (the Sierra Maestra in Oriente and Escambray in Las Villas, celebrated for their dense underbrush; then one dorsal chain around Pinar del Río) accentuate the relief here and there. However, the *proportion of plains* is much higher here than in the other Antilles, especially in Jamaica and Martinique, where it is hardly more than twenty per cent and risks being monopolized by the cities by the end of the century.

The sandy savannas have an agricultural potentiality that is much more limited, especially where they are not fertilized. But if they are planted with Pangola,[4] irrigated, and heavily fertilized, they can still produce four to five times more grass than the Norman prairies, which have been highly overestimated. If the rains have washed the sand from the soil, the damage has been very limited since clay is present. The phenomenon of true laterization or of surface formations of ferric crusts, which are so frequent in comparable latitudes in Africa, and which lead to the total ruin of the soil there, are unknown here.

Let us not hasten to conclude, as Christopher Columbus did when he disembarked, that this is a sort of earthly paradise. Hurricane Flora, from the sixth to the tenth of October 1963, the most destructive storm in five centuries, has just cruelly reminded us of the terrible caprices of the Caribbean Sea. In the Matanzas clay, in the province of the same name, good sugar cane has been grown continuously for two centuries, though it was not fertilized until the last few years, whereas many African soils have to lie fallow after two or three years' cultivation.

---

[4] A graminaceous tropical plant of high productivity, *Digitaria decumbens.*

However, the production per acre of Cuban sugar cane has never again reached the level it attained in 1938. There is therefore a noticeable reduction in this natural fertility with time, and it would be a mistake to believe it to be inexhaustible. Cuban agriculture has good tools at its disposal, providing that they are not abused.

Its geographical location, finally, constitutes another advantage which, if present political conditions prevent the Cubans from profiting from it, is nonetheless not canceled out for eternity. "Cuba is the closest tropical country to the most highly developed and the most affluent industrial zone [in the world]," the late lamented Juan Noyola wrote, pointing out how close Cuba is to the United States. Though ninety miles of sea separate it from Florida, transportation is much less costly (it is 1,386 miles by sea from New York to Havana) than from Mexico City (almost double the distance overland). The frost line passes just south of Florida but north of Cuba, where citrus fruits are no longer a "risky business." In Florida and Louisiana, sugar cane is really a marginal crop.[5] And the general ease of communication, the ports everywhere close at hand, orient Cuba toward very important exchanges with the outside, *rather than toward autarchy,* when there is no blockade.

Its known mineral resources, while not negligible, are nonetheless limited. There is no coal and little peat, and very little petroleum has been discovered; in this latter domain, it is difficult to predict future possibilities. Its potential hydroelectric resources are probably less than a million kilowatts; Cuba must plan on importing almost all the energy it needs. The most important mineral deposits are those of nickel and of cobalt, then of chromium, manganese, copper, and iron. But these possibilities have not been sufficiently explored, and Soviet experts are investigating further: agreeable surprises may very well be forthcoming.

---

[5] R. Dumont, *Les leçons de l'agriculture américaine,* Flammarion, 1949, Chapter 6.

2. Long Spanish abandonment, followed by a plantation economy

This archipelago was long considered by the Spanish mother country to be largely a naval and commercial base. Its geographical position, at the entrance both to the Gulf of Mexico and the Caribbean, made it the strategic key of the communication network of the Spanish empire. This empire extended from California to Chile, from Florida to Argentina, leaving the vast expanses of Brazil to Portugal. The splendid roadstead of Havana was a rendezvous point for galleons carrying the rich treasures extracted from the gold and silver mines of Peru and Mexico which were to lead to the economic stagnation of the Iberian peninsula. Its men-o'-war did not always protect these convoys from English, Dutch, or French pirates.

Aside from its tobacco and its famous cigars, the island was content to grow only the foodstuffs necessary for a population that in those days was sparse. The most extensive cattle-raising, of sturdy *criollo* herds imported from Iberia, was carried out more or less in complete freedom, on a few immense ranches with no visible markings of their boundaries, each owner's property being laid out in a circle around the ranch buildings, the *batey* (sugar mill). In exchange for this land, the grantee had to supply the *municipio,* the neighboring town, with meat at a specially regulated price. It was practically impossible to fix the boundaries of these lands and get them on the land register. The *llanos* of the Venezuelan Orinoco, even in 1956, still provided a rather good picture of this sort of use of the land.

The circles could not intersect, and the peasants who came later were permitted to practice their subsistence economy in the interstices, the *realengos*. Others were granted permission to dig in the earth with pick-axes to cultivate corn and beans, inside the boundaries of the large ranches. They shifted fields as the Venezuelan *conucos* and the Brazilian *caboclos*[6] still do today; when they were through working a field the grass grew back

---

[6] R. Dumont: *Terres Vivantes,* Chap. 2 and 4.

more thickly than before. But these squatters, simply tolerated, did not pay rent and could be put out on the *camino real,* the main road, from one day to the next: it was broad enough so that their cow would not die of hunger along it, but the cow could not supply milk for the children all year long. But let us not get ahead of our story.

The cultivation of sugar cane did not develop on any real scale in Cuba until the end of the eighteenth century; it was therefore a good century behind the Antilles, and two centuries behind the Brazilian northeast. The sugar cane was grown on plantations, worked by black slaves imported from Africa,[7] who often had to be replaced, for they suffered from a high death rate. Sugar cultivation did not really prosper until after the revolt of the blacks in Haiti, which brought on the ruin of production for export because of the departure of the French colonists, certain of whom settled in Cuba, especially in Oriente. The great European demand for sugar and coffee caused a parallel development of these two crops; it was not until 1830 that sugar was clearly predominant. The Cuban colonists had not revolted from 1810 to 1820 as had the other Spanish colonies of America. They were fearful that if they did rebel it would set off a revolt by their black slaves, inspired by that in Haiti. These colonists would certainly have liked to free themselves, however, in order to further exploit the blacks. Having remained the principal colony of Spain, Cuba then "went white," especially in its western half because of the massive arrival of immigrants, of Galicians and *isleños* (Canary Islanders) in particular.

Cuba gave signs of being an advanced country; the year 1837 saw the construction of the first railroads; the ports underwent large-scale expansion; sugar factories were built each year. But the economic crises of 1847, 1857, and 1867 shook the Cuban economy, which was coming to be linked more and more closely

---

[7] The native Indians, the Siboneys, were decimated by European diseases, repression, and exploitation by the Spanish, and by forced labor on the *encomiendas* (estates granted by the Spanish king). Elsewhere the Spanish imported fewer African slaves than the Portuguese, for their "Andean" colonies were abundantly populated.

to that of the United States, which absorbed 40% of the island's exports, as against 12% going to Spain.[8]

For the United States had rapidly become an enormous economic power. The "widely distributed" land belonged in part to Spaniards, but already the Creoles, soon called Cubans, owned a majority of it. The undercultivated feudal latifundium gives way to the sugar plantation oriented toward the market much earlier in Cuba than in the rest of Latin America.

In these beginnings of capitalist development, Noyola points out,[9] the influence of American independence and liberal ideas in Spain made the task of the large landowners of Oriente easier when they launched the uprising of 1868 in Bayamo. This ten-year war had a ruinous effect on the economy, for the "rebels" burned the sugar cane and half of the sugar mills, which were still semimanual—those which did not obey the order to stop work that was given with the intention of ruining the colony. Thus the production of sugar, which reached a million tons from 1,500 sugar mills[10] in 1850, was raised at the end of the second war of independence (1894–1902) to no more than a million and a half tons. Not all the industrialists were able to replace their burned *ingenios* with modern sugar factories, for this required large amounts of capital, offers of which were to come from the United States. In spite of the abolition of slavery, this second half-century was thus marked by both demographic and economic stagnation.

In 1883, the great leader of independence, José Martí, warned of the danger of too extreme a sugar monoculture: "A people that puts its trust in a single product in order to subsist is committing suicide."[11]

---

[8] Jacques Arnault: "Cuba et le marxisme," a special number of *La nouvelle critique,* 1962.

[9] "Problemas de desarrollo económico de Cuba," mimeographed lectures, September–December 1959.

[10] From 1950 on, 161 sugar centrals have been able to produce seven million tons annually.

[11] In 1960, portraits of Martí and quotations from his works were everywhere in Cuba, from the edges of the highways to meeting halls. In 1963, there were more of Lenin, thus underlining the political evolution of the country.

Since 1891, according to Jacques Arnault, 95% of the sugar and 87% of other Cuban exports have gone to the United States.

On the political plane, "the colonial authorities, representing the mother country, ran the country until 1897; the administrative cadres were entirely Spanish. The Cortes refused to seat deputies elected by Cuba. Made to submit to the arbitrariness of a Captain General named by Spain, the Cubans never had any real practice in government, *and educated themselves instead in the art of revolution and improvisation.*"[12]

Thus on the eve of the "independence" of 1902, in addition to the *specialization in sugar,* which is a familiar fact, we must emphasize the *corruption* of Spanish bureaucrats, and the habit of using sugar profits to pay debts of the mother country, rather than to develop Cuba. Then too, there was the absence of *administrative cadres* and the tendency to improvise, which were to be two essential causes of the political instability of the so-called "Republican" period from 1902 to 1958.

3. The Republican period: the failure of neo-colonial development

Juan Noyola[13] showed that the rate of demographic[14] and economic growth of Cuba was very rapid: perhaps the highest in the world within a framework that was now "neo-colonial." In their disorderly retreat, the Spanish owners of large estates gave up their domains for a mouthful of bread, sometimes less than a hundred *pesos*[15] per *caballería* (33½ acres). During the three

---

[12] "Problemas de la Nueva Cuba," *Foreign Policy Association,* New York, 1935.

[13] He wrote: "I am one of the numerous millions of Latin Americans who consider the Cuban Revolution to be our common patrimony (as was the Mexican Revolution in its time) . . . All those who wish to see the economic development of their country and social justice take it as a personal matter."

[14] The population increased from 1.6 million in 1899 to 2.9 million in 1919, beginning the 3% increase in the birth rate that from this time on has been tragically the rule in Central America.

[15] Until 1958 the *peso* (100 *centavos*) generally remained at parity with the dollar.

years of Yankee occupation, the buyers were often American. The lands of the Cuban patriots, confiscated by the Spaniards from 1868 to 1877, had already been bought up cheaply, often by Yankees. Thus, in 1903, Americans held a tenth of the appropriated lands, but a proportion larger than that of land under cultivation and often the best sugar-cane lands and the best cattle ranches. "The American Tobacco Company at this time controlled 90% of the tobacco exports," Jacques Arnault reminds us.

On the departure of the occupation troops, political independence remained highly limited because of the Platt Amendment, under the terms of which the United States could intervene militarily in Cuba "when, *in their judgment,* lives, *property,* or individual freedoms were endangered." Note the interesting priority: property comes before freedom. And at the same time, the reciprocity agreement let North American products enter freely, thus long interfering with the possibilities of any large-scale indigenous industrialization.

On the other hand, capital flowed in in a heavy stream, and the central railroad was finished before 1914. Sugar centrals, at last as modern as those in Europe, and often of a greater capacity, were built. "Without sugar there is no country"; and the American market seemed unlimited. From 1.5 million tons in 1901, sugar production went up to 4 million tons in 1920, with a factory capacity of 5 million tons. Thanks to the influx of American capital and of immigrants from the Caribbean islands, helped along by a dense transportation network, Cuba was able to increase its sugar production much faster than her rivals—Java, Brazil, and Peru. Frozen during the war, when this product was in such short supply, the price of sugar went up in 1920 to twenty-two cents a pound, a price that recalled the good old days of the eighteenth century. Sugar beets, largely from Europe, furnished 40% of the world's sugar in 1914, but only 20% in 1919–1920.

Cuban millionaires went through a short period of splendid prosperity, referred to as "the dance of the millions." That year, Cuba broke the world's export record per capita (close to $400 per inhabitant), surpassing even the United Kingdom. Its per capita income equaled that of Australia, was half that of the United States, and surpassed that of all the other tropical and Latin American countries. Beginning in December 1920, sugar at four cents a pound ruined the cane producers (*colonos*), the sugar industry, Cuban and Spanish banks, and even the Cuban National Bank. Almost the only banks left were branches of American ones, which now provided eighty per cent of banking services. It was to take many years to re-establish a national issuing bank, a Cuban bank for foreign commerce.

This relatively high standard of living of 1920, and the amount of sugar exports per capita, have not been equaled since. The "ruling class," born in the sugar sector of the economy, now went into banking and commerce. There were thus hopes that a Cuban bourgeoisie would develop, and engage in heavy industrial development of a capitalist type. But the economy was too specialized, and an excessive proportion of foodstuffs and manufactured products was imported. Had it not been for the hard blow of the 1921 crisis, however, there would have been hopes of quickly remedying this situation.

This crisis was to put off all hope of a real autonomous development for a long time. The weakest sugar centrals, those that were recent or had no reserves, went bankrupt and were bought up, most of them by Americans. The national reaction came in the timid form of the imposition in 1927 of customs duties, which made it easier for Cuba to take a few steps toward agricultural diversification, and build up certain industries, for instance the milk-processing plants of the Nestlé trust, at Bayamo (Oriente) and Sancti Spiritus (Las Villas). The Carretera Central, the great highway running the length of the island, was finished in the same year, giving Cuba a denser communications network than any other Latin American country except El Salvador. Incomes in Cuba were also a little less badly distributed, and salaries remained higher. The differences in income were greater, however, in the country than in the city, where the trend was toward less inequality.

In the political order of things, the Cubans, obliged to learn everything about administration on their own, without the slightest preparation, soon experienced political corruption in every form: buying of votes; *votelleros* or beneficiaries of superfluous public jobs they did not work at; *colecturías,* enjoying a well-paying monopoly on lottery tickets. The crisis of 1921 favored the arrival in power in 1924 of a military dictator, General Machado; in order to remain in power (until 1933), he did not shrink from extending his repression to the murder of students and journalists.

The United States thus deprived Cuba of *the initiative for its own economic development.* It was carried out, not according to the needs of the country, but rather according to the needs of the American market. Its highly specialized production (sugar) was directed in the main toward a single market. American capital, which predominated—the dollar circulated in the country for a long time, and then the *peso* was pegged to it—controlled the financial circuits and channeled almost all credit toward activities having to do with sugar. The Cuban farmer wanting to produce something other than sugar cane generally was unable to secure any credit. Wanting in foresight, like many South Americans, he was always strapped for money, and this prevented him from doing anything on his own to meet the needs of the country.

The crisis of 1929–1934 was very severe in Cuba, which had 50% of its working population unemployed in 1933, when the United States believed it was "at the edge of the abyss" with 25%. One day in 1932 sugar went down to the unbelievable price of .57 cents per pound and Cuban cash receipts fell to one-sixth of what they had been. This was because the United States, as the crisis grew worse, increased the protective tariffs that favored their producers (sugar beets from Colorado, cane sugar from Louisiana) and their dependencies (Puerto Rico, Hawaii, which today has become a state, and the Philippines). At the same time, Cuba subscribed to the international agreements setting up quotas. Concentrating its economy on sugar, this country thus allowed itself to be strangled by progressively reducing its rights to sell what was almost its only crop.

The extremely high rate of unemployment is explained first of all by a very high rate of immigration that had been deliberately sought, proportionally superior to that of the United States and destined to put a brake on higher salaries. There next entered into play the combined factors of cyclical depression, an overly rapid natural increase in population, and the seasonal character of the heavy work in the cane fields, concentrated mostly in the months from January to June, during *la zafra* (harvest). Until the advent of Keynes and Roosevelt, classic economists taught that no one could be unemployed against his will: the worker had only to accept a decrease in salary—though no one specified how low this salary might go. A deliberate policy of full employment is only about thirty years old; in Cuba it was unknown before the Revolution.

In reaction to a similar crisis which had likewise deprived it of five-sixths of its exports because of a falling off of the supply of natural nitrate and economic difficulties, Chile began to build up a powerful native industry, partly with capital provided by the state. The Cuban revolutionaries of 1933, having overthrown Machado and abolished the Platt Amendment, did not prove to have that much economic imagination. They could scarcely conceive of possibilities of growth other than by increasing the amount of sugar they supplied to the United States. The United States did in fact allow them to fill sugar quotas at advantageous prices, but the decision was made unilaterally by the United States, and since it was not a bilateral commercial treaty that country was in no way prevented from going back on this decision in 1960.

Whereas Chile and Mexico protected their young industries by foreign exchange controls and by customs duties, Cuba lowered its duties in exchange for the "quota," and maintained freedom of foreign exchange. Thus it could not intensify its effort to diversify, to transform its economic structure, an effort which had reached no more than the planning stage as late as 1927. The absence of a bank, of a really national currency, and a sufficient domestic food supply stood in the way of an eventual devaluation: by raising the price of imported products, such a devaluation would have lowered real salaries in a period of massive unemployment.

Thus Cuba still had the same essential weaknesses as it entered the period of the Second World War. Noyola catalogues them as follows: chronic unemployment, overcapitalization, and excessive concentration on land which, as we shall see, was underutilized. The Second World War accelerated the process of industrialization already given impetus by the great depression, especially in Mexico and Brazil. Cuba did no more than partially correct certain economic deformations, by increasing its output of animal products and fruits and vegetables. But its industrial development, limited mostly to consumer goods, textiles, and food products, remained far behind that of Chile, even though the average income of that country was 30% lower.

The new prosperity of the sugar industry in 1940 was to be less sudden in its effects, but it was to persist, in attenuated form, after the Second World War and on up to the "boom" brought on by the Korean War. This boom allowed it in 1952 to harvest, for the last time until 1961, all the ripe sugar cane, a record crop of over 7 million tons. But in the other years from 1953 to 1960 a fifth or even a quarter of the cane had to be left standing in the fields for lack of markets, and thus only 5 to 5.8 million tons were processed. In 1925 and 1929, the figure of 5 million tons had twice been surpassed, and in the interval the Cuban population had practically doubled. On the eve of rebellion, this state of affairs had resulted in *much less cash and work per capita.* What little work there was was apportioned by quotas, and the right to work was bitterly defended; the unemployed were thus thrown into the most severe destitution. In 1933, thanks to the trade unions, the use of machines was forbidden in the manufacture of cigars; the American factories therefore emigrated to Tampa, Florida.

4. *A foreign-dominated, unbalanced economy*

A few sporadic efforts had been made, in particular around 1927 and 1953, to diversify agriculture and reinforce the industrialization of the country. The Cubans redoubled their efforts to improve their breeds of cattle of Spanish origin by crossing them with zebus that resisted tropical diseases, and then with Schwytz, Holstein, and even Charolais cattle of Swiss, Dutch, and French origin, which produced more milk and meat. A definite effort was made to develop the cultivation of rice through the use of techniques from Arkansas and Texas. Thus, on the eve of revolution, this crop filled half of Cuba's needs. Tomatoes for export to the United States market were also being grown in larger and larger numbers.

Though not negligible, *all this was quite insufficient.* With natural conditions very favorable to horticulture (the absence of cold weather, the possibility of irrigating, fertile soils), Cuba in 1958 imported from the United States *almost half its fruits and vegetables,* both fresh and canned. As late as 1960 I found almost no fruit juice in Cuba that wasn't from California. *Insufficient food production and the absence of industrial crops* other than sugar cane obliged Cuba to spend more than 200 million dollars in 1958 for the purchase of foodstuffs and raw materials that come from agriculture, not to mention all the manufactured products it had to buy. And there was less progress made in equipment than during the first twenty years of this century, though the increase in population was just as high. American doctors advised their patients not to eat animal fat, but the only thing Cuba had was Chicago lard—bought very cheaply.

The few going industries were often poorly tied in with domestic demand. American industrialists came to Cuba in the main to profit from cheap labor and escape the increasing rigors of the United States Internal Revenue Service. But outside of stone, cement, and glass, most of the raw materials were American, as were the engineers, who used Yankee machines and techniques. There were not enough trained Cuban cadres able to use these modern processes. Mines were "placed in reserve" by certain individuals, and others were "not exploited, as befits a good father," while the most productive deposits were worked ruthlessly.

After the Second World War, the tourist industry became an important source of cash for Cuba. Rich Americans came to Cuba looking for sun and wintertime beaches, for casinos and nightclubs, if not brothels. Arnault emphasizes the fact that the island had more prostitutes (11,500) for whom taxi drivers drummed up trade every night, and more croupiers (27,000), than miners (10,000).

This activity was concentrated largely in Havana, the microcephalic capital of a small republic, with its deluxe and lucrative trade in pleasures and vices. Thus in the capital there was a growing bourgeoisie, more numerous than in other Latin American countries, made up of tradesmen, service personnel, those who made profits on leisure-time activities, men in the liberal professions,[16] people with independent means, and privileged functionaries of the regime. Those who were rich contracted habits proper to the life of luxury, in their air-conditioned villas, with their sumptuous automobiles and their trips abroad.

These people were the ones who took out one-sixth of the cash revenue brought in by 200,000 American tourists. To speak of an average per capita income of $400 per year, which is thus more than Japan's, is to average out the rural unemployed, the *guajiros,* and the millionaires. If there was less of a gap between them than in Mexico, it was nonetheless much larger than that in Europe. The privileged classes of the city were a violent contrast with the miserable peasants, those squatters occasionally chased out of large land holdings by the famous rural police force, and the cane-cutters, who were dismissed the moment their extremely hard work was over, who were employed an average of 135 to 180 days per year, and who were on occasion the objects of "raids" in the mountain villages and thus torn away from their poor subsistence farming in good years.

But the United States often paid more than the world market

---

[16] Whose lot was sometimes a hard one, as Castro emphasizes in his "History Will Absolve Me."

sponsibilities, the average cultural level of Cuba was really surpassed only by Argentina and Uruguay, and this island "even exported doctors to the United States,[23] and accountants to South America." In 1959, Noyola found a concatenation of *conditions favorable to development:* by modifying the nature of imports and accelerating the formation of reserve capital, he estimated that it would be possible to invest 20% of the gross income, and to assure a rate of increase of raw production of 10% per year for five years, then 8% in the following five years, and thus to multiply Cuban production two or three times over in ten years. This was excessively optimistic, a shortcoming that was all too common in 1960. Thus the conditions that this Revolution was faced with in the beginning *might have appeared to be less bad* than in most of South America, especially in the Andes. But the fact that it was an appendage of the Yankee economy made the problem more difficult. However, after reaching 52 tons per hectare in 1938, a good year, the 1950–1958 average per hectare was not quite 40 tons of cane and 5 tons of sugar. A bare quintal of fertilizer per hectare was used, against often a ton in Martinique, and sometimes two tons in Puerto Rico. And the canes were replanted only at intervals of time that were too long, often ten years, but sometimes twenty-five years or more, even though it is not a good practice to let them grow longer than six or seven years. With annual replanting, cultivation by the Indonesian peasant, the technical proficiency of the Dutch agronomists, and the widespread irrigation of fertile soil, Java harvested an average of 17 tons of sugar on each of its 500,000 hectares of cane in 1934. In 1960–1963, with independence, this country's production went down to an average of around 11 tons. The cultivation of sugar cane had begun around Havana, which has recently incorporated a sugar mill within its limits. And the development of the east of the country, Camaguey and Oriente, did not really get under way until the twentieth century. To cut its cane, Camaguey must

---

[23] Who were looking for higher salaries; meanwhile Cuba lacked doctors.

still call on a Las Villas that is "overpopulated" because of insufficient development, and on Pinar and Havana.

The great sugar estates thus occupied hundreds of thousands of hectares of fertile soil without cultivating them. With the manual harvesting techniques still in use, sugar cane demanded, certainly, almost all the rural labor available in the *first half* of the year. The diversification of 1960–1964, by requiring other agricultural work in this period of the year, was to force mechanization. But the majority of agricultural workers were unemployed during the better part of the second half of the year. A short-cycle crop, such as corn or beans, was nonetheless still possible, and also intensive grazing. For if the "Cuban" rate of consumption of meat and milk was appreciable,[24] the distribution of it was not satisfactory, for these products rarely had a place on the family table of the cane-cutter or the little coffee-producer of the Sierra Maestra; once again, averages are very misleading. Imported fruits and vegetables went to the cities, and country people rarely ate anything but *"viandas,"* that is to say tubercules and cooking bananas, as in Africa. The luxury and the wastefulness of the capital came close to equaling the shortages in the country. And while the city had eleven per cent illiteracy, the country had more than forty per cent.

"The farmer looks for the greatest net product, but the nation is interested in the highest gross product," Arthur Young explained as early as 1788. With its government leaders and its landowners who cared little about the interests of the nation, *Cuba had in large measure lost the lead it had in the beginning of the century,* and its development had slowed down. Economic crises favored a more and more intolerable dictatorship in Cuba, where torture went hand in hand with corruption and even downright gangsterism, but the United States kept it going.

---

[24] About 40 kgs. of meat and only 7 kgs. of fish, in one island; 75 to 80 liters of milk, plus 35 liters of milk products, half of which were imported (J. Coléou).

6. A "rebellion" of students and peasants

Note the official term "rebel army" that the two or three thousand *barbudos* used, since their number never went beyond these figures. After the failure of the assault on the Moncada barracks at Santiago, Cuba, on July 26, 1953, by Castro and his 150 companions, the magnificent speech of Fidel, "History Will Absolve Me," shows us a revolt by *idealistic* nationalists, rebelling against an oppressive and corrupt regime: "We were born in a *free* country . . . today men who put in practice the ideas they learned in the cradle are murdered and imprisoned."

The democratic program then put into effect, a mixture of the principles of 1789 and utopian socialism, was not at all that of a socialist revolution. It planned to *give sovereignty back* to the people, *re-establish* the (relatively advanced) Constitution of 1940. In the domain of agriculture, this constitution did away with the latifundia, and was to hand over ownership of the land to all the farmers, tenant farmers, and squatters with less than sixty-seven hectares, or five *caballerías*. It was more a reform than a revolution, since it proposed to give the owners, as an indemnity, a sum equal to ten years' rent. The sugar-cane producing farmers received fifty-five per cent of the price of the sugar obtained, and the workers thirty per cent of the profits of large enterprises. Goods acquired illegally were to be confiscated . . . Basic economic notions did not worry Castro particularly; not a word was said about investments at this time. This idealistic reformism aimed at a rather vaguely defined social justice, and had as its goal the procuring of "work and a decent life" for all. But it in no way foresaw the overturning of social structures that was to take place after 1959. The creation of cooperatives was intended only for "the use in common of costly machines and refrigeration equipment." There was no mention of production cooperatives, and the only nationalizations then planned were those of electric companies and the telephone company.

In February and May, 1958, Castro was still insisting that he had no intention of nationalizing or socializing either industries or foreign investments. Law number 3 of the Agrarian Reform of October 10, 1958, promulgated in the Sierra, insists on the necessity of *giving the land to the person who cultivates it,* but does not speak of production cooperatives. All this is of a piece with the social standing of Castro's first supporters, a group composed of a small minority of students, intellectuals, middle-class and lower-middle-class bourgeois city dwellers (Cuba is fifty-seven per cent urban). "None of us had a past as workers or peasants," Fidel was to declare.[25]

The majority of the peasants of the Sierra were long to regard them with a certain mistrust, because of all that they had suffered. And Castro was to go so far as to say that his rebels had been "cruelly abandoned by our fellow citizens who systematically (if not criminally) refused to aid them, even though they had the means to do so."[26] But he had read Mao, and his *compañeros* were soon to gain the confidence of the peasants and agricultural workers (who were even more deprived of their birthright), first of all by respecting them—and not stealing from them and harassing them as had the soldiers of the regular army. Then, they said, "we will build a country hospital, a school—the first the Sierra will ever have had" (J. Arnault). Thus "more than three-quarters of the rebel army formed in the Sierra Maestra was made up of peasants."[27] And on the twenty-sixth of October, Fidel was to declare: "The peasant detachments are the most efficient units in the army. *The peasants are the best soldiers of the revolutionary army.*"

Their headquarters staff made up of students from the wealthy cities, from the middle class and also from the lower

---

[25] *Obra revolucionaria,* September 16, 1960. By "us" he was referring to those who had attacked the Moncada barracks, those who had disembarked from the *Granma,* and those in the government.

[26] According to Th. Draper, *La Révolution de Castro,* Calmann-Lévy, 1963.

[27] Charles Bettelheim, "La planification cubaine," *Recherches internationales,* August 7, 1962. "Peasants" here includes agricultural workers, and sometimes workers in the sugar factories.

middle class (as César Rodríquez explained to me when I arrived in May 1960) was greatly impressed by the extent of peasant poverty, which was still more marked in the Sierra and which it had not suspected of being this severe. *This contributed to radicalizing them, to pushing them toward the left.* On January 23, 1959, a little after the victory of the rebels, won on New Year's Day, 1959, Che Guevara declared: "It was the peasants who forced agricultural reform and the confiscation of cattle on the Revolution . . ." The leaders who had come down from the Sierra, where they had also read Marx, no longer reasoned as they had on December 2, 1956, when they had clambered so clumsily out of the "old tub" the *Granma,* and into the mangrove swamps in the middle of a storm.

The urban working class, which was too Americanized, and its "avant-garde," the popular Communist-Socialist Party, stayed rather aloof from all this. They advised Fidel against the landing. Urban resistance, which suffered so under the Batista reign of terror, was organized in the main by the intelligentsia and the liberal—I was about to say bourgeois—professions. Excessive torture made people turn against the dictator, especially when it was learned that he was "giving up" and preparing to flee. Batista's 50,000 mercenaries melted away before partisans who had many fewer arms but were led on by an idea that they were ready to die for, as they had so often proved.

7. *April 1959: The United States interferes with the "decolonization" of Indo-America*

Fidel, who did not assume a power that he was not seeking, landed in Caracas with a few *compañeros* armed with loaded machine guns, to pay his respects to his fair-weather friend Romulo Betancourt. On the fifteenth of April, 1959, he declared in New York: "We haven't come looking for money, but rather for understanding of our Revolution." It was perfectly evident that he was not seeking a confrontation with his powerful Northern neighbor whom he found hard to put up with in every way, shape, and form. And if he for his part failed to ask for aid after the nasty insinuations of the American press, the United States for its part offered him none, though as Claude Julien[28] pointed out, it had proffered help to so many others, Batista included.

In Central Park on April twenty-fourth, he said he belonged to "a sincere democracy that does not forget the rights of man— [that wants] no bread without freedom, no freedom without bread, no dictatorship of one man, one class, one caste, no oligarchy. Humanism is freedom with bread [and] without terror."[29] Because of this statement, the New York newspapers accused Castro of insinuating that other visitors from Indo-America had come begging. The reaction of the press, which had protested the execution of Batista's killers much more than it had protested Batista's atrocities, was generally hostile from January on. Though the reaction of official circles is not clear, it apparently was not very favorable. Thus when Castro came back from the United States *he was very bitter, and more hostile to the Yankees than when he left.*

During these ten days in April of 1959, the United States passed up an unexpected historical opportunity to revise its policy toward the south of the continent. Recognizing the Cuban Revolution was in a sense tantamount to accepting a radical form of decolonization, analogous in certain respects to that being carried out by France in Africa during this same period. This meant chalking up to profit and loss a certain number of investments in Cuba, many of them too highly amortized. The French did not ask Mali to reimburse them for the money—a considerable amount—expended on the hydraulic, agricultural, and industrial improvements made by the Niger Authority. To ask for reimbursement at 1958 prices of latifundia, part of which had been bought for a few dollars per hectare in the period from 1900 to 1910 seems, at the very least, to be a curious form of "aid to underdeveloped countries." *And the opportunity to establish a humanist socialist*

---

[28] *Terre entière,* September–October, 1963.
[29] For the period 1958–1960, read this same Claude Julien's *La révolution cubaine,* Julliard, 1961.

regime, in large measure independent of the U.S.S.R., fell through.

"Imperialism is such that by its very nature it cannot accept such a sacrifice," my Cuban friend René Alvarez Ríos said, more or less, at the end of a lecture in 1960 to students of Economics and Humanism. I don't believe that imperialist regimes have an intrinsic and immutable nature, and some of them have shown that they know how to adapt to a situation better than others. In 1946–1947 England was more intelligent in India than France in Indo-China. In 1958–1960 even De Gaulle had been more clever—as it was also easier for him to be—in tropical Africa than in Algeria, and so on.

This amounted, granted, to a very serious decision, an "agonizing reappraisal" for the United States. For the other countries of Indo-America, if not of the rest of the world, might have sought similar advantages, such as "most favored nation" status. Negotiation concerning how much was to be sacrificed was still possible, in Cuba as elsewhere. But in order to enjoy good chances for success, a real change of mind would have been required, the acceptance of an economy turning toward socialism as a peaceful neighbor—a prospect which was considered to be "diabolical."[30] A day will come when people in the United States will regret (as people in France already regret what happened in Algeria, where our young people died for nothing) that nation's intransigence in April 1959, and it will again be too late.

More up in arms than ever against these uncompromising Yankee imperialists, Fidel was already less reluctant to entertain the idea of taking more revolutionary measures and drawing

---

[30] On the plane from Miami to Havana in May 1960, a Cuban agronomist who had a degree from the Maison Carrée in Algeria explained to us that the only supporters of the Revolution were "hoodlums and Negroes." When my seatmate on the flight to Paris at the end of May, an American officer, learned that I had had dinner with Fidel the evening before, he quickly moved away from me. This is the fundamental obstacle, comparable to that which prevents desegregation of the South of the United States.

closer to those like himself who were arrayed against the United States. Certainly he admitted, on December 2, 1961, that he had been more of a Marxist-Leninist than he had publicly confessed to being. I continue nonetheless to believe in a progressive and normal evolution of the Cuban leaders by way of the press of events and the experience they have acquired. But history never repeats itself. At the end of 1958 the semi-colonial economy of Cuba had become a veritable caricature of capitalism: organized theft, backed up by repression and torture. The treasury had been emptied by ministers who had fled the country, the public debt was over $1,200,000,000, the budgetary deficit $800,-000,000. With the same income, the municipality of Havana was able to build thirty-eight school complexes in 1959 (there were none built in 1958); the sum was equivalent to money paid out in bribery in 1958 . . .

At the beginning of the Cuban Revolution, the natural and economic conditions none the less appeared to be quite favorable, even in the eyes of foreign experts who examined them in 1960. To different degrees, we underestimated two essential difficulties at this time. The first was that it was not a question of an autonomous economy but of an American appendage, which, once it was suddenly separated from the mother-economy, was to have much more difficulty organizing itself alone than had been foreseen: imagine Florida or Mississippi suddenly cut off from the rest of the United States.

The second difficulty was that the whole of the population, including the leaders, was not as aware of economic problems as they should have been in order to accelerate Cuba's development. The European situation is the result of several centuries of precise calculations at the state, local, and management level. There was, therefore, a contradiction between the needs for development, which require a strict accounting at all levels, and the underdeveloped reality, which had no knowledge of such a thing. And this was a profound social phenomenon, which was to be very difficult to get around, despite the good will of the Cuban leaders. Thus armed, we can better understand the difficulties that confronted them.

2

1959–1960:
Agrarian Reform Amid Revolutionary
and Romantic Anarchy

1. The "takeover" of the economy: the reformist law, a revolutionary accomplishment

Fidel Castro did not take the government into his own hands on his arrival in Havana on January 8, 1959. But the "bourgeois" cabinet was too timid, doing nothing that the rebels had hoped it would do, and had fought for, and everyone called on Castro to countermand its decisions. In order to avoid this duality and prompt really revolutionary actions, he was led to take over completely, assuming the duties and responsibilities of prime minister, a post that he has held ever since. He had already attacked the United States and its imperialist monopolies. When José Figueras of Costa Rica stated that it was in Latin America's interest to line up on the side of the United States, and not of Russia, Castro did not let the statement go without a brusque reply:

"Rather than an ideology, Fidelismo, a movement that is at once a peasant movement and an intellectual movement, makes its appearance as a revolutionary and romantic aspiration to honesty and justice."[1]

But theoretician Che Guevara already was looking farther ahead, and on July 27 he announced a program that was plainly revolutionary. "If Agrarian Reform were to have to pay in-

---

[1] *Fidel Castro parle,* commentary by J. Grignon Dumoulin, Maspéro, 1961, an interesting book if the reader wishes to follow the history of the revolution down to July 1961. The complete text of the law of Agrarian Reform can also be found in it.

demnities to owners, it would take effort slowly and at great cost . . . peasants must engage in collective action and democratically *demand* that this principle be waived."

The second law of Agrarian Reform,[2] announced like the first in the Sierra so as to stand as a symbol, on May 18, 1959, was, however, much more mindful of the Italian laws of 1949–1950 inspired by Christian Democratic principles, than of those of the popular democracies of Eastern Europe passed around 1945. The only property expropriated were estates of more than 402 hectares (30 *caballerías*), whereas from Poland to Bulgaria the maximum limit varied from 20 to 50 hectares.[3] These properties in principle were to be paid for in interest-bearing state bonds. The best cattle-raisers and those efficient growers of rice and sugar cane whose yields were 50% over the average for the region, could even keep 1,342 hectares! Long afterward, President Dorticos was to stress the reformist aspects of this law: the rate of interest provided for, 4.5%, was higher than that granted by the Japanese law that had been passed under Mac-Arthur's tutelage. And the twenty-year term of the bonds was less than that in Formosa (twenty-four years!).

All rented lands were expropriated, however, no matter how large or how small, and if the tenant farmer cultivated less than twenty-seven hectares, he was given full and free title to this land for nothing. Twenty-seven hectares of mediocre pasture land or thick underbrush on the poorest sandy savannahs lying over serpentine rocks was not really very much. On the other hand, at San Luís, near Pinar del Río, I examined a tobacco farm of 10 hectares that was rented for $1500 per year and was worth more than $40,000. It employed 20 workers who cultivated the tobacco for four months a year, and 100 workers during the one week's harvest, and this land had been given free to the man who was getting the profits from it. It was not a case here of giving the land "to the man cultivating it." In this case

---

[2] The first law, a provisory and tactical step, had been made public in the Sierra on October 10, 1958.

[3] If 400 hectares had been left to the owners, there would in some cases have been almost nothing left to take; the conditions were different.

the elderly proprietor needed to have an income to live on, and his capitalist tenant was much richer than he was. Thus in Pinar del Río there were a number of small landowners who did not do the actual farming: "They give promise of opposing seizure by every possible means . . . Certain zone leaders are decreeing that large estates with high yields must be broken up, instead of beginning, as the law provides, by distributing non-cultivated lands."[4] *Instead of doing away with ground rents, it would have been better to confiscate them for the benefit of the nation,*[5] in order to increase its investments.

Large-scale farms being exploited with no intermediaries were handed over undivided to cooperatives. The Minister of Agriculture, Sori Marín, resigned because he wanted the law to be applied with less severity.[6] The law provided for "the adoption of the most appropriate measures to eliminate difficulties and facilitate general progress"—which was vague, and therefore allowed of loose interpretation. The execution of this moderate law was turned over to an organization especially set up for the purpose, the National Institute of Agrarian Reform, or INRA, for the old administrative bureaus were mistrusted. This was done "in coordination with the rebel army," which put another color entirely on the matter, especially since Fidel took over the office of president of the Institute.

Arriving in Santa Clara in May 1960, Major Luís Borgés, a former student of dentistry, was the provincial head of the INRA, in charge of administering the requisitioned estates. He boasted to us that all he need do was "sign a little paper" every time he wanted to acquire this or that installation, studio, factory, store . . . He was obviously carrying out these expropriations with no preconceived plan, more or less as the whim seized him, without examining whether such a move was really useful, and with no thought as to whether the INRA was

---

[4] *Fidel Castro parle,* op. cit.
[5] As the *Communist Manifesto* of 1848 proposed.
[6] Arrested subsequently, he was later shot after the April 1961 invasion, for the Cubans in exile announced that he would have a post in the "free" Cuban government.

capable of administering them well. The takeover of the terrain and of economic power had to be rapid; it could, however, have been more orderly. It was held to be yet another battle, with no thought of how efficient it would be economically—a notion that did not often occur to Fidelistas. For outside their lives as students, Fidel's young men had little experience of anything but guerrilla warfare. The absence of any sort of professional experience in the case of the youngest of them, and of training in economics, in the case of the majority of them, was soon to be felt as a sore lack; almost before they knew it, they were swept into political power, and therefore into economic power. They had experienced an exceptional solidarity in the underground; they believed too readily that it could be brought over into daily life just as it was.

No one spoke of paying even the smallest indemnity—fortunately, for that would have enormously reduced the state's possibility of investment for many long years. A number of landowners could not secure a receipt for their holdings, a piece of paper that they still hoped would entitle them to claim indemnity, but only after a change of policy, and therefore of government. Though in the summer of 1959 some of these landowners who had financed the revolution handed over surplus lands with great good grace, there were lowering clouds long before the end of the year.

The rebels' takeover of the Cuban economy, Marc Balin reminds us, was never clearly formulated, but rather seemed to have been inspired in the beginning by three concerns. It was necessary to attack the great fortunes, which were fruits of political corruption and speculation in sugar. Once the "bourgeois Fidelistas" who were opposed to it had been excluded from the government in November 1959, a law confiscating the ill-acquired possessions of the profiteers of the preceding regime was put through in December. A combined exposition and sale of this property in the immense hall of the Capitol in Havana was quite picturesque. Since the goods on view had been improperly appraised, Yankee antique dealers turned a handsome profit.

The two succeeding steps were to attack the control of the economy by American interests before poceeding to the general socialization of the principal means of production. The pace of this socialization was in no sense established before the fact in the minds of the revolutionary leaders, who did not necessarily all have the same ideas on the subject. It was to be partly determined by the march of events. The communists in the popular Socialist Party often had a better notion of the needs of production. When I reminded the INRA, in a talk I had with its leaders in May 1960, of the most elementary necessities of organization, account-keeping, discipline, and work, and stressed certain paths that would lead to higher farm yields, their economic representative, Carlos Rafael Rodríguez, insisted that I lay these ideas before Fidel himself.

"These Fidelistas," he more or less told me in so many words, "are excellent when it comes to stirring up people politically or creating militias, but they are less well prepared to organize the economy; this might harm the Revolution, and we want to prevent this." It is understandable why Fidel tried to give communists more places on the boards of labor unions. He thought that they would be better at making workers understand the necessity of production, of discipline. Our "Major" had great political and economic decisions in his hands, and this was not without its risks. For Fidel, whose sincerity and devotion are as obvious as his gifts as a teacher, wanted to do too much himself, busied himself with petty details, and wasn't as good as he should have been about delegating authority and sharing tasks with others. He was excessively mistrustful of technicians who had not been fighting guerrillas. Nuñez Jiménez, his delegate in the INRA, put journalists such as Pino Santos, who soon had to be removed from the job, at the head of the technical directorates of the state. This was one of the things that was to lead many technicians and agronomists to leave; they were also attracted by American offers, for the INRA underpaid them. By 1963, Fidel had made progress, but he is still solving problems whose technical bases he is not familiar with (Chapter 4, 2).

2. *Intelligent innovation: the large estates are not broken up*

Existing small farms are just managing to hold their own, though their tenants no longer pay rent and thus have a chance either to invest more or live well while working less. Contrary to preceding agrarian reforms, Cuba has not set up new farms, nor has it extended its "peasantry." There are good reasons for this: in Eastern Europe the parceling up of land in 1945–1946 noticeably diminished the marketable production of the best-cultivated large estates. In the case of that of Prince Esterhazy in Hungary, the yield has supposedly fallen to half of what it was, and certain people maintain that it has fallen to one-third of what it was.[7] Subsequently these neo-peasants definitely resisted the regrouping of their minifundia, after the "turning point" of 1949, into production cooperatives of the kolkhoz type. From this there resulted a prolonged stagnation of agricultural production; in 1963 Czechoslovakia was just barely regaining the previous high point of production that it reached in 1938, and it amounted to much less per capita.

"Previous experiences in Bolivia and Mexico had amply proved that the rapid development of a small-farm agriculture posed problems that were extremely difficult and thus far insoluble insofar as mechanization (and often credit) are concerned," Michel Gutelman writes.[8] We have seen that in Mexico the small-scale farmers who got land through the Reform have progressed much less rapidly than the former proprietors, within the framework of an agrarian reform that in general was "sabotaged."[9]

In a study carried out for the International Food and Agricultural Organization of the United Nations in the summer of

---

[7] On the other hand, on-the-farm consumption increased. And on neglected pasture land, such as the *puzta* of Horto-bagy, "peasant" labor cultivating wheat and corn easily increased production.

[8] *Etudes rurales,* January–March, 1963; an interesting work, to which we shall frequently refer.

[9] R. Dumont, *Terres vivantes,* Chapter 6.

1962, I showed that the Jamaican "reform," which had begun as early as 1938, had barely managed to increase the number of inefficient minifundia, impossible to modernize, by 30,000 units, at very great expense to the State. Though some people ate better, this did not really resolve a very acute agrarian problem. Certain Cuban experiences also made it advisable not to proceed to divide up the land and the cattle. When the stock of a latifundium seized from a supporter of Batista on the plains of Oriente province was divided up among the poorest peasants of the Sierra at the end of 1958, it soon became evident that the majority of the draft oxen and the milch cows had been slaughtered for food, or if not, had been very badly cared for.

Moreover, hired agricultural workers, who made up the great majority of the possible beneficiaries, had neither the capital, nor the livestock, nor the knowledge necessary to become the leaders of an agricultural unit with very many chances of succeeding. The Cuban leaders also said that these "non-peasant proletarians" did not want land; according to my research this was true, however, of only a part of them. But the majority, accustomed to obeying someone else, would have managed to set up little more than subsistence units. Certain of them would even have had a tendency to prolong the enforced periods of idleness they had known previously. What is more, the revolutionary leaders' desire for equity (that was often pushed to the point of egalitarianism) could not have been satisfied by just any sort of division, especially when it was a question of lands that varied as much in their fertility as in their mode of exploitation.

How to economically cut up a pastoral latifundium based on a technique of extensive cattle-raising, which cannot be changed with one wave of a wand in the course of a single year? The disciple of the sugar plantation, moreover, had to be maintained if there was to be a steady supply of raw cane to the factories. Beginning in 1959–1960 a distinction was maintained between farm lands and cattle lands. Cooperatives were established only on farm lands, where work was really the principal source of the wealth produced.

But from the beginning this formula was rejected for the cattle latifundia, *where this sort of work was almost totally absent from the process of production,* and in any case negligible. Dividing up the product of 6,000 hectares of an estate in eastern Camaguey among its ten workers (eleven with the foreman) would have merely been tantamount to transferring privileges. This became all the more true in the absence of ground rents that could benefit the State, and of interest that could be spent as development capital. The net product, in fact, came first and foremost *from the land and the cattle-capital;* attributing it to work alone, which was by far the least important factor in production, would have thus been particularly absurd in this situation. However, the overexclusive primacy accorded by certain Marxists to work in the process of creating wealth interfered with or delayed the adoption of economically practical measures, such as ground rent and interest. It was therefore decided from the beginning that certain kinds of State farms would be set up for the exploitation of these cattle estates. This was a formula that was subsequently to be overexpanded, but let us not get ahead of our story.

3. A series of nationalizations, brought on by the anti-Yankee reaction

From the summer of 1960 on, events occurred one on the heels of the other. The Texaco, Shell, and Esso refineries, which refused to treat crude Soviet petroleum that had been acquired in exchange for sugar and was less expensive than that from the Gulf of Mexico, were seized on the 29th and 30th of June. In retaliation, President Eisenhower on July 6 canceled the last shipments under the sugar quota at a preferential price, amounting to 700,000 tons of sugar. On July 7, a decree confiscated $800 million in American property out of the $1,100,000,000 invested in Cuba: sugar factories, the principal companies (mines, electricity, petroleum . . .) and property "spared" by the law of May 1959.

These measures were essentially a retaliation against the financial maneuvers and the economic power of the imperialist enemy, giving back as good as one had gotten, amid the joy of the populace and the bitterness of the middle class. Symbolic coffins "burying" the monopolies were thrown into the sea in happy celebration in the capital. But this reaction *was to prompt a speed-up of the global process of socialization,* which doubtless would not have taken place in a less tense international atmosphere. In reply to the furnishing of American arms to the counterrevolutionary underground groups in Escambray, decrees on the 13th and 24th of October, 1960, nationalized the banks (except two Canadian ones, which were soon bought back) and all the large- and middle-sized industrial and commerial enterprises, department stores, luxury hotels, and movie theaters, as well as factories of all sorts, including those manufacturing food and textiles.

The Soviet Union had seen its industrial production go down to eighteen per cent of the 1913 level in 1918–1921, as a consequence of the civil war, but also because of nationalizations that became the general rule too hastily, and because of the departure of enormous numbers of technicians. Learning from this experience, China for the most part followed the formula for mixed-economy societies[10] from 1949 to 1956. If several thousand "national capitalists" were thus allowed to enjoy a higher standard of living for a few years more, the fact that production was maintained at the same level and then increased thanks to this measure was much more important than this temporary overconsumption. Cuba could have taken a lesson[11] from China in their handling of non-Yankee property, whether Cuban or European. To have slowed down the nationalization of installations that no one was yet able to administer efficiently

---

[10] In 1952 the private sector still controlled more than a third of the modern industries, more than two-thirds of the commercial establishments, and all of the agricultural production in China, according to Hugues and Luard in *Le développement économique de la Chine communiste,* Les Editions Ouvrières, 1962.

[11] A part of the Cuban middle class with ties to the United States dismissed its workers, did not renew its inventory, and slowed production. The expropriations, it seemed to me then, could have been more discriminating: for certain enterprises seemed quite disposed to collaborate with the new regime.

seemed all the more necessary economically in that the policy followed in regard to the peasants was radically different from that of the other Communist countries, and not only because some latifundia had not been divided up.

4. The dangerous generosity of the Cuban revolutionaries

The Soviet Union had largely financed its industrial investments by underpaying peasants for their work, a practice that lasted until at least 1953. This was accomplished by requisitions, first of all, that practically speaking were not paid for; then by making delivery of farm products at low prices obligatory and then selling these farm products to the consumer at a high price, which allowed the large difference to be invested. The kolkhozes themselves took care of 85% of their investments, and paid the State in taxes 12.5% of their net production of the "value added."

From the beginning of its revolutionary power, Cuba proved itself to be generous with its peasants, even more than it could afford to be; this was to have dangerous consequences. The true revolutionary must be *pure and tough*. The revolutionaries' purity cannot be questioned, but they reserved their toughness for enemies of the people. In 1959 the rebel army began to erect buildings for the permanent agricultural workers, who were now "cooperators," and without worrying overmuch about costs, built them fine, comfortable houses, often with five rooms. Too handsome for the resources of the country, for they required the massive importation of beams and timber, and quantities of plumbing and other fixtures. Because they required too much work, not enough of them could be built, thus leaving others in their miserable shacks for long years. The matter was rectified later, when the leaders became aware, too late, that it is never possible to do everything immediately. Ania Francos did not see this very well when she wrote: "For once it's true that nothing is too good for the proletariat."[12] It is *too* good, on the other hand, if it means reducing the proletariat's rations two years later.

---

[12] *La Fête Cubaine,* Julliard, 1962.

Cuba wants to be an example of *revolution;* especially for the peasants of the other countries of Indo-America. They were thus shown other modifications than a simple change of government personnel, and thus of profiteers. This time it was unquestionably—the houses and the popular tourism were there to testify to this—if not a regime *directed by* the people,[13] at the very least a revolution *made for* the people.

Before many of these houses had been erected, people's stores—*tiendas del pueblo*—were set up throughout the island. Remote parts of the country had previously been taken care of by shopkeepers who often enjoyed a sort of de facto monopoly and took unfair advantage of that state of affairs. The tradesman of the Sierra Maestra bought the coffee, made advances that amounted to usury to assure delivery of it, and sold on credit, which is to say at much higher prices—another form of usury. Set up by the INRA, the *tiendas* sold things at their cost price plus expenses; shaving things too fine (by reckoning the wholesale price and adding twelve per cent), those *tiendas* in places where there was little demand incurred a deficit.

These were not consumers' cooperatives, but administrative stores, whose management was often questionable. And the lower prices thus obtained greatly increased rural buying power. But the absence of "sugar" dollars made the task of supplying them with goods more difficult. It would thus have been necessary to reduce consumption by raising prices, or to ration, early on, those things which were going to be in short supply: household linens and clothes, meat, and fats; this would have allowed the leaders to make such rationing less severe later on. On the contrary, the number of cattle slaughtered went from around 750,000 in 1958 and 1959 to 1,000,000 heads per year in 1960 and 1961, despite the warnings of Chonchol[14] and

---

[13] Decisions tend to be explained to the people rather than permitting them to participate in formulating them and carrying them out through elected representatives. But the contacts between leaders and popular masses are much more direct and trusting than in the other Socialist countries.

[14] Chonchol was then an expert from the United Nations Food and Agricultural Organization (FAO).

myself. This imprudence ate into the cattle-capital, which should have been increased instead. As a result, in 1963 only 250 grams of dressed meat per week (plus chicken, tripery, and fish) could be issued, up until the hurricane.

The demand was increased even more by the *raising of rural salaries,* which went up around 20% between 1959 and 1961. If account is taken of the increase in the number of work days, which often went from 160 to 200–240 days per year, salaries in general were perhaps raised more than 60% in two years.[15] This created an inflationary situation, which would have required a parallel rise in production in order to meet a demand that had increased so suddenly and so sharply.

5. Buildings and ill-considered clearing of land: an act more social than economic

Important investments were made in agriculture in order to reach this goal. The twenty-eight zones of development were turned over to guerrilla fighters who were to direct these new pseudo-cooperatives, though they had little competence either technically or economically.[16] Like many agriculturalists starting out without training in economics, they began by building immense pig-sties and poultry-houses, copying the way America raised pigs and poultry, but with a vastly inferior technique. Certain pig-sties were much too large. "The sows will be better," Mazoyer was told when he stressed how wasteful this was! Because the feeding trough was sometimes located inside

---

[15] Salaries distributed in January–February 1959 were already estimated to amount to 123 million *pesos,* and the figure reached 183 million in January–February, 1960.

[16] "At the beginning of 1961, Raúl Castro discovered that things in Oriente province were in a mess. Everything worked *por la libre* [as people pleased]. Everyone struck out on his own. In the cooperatives, the most responsible peasants tried to fight against anarchy, but individual efforts were lost in the crowd. It was often necessary to go to Havana to settle minor problems . . . *The excess of enthusiasm and Cuban madness are causing us to lose time and money."*— *La Fête Cubaine.*

the sty, the farmer had to go inside to fill it; Mazoyer wondered whether the drafter of the plans were not a saboteur—or an ignoramus. Because an enormous number of animals were grouped together, very well-prepared rations were necessary, a continuous supply of quality feed had to be assured, and the animals were exposed to the risk of epidemics, especially in view of the fact that there were not enough veterinarians. The technical milieu was not capable of *skipping stages in this fashion as it progressed.*

As for cultivation of land, fields were cleared in a frenzy; Fidel confessed to me how much he "hated" marabou, a sort of spiny tropical acacia that invades the sandy savannas; the guerrilla fighters had burning memories of it. Hatred is not a good counselor in agronomy, for these savannas were often very poor in quality.[17] If in addition they were on a slope, erosion began immediately, to the point that an old Cuban agronomist called 1960 not only by its official name, the year of the Agrarian Reform, but also the year of erosion. When a thin layer of fertile soil covers a zone of iron granules, called *perdigón* (bird shot), deep scraping with a bulldozer which pulls up the bushes and the fine palm trees brings this infertile zone too close to the surface. In order not to remove the thin fertile layer, clearing should be limited to the dry season alone.

At the western tip of the island, a professor of rural economy at the Havana agronomic institute—an armchair economist rather than one who goes out into the field—who was responsible for Zone 4 in Pinar del Río, was clearing lands dotted with outcroppings of hard calcareous rocks called *dientes de perro* (dog's teeth). These pointed rocks should obviously be left buried in the middle of the forest, since it is not possible to cultivate the little hollows of earth except with a hoe, as the

---

[17] A machine to pull up and then shred marabou leaves, developed in 1963 at Ciego de Avila, makes a product similar to alfalfa meal from them. Thus these "fallow fields" can yield infinitely more forage, of better quality, than the immense majority of the natural grazing lands of the island. At this time I insisted that all clearing of marabou be forbidden, whereas I had merely advised against it in 1960.

Indians used to. As soon as the forest humus was burned, its fertility would disappear. And during this time the richest prairies of Camaguey, where the soil is so fertile, needed only a simple ploughing to furnish an increase in production, at far less expenditure than that required by pasture lands, that would be much higher than that that could be anticipated from cleared savannas. Closer ties between the cultivation of land and the raising of cattle, using forage sub-products resulting from the cultivation of the land, would have allowed production to be increased faster and at less expense than through the creation of new farms.[18] Likewise the full use of the unused capacities for production, such as that in the factories making textiles and processing food, was more pressing than the creation of new factories. The former guerrilla fighters were thinking in social terms, wanting to give everyone wealth and work, without having the economic bases that would have opened up better paths for reaching this goal.

6. The failure to publish critiques slows down the recognition of errors

Fidel said in 1960 that it would not cost any more, or at any rate not very much more, to transport workers' children to the beach in luxury cars (abandoned by the wealthy middle class leaving the island) than it would in a bus. And he raised crocodiles in the Ciénega de Zapata, with detritus from slaughterhouses that would have been more useful if it had been used to feed pigs and poultry, at least so long as elsewhere in the world there are crocodiles on the loose that can be killed with one bullet. The development of popular tourism was less pressing than assuring the right long-term nourishment of the whole of the population, which seemed to me to have already been compromised; but those Cubans responsible weren't as aware of this as they should have been, despite warnings.

No revolution is possible without a takeover of the territory,

---

[18] This is true, but this intensification requires a great deal of technical knowledge, and careful, really interested peasants, and in 1964 the U.S.S.R. had not yet reached that point.

in the course of which such errors are inevitable, and Cuba has made fewer than the U.S.S.R. But it could have profited more from the Soviet experience, and it is especially important that Cuba put itself in a position to correct its errors as quickly as possible. On May 20, 1960, after the peasant meeting at Pinar del Río, I had an interview with Fidel in circumstances that were rather exceptional.[19] Having been given a political role by this fact alone, I was asked to hold a press conference the next day.

After a delay of two hours (they had forgotten to tell me where the conference was to be held, which was nothing out of the ordinary), I outlined for the journalists the principal difficulties of the situation. Each of them was persuaded that everything was going along fine, especially since day after day *Revolución* was publishing the occasionally ill-considered praise of Jean-Paul Sartre,[20] who saw all kinds of good qualities in the Cuban leaders and therefore risked giving them a sense of false pride. Thus Fidel the evening before had brusquely accosted me: "All the foreign friends that visit us have nothing but compliments for us, whereas all you ever seem to do is criticize. Why do you criticize us?"

At the end of my speech to the press, in the midst of general consternation, I was asked if I would repeat these facts in France. I replied that I would, but that I would add other explanations, so that the objective causes of the situation would be better understood. They protested that criticism ought to be kept within the Revolution and be confined to the leaders, not set forth publicly. And one journalist exploded: "If things are going badly, we must shoot one of the twenty-eight zone leaders." Conjuring up a picture—in my own mind only—of the "dog's teeth" in Pinar,[21] I protested that these "bush-

---

[19] *L'Express,* 15 septembre, 1960.

[20] Which had first appeared in *France-Soir* under the title *"Ouragan sur le sucre"* [" ATempest over Sugar"], then in a book published in New York, although not in Paris.

[21] I for my part would only have "condemned" the man responsible for this stupidity to having his pupils make an economic analysis of his administrative errors: this would have been interesting for both the professor and his students.

rangers" were struggling in the midst of very difficult conditions, and that those most responsible were the big bosses, the ones in the capital.

After having left the latter to reflect on their responsibilities a little bit more than they usually did, I added that the acting president of the INRA, and therefore the man primarily responsible, was Major Fidel Castro. There was a general silence, and I did not propose that he be punished! The leaders of the Revolution are dedicated men who are having a hard time of it and can also be mistaken—a fact which Fidel is more aware of now.

The next day, Havana journalists didn't even mention this conference, though they were the ones who had asked for it. Yet I had not criticized any political choice of the government, or any important economic direction being taken: I had criticized nothing but methods of application, ways of carrying out the Revolution, with the aim of bettering them. I had made a special point of reminding them of the need to think these projects through, to get the account books in order, and impose discipline on the job, pointing out everyone's responsibilities, so as to put a brake on expensive caprices. If those responsible stifle criticism of this sort in this way,[22] they can put off rectifying their mistakes a while longer. This is indeed what has happened since in Cuba, which has already paid too high a price for disorder. The U.S.S.R. has suffered severely because it was late in recognizing the usefulness of self-criticism, and in this regard it still has not progressed enough, has not really taken a good look at itself.

The man primarily responsible for the bad management of

---

[22] Later on, criticism of details, of the way orders were carried out, was permitted, but the questioning of major decisions was never permitted. See the speech of Raúl Castro on January 5, 1961, at the University of Havana: "Certain people do not like to be criticized, and like even less to criticize themselves, but are not averse to gossiping when their adversary has his back turned." "You can't dish out serious and severe criticism every day to people who are having a rough time of it," a Cuban woman friend tells me. But if more criticism had been allowed in 1960, the going would have been less rough in 1964.

the INRA was its executive director, the geographer Núñez Jiménez. He seemed better qualified for holding a meeting, or occupying the lands wrested away from United Fruit on horseback, banners flying in the wind, than for rationally organizing the agricultural production of the socialist sector. In August of 1960, he never left me alone with Fidel, for fear that I would ask Fidel to assign him to a job more suited to his abilities. He thus continued as head of the INRA up to the end of 1961. In 1963 his thoughtlessness was costing dear: we shall see the errors that resulted from his irresponsible demands for palm seeds, Para rubber plants, and coconuts.

In 1963 he was the president of the Academy of Sciences, which Fidel did not take very seriously. He had already recruited a team of three hundred administrators, before he had any scientists in the organization. He gave his *Geography of Cuba* a revolutionary color, but his book is often quite inferior to that of Leri Marrero, who had preceded him—and has not been republished. The carelessness of certain administrators was the object of excessive punishment in 1963; their negligence certainly did not have as much effect on the Cuban economy as the disorientation of certain responsible leaders.

During this same period, in a very small department of the INRA, there was a minister of agriculture, Major Pedro Miret, who was doing an excellent job of reforestation, administering his material and his personnel economically. Working at his side was a discreet agronomist, Alonso Olive, whose encyclopedic knowledge even then was being underutilized.

7. Disordered diversification, insufficient popularization, absent autonomy

The cultivation of sugar cane was said to be neo-colonialist, and certainly it had been wrong of Cuba to limit itself to this one crop. It had, however, brought Cuba enormous resources, and it is highly suited to the country's good land, especially if it can be cultivated more intensively, as was already being recommended in the last century by the great Cuban economist Avaro Reinoso.

I had therefore suggested that it be replanted more frequently; that the drainage, the weeding, and the fertilization of it be improved; that it be moved to more favorable zones. This would have allowed *the yield to be increased,* and then *the acreage devoted to it to be decreased* if the market for sugar remained constant.

A certain diversification was thus indicated *on the national scale* so as to grow all crops fairly well adapted to Cuban conditions, but I set three conditions for the proper implementation of such an agrarian policy. The new crops were to be parceled out logically, *by specializing each region,* and even more so, by specializing *the growing of each crop.* A denser belt of truck farms should first have been set up around the capital, pushing sugar cane and poor grazing lands much farther away from the outlying suburbs. Then in a second concentric circle, the cultivation of intensive forage crops could have assured both the production of fresh milk and that of bananas, for in 1963 these latter were still coming from far-off Oriente, at the cost of enormous freight bills and heavy losses.

Fruits and tubercules (potatoes, manioc, tara, sweet potatoes, and yams) which were in short supply in the Cuban capital in 1967–1968 would also have to be produced there. Industrial crops, primarily cotton, *kénaff,*[23] and peanuts, should have been *concentrated* in zones that suited them, in the middle of which corresponding factories to process them should have been set up. Fruits and vegetables logically grow close to the city, the port (for shipping winter fruits and vegetables and tropical fruits), and factories to make juice and jam.

Each region and each area, which up to that point had been too specialized, was now seen to be trying to grow an excessive number of crops and trying to raise too many cattle, all at once. If it was too early to work out a real national plan, a program of regional agricultural orientation might have avoided such a dispersal of effort. By keeping sugar cane for export, the business of feeding workers better could have been attended to. This

---

23 *Hibiscus cannabinus,* a jute substitute.

would have led to the development of a horticultural section, a garden and an orchard on each cooperative, and milk production for on-the-spot consumption, while commercialized crop production would have continued to be specialized. This is indeed what Fidel recommended in his speech of August 11, 1960, which was inspired in large measure by my May report, though he did add the poetic elements which my report so sorely lacked.[24] The second condition for the success of this movement was the diffusion, both prompt and widespread, of each of the thirty new crops (including forage crops), of the fifteen or twenty essential fruits and vegetables, plus a dozen kinds of husbandry, and of fifty-five to sixty introductory pamphlets. Each of these latter should have been drawn up on two levels, one on a more technical and detailed level for the leaders responsible for the farms and for educated farmers, and another simpler one full of pictures and drawings for almost illiterate agricultural workers and peasants.

These pamphlets were indispensable if the country was to avoid gross technical errors on the part of rural workers who had almost no notion of how to grow such crops, because what they were most familiar with was sugar cane and cattle raising, with perhaps a little knowledge of horticulture. Even in 1963 these pamphlets, certain of which were still to be found in the offices of the INRA, had often not turned up yet on the site where the work was going on. And even if they did turn up there, very few people read them, for a taste for such reading must be instilled in them. This shortcoming, and all the disorganization that went along with it, cost the Cuban agrarian economy hundreds of millions of dollars. Instead the INRA published vague propaganda articles about agriculture, written

---

[24] On this date Fidel proclaimed that it was no longer a question of reform, but of agrarian revolution, which meant that it was no longer a question of paying indemnities. Then he went on to paraphrase the Gospels, for the bishops had severely attacked him on August 7, and concluded: "To betray the poor man is to betray Christ." As regards the Catholic problem, see the study of Claude Julien in the previously cited issue of *Terre entière*.

by journalists whose very limited technical knowledge made them more dangerous than useful.

The third condition, which was still more important, was the creation of real units of agricultural production, with an appointed head who would be responsible, with an elected steering committee that was a juridical entity, and above all with a *broad autonomy,* both financial and managerial. But the pseudo-cooperatives established in 1959 and 1960 received their gifts in kind from various sources, and cash money only for salaries. It was impossible to draw up a balance-sheet, a calculation of costs, and therefore to have some idea of their efficiency. Orders came from several different technical boards having to do with farming and cattle-raising; these orders were sometimes contradictory, and had no unity of conception.

The last paragraphs of my first report[25] to the Cuban government (May–June 1960) were entitled: "The pamphlets for popular consumption, a primary tool . . . The financial autonomy of the cooperatives. A Socialist ground rent." In it I wrote specifically: "At present no one is in a position to really pin down the real costs of production . . . the moment has come to develop a tool able to point more quickly to the economic errors of certain cooperatives . . . The lumping together of expenses prevents the economic efficiency of each 'individual' cooperative from being measured. Financial autonomy must be arrived at soon." This does not mean that I had come to the right conclusions about all Cuba's problems: I had (in particular) overestimated the possibilities of increasing the yield in sugar cane. But I had asked (in vain) for criticism of my propositions, whose inadequacy I emphasized.

My second report, in August 1960, stressed that: "The Cuban agricultural situation in the summer of 1960 is *more serious than it appears to be to many responsible people . . . A production unit must not be managed like an administrative bureau,* with civil servants, and in particular it must not be run

---

[25] Reproduced in part in the 1962 *Études de Tiers Monde:* "La réforme agraire à Cuba, ses conditions de réussite," especially pp. 25–29.

with a bureaucratic mentality. Errors must come to notice faster so as to be corrected faster . . . announcing on all sides that everything is going very well is not the best way to reach that goal. It is necessary to pass from the frame of mind in which certain claims are made, which easily leads to demagoguery, to the frame of mind of the State, which can distribute only what has actually been produced, and must therefore make production its prime concern."

These elementary cautions were not heeded enough, for the cultural milieu did not always allow their importance to be realized, or these prescriptions to be followed. The highest priority should have been given to speeding up the education of those cadres necessary for the management of the nationalized economy. Cuban revolutionaries work hard, but they have not always caught on quickly to the difficulties of development, or even to the difficulties of understanding Marxism well: and this observation is not limited to Havana!

8. If the U.S.S.R. exploits its peasants, Cuba spoils them too much

"As often as possible," the constitutional law of Agrarian Reform states, "the INRA will create agricultural cooperatives to be placed under its direction, will appoint their administrators . . . [and] will see to it that they accept and respect the aid and the technical orientation which the INRA *will dictate* . . . This latter entity will mobilize the funds necessary to the creation of the cooperatives, long-term credits with minimum interest, [and] short-term credits . . . *being careful to guarantee, from the beginning, a suitable family income."*

This was in total contrast with Soviet agrarian policy, except for the guardianship over cooperatives—which was indispensable if workers were to be educated. For all the credits are here furnished by the collectivity, which in observance of the law pledges to "improve the conditions of life, health, and education of the rural population." This is a praiseworthy concern, but social expenditures, which in Marxist terms are referred to as nonproductive, were to increase much faster than investments for production in Cuba in 1959–1961.[26] The most essential difference as compared with the kolkhoz was the *guaranteed daily salary;* compensation for the *troudoden* or average work-day was for a long time, and still remains, much less than the legal Soviet minimum salary. *If the U.S.S.R. went too far in one sense, Cuba went to the other extreme.*

The law made the INRA responsible for drawing up the statutes of the cooperatives; in August 1960, these statutes were still in the planning stage. When I visited a cooperative in the province of Las Villas at that time, the workers questioned me about them, in more or less these terms: "All of us here are completely devoted to the Revolution, ready to follow Fidel wherever he tells us we should go, to accept all his proposals. But when you see him, tell him that we'd like to know where we're going, and that we'd like to be told how our cooperatives are going to be organized." I was all the more embarrassed in that I had in my pocket the draft of the rules governing cooperatives, but had been forbidden to pass them on, whereas a true democratic centralism would have required that the base—the workers and their representatives—be consulted about these proposed rules.

They could have made some interesting suggestions; though they could not have been given everything they wanted, the discussion would have provided an opportunity to explain why. Some of the workers, who had thus been promoted to "members of cooperatives," tried to organize a defensive union clearly aimed *against* their own cooperative: a clear proof that they did not feel it to be "theirs," that they did not feel "at home" in it. But the Cuban tendency is to make decisions at the top. In 1963 the proposed reorganization of the INRA, worked out by four administrators, was not passed on to the heads of the *granjas;* the advice of these "boondockers" was nonetheless essential.

---

[26] On September 26, 1960, at the United Nations, Fidel himself was to demand "public investments for Latin America aimed at economic development, not at 'social development,' this latter being a calculated invention aimed at hiding the real needs of economic development."

In my report to the Cuban government, I had stressed the danger of this projected reorganization, which placed great emphasis on the distribution of profits. I pointed out in particular that the combination of guaranteed salaries, "the price for sugar (which was at that time being sold at a very low world figure), and a low technical level of certain units growing sugar cane did not preclude the possibilities of a deficit." In reality, it was a question of administrative units, entirely in the hands of the INRA, that were very far from being kolkhozes. The absence of financial and administrative autonomy made their organization much more dangerous economically than that of the sovkhozes, which are already often on the road to ruin. Their deficit was to increase: in August 1962, out of 620 sugarcane cooperatives, only three could come up with even the appearance of a profit, these three being the only cooperatives to oppose—in vain—the adoption of an entirely State-imposed formula.

I was to find the same singleminded hope of marvelous profits to be shared in December 1962–January 1963, in Algeria, on the autonomous farms that had recently been taken over from colonists; in all the meetings we had, I therefore stressed the much greater probability that there would be deficits.[27] The proposed Cuban statutes, which were later confirmed by a congress of "members of cooperatives," provided that eighty per cent of the profits of the first five years would go toward reimbursing the construction costs of the dwellings for members of cooperatives that had been advanced by the INRA, and that the rest would be divided among them. Nothing was set aside for productive reinvestments; this was willingly left up to the State. I greatly surprised the zone leaders by reminding them that "their" cooperatives, which had been built up on the golden eggs laid by the goose of the budget rather than the invested work of members of cooperatives, ought to be able to

---

[27] In the autumn of 1963, the majority of these farms had not paid back the credit extended them, and often they did not even know how much these loans amounted to.

pay back all the capital that had been so generously invested in them. But this reimbursement seemed to them to be no more than flowery rhetoric: this was a happy time for these builders with apparently unlimited resources—the future belonged to them. Why should they have listened to Cassandras predicting rude awakenings?

9. *Discussion with Che Guevara*

In mid-August of 1960, I asked to discuss this problem with Che, who received me very early (it was only 10:00 A.M.) as a special favor, in the office he occupied as president of the National Bank.[28]

At this juncture everyone pointed to him as the man most responsible for Cuban economic policy. Not being very well acquainted with him, I had come to see him in the hope that he would get Fidel to understand the requirements of the economy better, but he immediately protested: "You can't get him to do everything you want him to do," and it did not take me very long to realize that this was true.

I outlined to Che the necessity of increasing the work put out without increasing base salaries just as fast, and proposed that members of cooperatives participate in the building of their houses without pay, especially during the second half of the year, which is the slow season on the farms. This would have allowed full employment to be attained more quickly, and would have allowed the diffusion of technical knowledge to have been the most meaningful part of the project. Since their owners would have had to make a noticeable sacrifice, their houses would have been appreciated much more and therefore

---

[28] Where he denounced the fact that he had more than one hundred extra employees, but their number has since increased! A Cuban anecdote tells how he was appointed to this post. At a Council of Ministers, Fidel asked: "Is there anybody here who's an economist?" Che, who was dozing (he doesn't get enough sleep), thought he said: "Is there anybody here who's a communist?" Since he claimed to be one, he raised his hand before anyone else and got the job.

would have been kept up much better, and above all they would have cost less within the framework of this "beaver" policy.

I also proposed that the members of cooperatives *invest work in them,* during the season when heretofore they had been out of work. A part of this work would be "paid for" in the form of shares of stock as members of a cooperative. There is no real cooperative without a minimum of contributions by members. They had scarcely any money at this point, but still had a great deal of leisure time, for there was still unemployment; they could thus contribute by working. According to my plan, these shares would have borne interest, and thus would have constituted a form of *forced savings.* They would have been redeemed in cash—which was necessary, so as to stress their real value— only when members left the cooperative. I stressed my general impression, received from members of cooperatives, that they did not appear to be *a part of an enterprise that really belonged to them.*

Instead they felt that they had become salaried employees of the government, quasi-functionaries, and for this reason some of them were already not putting forth their best efforts.

If someone in a small collective based on autonomous work malingers, it is friends and neighbors who suffer from your negligence, and they'll make you aware of this. But if it's a question of the State, the collective entity is immense and far away. It is generally admitted, even in the U.S.S.R. today, that everyone can steal from it without going against generally accepted moral standards. The few lazy louts earned as much as the others in 1960, and I therefore found that there were even more of them in 1963. In my opinion, this participation, which corresponded to what a member of a cooperative classically contributed, would reinforce the social capital and would give the members the impression that the cooperative really belonged to them, *a sense of co-ownership,* and a personal attachment to their work collective.

Che reacted violently: "You have put too much emphasis on the sense of ownership that is to be given to members of cooperatives. In 1959, there was a marked tendency here toward

"Yugoslavism" and workers' councils. It is not a sense of ownership that they should be given, but rather a *sense of responsibility*. In this way, the necessary changes in policy will be easier." Che later emphasized that it was an *ideological* error to have set up cooperatives, which were acceptable only in the case of Russian or Hungarian peasants, but not at all acceptable in the case of Cuban agricultural workers, who were really proletarian. Because of this, these workers don't feel that they are working for themselves, but instead only for an entity, the State, that was still too abstract in their minds, even though it had been rebaptized "all the people." In 1963, Titoism was considered real heresy in Havana.

Che therefore outlined a position that was very interesting in principle, a sort of ideal vision of Socialist Man, who would become a stranger to the mercantile side of things, working for society and not for profit. He was very critical of the industrial success of the Soviet Union, where, he said, everybody works and strives and tries to go beyond his quota, but only to earn more money. He did not think the Soviet Man was really a new sort of man, for he did not find him any different, really, from a Yankee. He refused to consciously participate in the creation in Cuba "of a second American society, even if everything belongs to the State." Charles Bettelheim rightfully emphasizes how dangerous it could be to set up institutions where *only the motivation of personal interest* would enter into play.

From another angle, *counting at present only on devotion,* not on a work collective with familiar faces, but on the whole of society more or less poorly envisaged, is to try to go on to communism immediately, like the Chinese in 1958; at the very least, it means skipping certain steps. And the Cuban economic difficulties of 1960–1968 suffice to show how inefficient this is, and therefore how dangerous. In short, Che was far ahead of his time—in thought, he had already entered a communist stage, which I did not think possible even in the Soviet Union of 1980.[29] Advancing the timing in this fashion interferes with

---

[29] Cf. *Sovkhoz, kolkhoz, ou le problématique communiste,* Le Seuil, 1964.

the functioning of the motor, and keeps certain of its developments from being truly adapted to the concrete situation in 1964.

Protestants had the merit of renewing the sense of personal responsibility that the old form of Catholicism had not stressed highly. Socialism needs to revive a sense of responsibility; but to believe that these moral stimulations can replace material recompense is *to deliberately and uselessly repeat the whole cycle of errors of the other socialist countries,* for which they have already paid quite dearly. *To have departed from the cooperative formula too much,* though it dominates the agriculture of the socialist countries, *was to my mind the basic error of the Cuban leaders,* and we shall see the many consequences of this.

I also explained to Che that the lowering of prices in the *tiendas del pueblo*—which were administrative units, not cooperative units—risked increasing rural consumption too much, and I proposed that at least half of this decrease in prices be recovered by the tax authorities, in the form of a tax on business receipts. "We are going to receive Soviet watches that cost us nine *pesos,* and we'll sell them for forty *pesos.*" He was not as aware as he should have been of the danger of rural overconsumption, when stocks were limited and imports had been reduced. Nor did he appreciate the niggling sums that would be brought in by a tax authority that would restrict itself to these durable goods, representing only a small proportion of workers' expenditures. An estimate was made of how much prices would have to be lowered in order for the regime to take root and affirm its socialist character, and the economic consequences of this drop in price were underestimated.

10. The granja del pueblo, *a "superior form" of ownership, decided on by Fidel alone*

I have already told about that other day, August 26, 1960, spent with Fidel, this time in his aluminum house in the middle of the Ciénaga de Zapata (how hot it was!). He started things off by showing me his crocodile farm. I forebore from mentioning what obvious economic heresy this was; I was still hoping to turn him away from another project that would have much more dangerous consequences for the Cuban economy. I thus considered it hardly diplomatic to begin by attacking him for a whim, for a hobby. After long discussions with President Dorticos on the subject of the instructions to be sent to Raúl Roa, who was slugging it out in a conference in Costa Rica, there followed a little relaxing but imprudent target practice with a heavy Czech machine gun along the surface of the water—he's a good shot. After having heard the essence of what I had to say, he outlined his project to me.[30]

All farms other than sugar-cane plantations, and all cattle ranches, were to be organized into people's farms—*granjas del pueblo.* He justified this by the advantages that would accrue because of the centralization of machines so as to ensure their full employment, and I vainly insisted on the full employment of men first of all. When he foresaw an area of two to three thousand caballerías, 27,000 to 47,000 hectares, for each *granja,* I gave a start of surprise. Taking from Fidel's hands the sketch on which he had already located the cowshed and its grazing lands here, the pig-sty there, and then the fields to grow crops, I drew lines to divide it into twenty or so *autonomous* groupings: each with its personnel, stock of cattle, and appropriate materiel. His *granja* would thus have been only a sort of *federation* of production units "on the human scale," each of them an individual unit with management of it within the capacities of the existing cadres. The group would have had at its disposal only the largest machines, bulldozers, and a part of the combines.[31]

---

[30] The first thing Fidel said to me was: "When I got the heads of the sixteenth zone together in Cienfuegos, I began things by telling them: 'Shut up, all of you, I came here to bawl you all out.' " One of the leaders, who had spent the whole night there, had already told me: "It was a real brawl."

[31] In my report I added: "In order to manage these units, *exceptional leaders* would be needed, with both technical and economic knowledge, with both authority and initiative, who would know how to 'stimulate' their fellow workers: this would be the greatest difficulty of all."

I reacted all the more strongly when he put off the eventual autonomy of management to an indefinite date. He spoke of the 100,000 chickens that each one of his hundred giant poultry farms would produce beginning in 1961, that is to say 10 million in all: a goal that would just barely be reached in 1967. He planned to sell them for thirty *centavos* a pound—once again less than their cost of production—as against fifty *centavos* per pound of beef. This would have allowed the number of cattle slaughtered to be reduced to a reasonable figure.

Why this decision to make a regular practice of establishing not real State farms but overlarge administrative farms?—a lack of proportion that would increase freight rates and general expenses, that would complicate the management of these farms, and prevent their being properly controlled. Giantism is not an article of Marxist faith, which merely condemns—rightly —the microfundium, which is an obstacle to modern technique. It is sought after, however, by socialist neophytes. China proclaims that its popular rural communes, "the radiant dawn of the rising sun," will permit it to arrive at communism even before the Soviet Union: a dangerous boast.[32]

It was necessary to train more solid cadres before the State could be put in charge of this enormous agricultural sector without danger. The 500,000 Cubans who had left the island since 1960 were not only capitalists, people living on their income, and tradesmen; there were also technicians and teachers, who were soon to be sorely missed. If from May of 1960 on, there had been some thought of organizing accelerated courses in accounting, with a simplified method of bookkeeping, such as that of J. Chonchal, the *granjas* could have been granted autonomy in accounting, and soon fiscal autonomy, in 1961. And agricultural production would not have encountered the same difficulties.

Fidel seems to have garnered from his reading about the Soviets the fixed idea that the cooperative is only an *inferior*

---

[32] As I became even more convinced by my trip to China in 1964. See *Chine surpeuplée, Tiers-Monde affamé*, by R. Dumont, Le Seuil, 1965.

form of production, that of a small group. Only the State farm represents the *superior* form of ownership, that of the people as a whole. Is it the magic of words, or the hope of surpassing others, that thus prevents the real problems—that of healthy management, of an efficient and rational economy—from assuming their rightful place? Many other experts will be able to martial ample warning, more enlightened than my own, against such a risky decision, but it will be in vain: *Fidel's* decision has been made.

For Che is right: it was really a question of a personal decision; even if this decision was talked over with others; and it doubtless was less of a group decision than in Mali or China. It was definitely not a question of a dictatorship of the Stalinist type, for popular support was evident, especially in the form of peasant demonstrations. The bourgeois elements, which were losing out more and more, were emigrating or drawing apart, which made Fidel draw closer and closer to the communists. In this period, he was to publicly estimate his partisans to be 94% of the rural populaton, but to be 71% in the cities: these were obviously optimistic figures, but the gap between them was a fact; the great majority of the rural inhabitants was with him.

Fidel is seeking with all his heart—as can be seen in Chris Marker's film *Cuba sí*—what is good for the people; he listens, he works, he thinks, he explains, he concerns himself with the questions that arise—and often even with problems that are minor. He receives more foreign friends than experts. It is not a question of the "direct democracy" evoked by Sartre, for in the last analysis he reaches the big decisions alone, after having discussed them. And he turns the other decisions over only to the men on his team, the men he trusts. Each essential idea must be thought over and assimilated by Fidel before he accepts it.

When certain questionable aspects of the Cuban revolutionaries are underlined, don't they thereby become more human? Panegyrists who make much of premature successes and do not offer the slightest criticism[33] give them a sense of false pride,

---

[33] See *Cuba, éveil aux Amériques,* Editions sociales, 1962.

which is a mortal peril of those in power: all power corrupts[34] the revolutionary as it corrupts others, and it takes an uncommon force of character to resist this. Fidel (without whom there would not have been a revolution in its present form, for he was the very soul of it) has shown that he has a great deal of it; it is useless to ask too much of him.

At the end of 1960, the socialization of all the major economic positions was therefore practically an accomplished fact; but the word socialism was still very rare in public declarations. A Chilean friend, who had just arrived in Havana at this time, was questioned by a group of Cuban militants. Believing him to be a Yankee, they said to him: "You think we are communists, but we are anything but." Six months later, these same militants were to try to give this Chilean, who had long been a communist, lessons in Marxism-Leninism . . . This shows how rapid the political evolution was, and this in turn explains a certain number of difficulties.

---

[34] And absolute power corrupts absolutely, the English add.

3

1961–1963:
The Rush to Adopt Socialism,
and the Bureaucratization of Anarchy

1. The abortive invasion of the Bay of Pigs (April 1961) and the status of agrarian reform

The more than famous secret agents of the CIA[1] were doubtless Yankees who came from the cities, and therefore enjoyed a high standard of living, and came in contact by preference, if not exclusively, with the middle class in Havana. This middle class at the end of 1960 was largely hostile to the new regime. All those who lived on tourism and traded in luxuries lost their businesses. After the great landowners living off their income lost their estates, it was the turn of home-owners to have their property expropriated by the "urban reform" which turned their houses over to tenants under contracts for combined leasing and purchase. Less badly treated than the owners of latifundia, these home owners received enough to pay their personal expenses— up to six hundred *pesos* per month, or the maximum salary of the island. Some of them who had a fortune in furniture, or handsome collections, stayed on in order to keep them, for if they left, they lost everything, even their cars. The elderly hung on, attached as they were to their country and too old to start life over somewhere else.

The "little people" of the capital did not approve of every revolutionary deed, and their bosses were not at all averse to

---

[1] Central Intelligence Agency, a counterespionage agency, a veritable State within a State, whose head Kennedy finally dismissed after the failure of the stupid invasion attempt. Kennedy was, of course, assassinated later.

passing on their slightest criticism. In this hostile little circle, people took comfort in giving voice to their rancors and were quite ready to take their desires for realities. Reports to the CIA in Washington announcing a general popular disaffection toward the regime took shape in this atmosphere of wishful thinking, and there were people who believed it possible to repeat the 1954 "Guatemala coup" against Arbenz, who had dared to lay hands on the sacrosanct United Fruit Company.[2] And a group of Cuban exiles were trained militarily and psychologically, with great care and great excitement, for a military outing that they thought would triumph with no trouble at all, for the men took along dress uniforms so as to hold a victory parade in Havana!

At the Bay of Pigs, dozens of peasants and workers in the Cuban militia who at first had arms that were ridiculous, allowed themselves to be killed on the spot rather than retreat, and thus gave the army and better-equipped units of the militia time to hasten to the front lines, despite the inferiority of the Cuban forces in the air. Popular support of the regime was thus strikingly demonstrated to the watchful eyes of the whole world, and even the most reactionary Indo-Americans—including those who served the Yankees—were not all that unhappy about this defeat of those they had so often held in contempt.

From the very beginning of the attack, after the first aerial bombardment, Fidel proclaimed for the first time in his speech on April 16, 1961:[3] "Comrades, workers, and peasants, this is a democratic socialist revolution of the humble, by the humble, and for the humble." Even with the word *democratic* hanging in the air, in the ceremonies on May Day, 1961, in Moscow, Cuba was still considered to be a "sympathizer," though it had not yet officially joined the socialist camp.

---

[2] During the "Friendship Month" sponsored by France and organized in August 1963, at Montargis, the three Americans, who had done advanced graduate work far beyond the master's degree, did not even know of the existence of United Fruit, and what they learned about its conduct in Central America greatly surprised them.

[3] At the funeral of the victims of this bombardment.

By May 1961, four million additional hectares of land, more than forty per cent of the agricultural land that had been in private hands in the island, were expropriated. Unlike Mexico, where owners were able to select and keep the best lands, in Cuba the nationalized sector already included the vast majority of fertile zones. Four per cent of the lands nationalized at this time had been confiscated under the provisions of the law of December 1959, concerning illegally acquired property. Though the law of May 17, 1959, is the only law that is well known outside of Cuba, Gutelman emphasizes the fact that it furnished only 27% of the lands nationalized, whereas 7% was donated to the INRA and 13% came from "voluntary" sales. Forty-nine per cent, or almost half, was secured by expropriation decrees promulgated on July 7 and October 13, 1960, in reaction against the Yankees.

The first of these decrees was aimed at the lands of American owners or companies, or those in which citizens of the United States had an interest. The second of these decrees nationalized all the large companies of the country, which this time were essentially Cuban, along with the land belonging to sugar refineries. We have already emphasized our misgivings about such haste. At the end of 1960, these lands were divided up into 622 sugar-cane "cooperatives," 220 agricultural and cattle-raising cooperatives, and 500 farms—large estates devoted to the extensive raising of cattle—which were administered without intermediary structures.

At this juncture the Americans, faced with the failure of their undertaking, attacked the Cuban economy even more vigorously at three weak points that had resulted from the fact that up to then the Cuban economy had been too closely linked with that of the United States. Though much of the managerial personnel had come from the United States, there were nonetheless some Cubans among them. Moreover, professional personnel—teachers and engineers, doctors and technicians—from 1960 on found themselves being offered excellent jobs in the other countries of Indo-America. Since they spoke the same language, they felt less exiled there. An egalitarian trend often resulted in their being offered salaries in their country that were too low, especially those on the staff of the INRA managing agricultural production. And the rebels promoted to managerial positions were not always skillful enough to handle them.

Those who did not approve of everything the Revolution did—and it was open to criticism, especially in the technical field—were too readily branded counterrevolutionaries. At the University, the federation of students tried to take over entirely, and professors who demanded a minimum of respect were told: "If you're not satisfied, get out." And it was often the most competent who left. But the attack that left the most immediate and the deepest mark on the Cuban economy was the abrupt breaking off of economic ties, the sudden disappearance of a market for sugar since the world market was flooded at the time, and above all the economic blockade and the halt of the supply of goods from the outside.

2. A series of difficulties, the blockade, and a setback for sugar

The weight of this blockade was heavy to bear in a country where Miami, the point of departure of the ferry-boat, was Cuba's central depot, and where almost all the machines were American. The search for available spare parts in Canada or in Western Europe was not carried out as patiently as it should have been. Sabotage by the underground, the burning of sugar cane, the destruction of property, and bombings forced the militia to devote one or two million hours to guard duty each week. A man who has been up all night cannot be as good on the job the next day. Despite these obstacles, and the shortcomings that I have pointed out, the employment of new means and the momentum acquired nonetheless permitted a noticeable increase in industrial and agricultural production in 1959 and 1960. But this increase remained less than the increase in the means of production, and work productivity declined.

Cuba then boasted of having effected the only agricultural reform that began with an increase in production. This is true with regard to the group of socialist countries. However, in Japan and Israel the increase was much more evident, and production was maintained at this higher level afterward, without disruption. The real triumph was the *zafra* of 1961, when for the first time since 1952 all the ripe cane was cut. Even though the harvest lasted longer than it should have, it reached 6.5 million tons, thus underlining the fact that the cane had been quite well cared for in 1960, for one year's harvest is the fruit of the care of the preceding year. Full employment, however, had not yet been attained, and *each worker was still afraid of losing his job:* this made for each one's trying to do his best.

This was a temporary swan song for sugar, for in 1962 the tonnage went down to 4.8 million, and in 1963 to 3.8 million. The removal of the sugar quota and the drouth of 1961 and the beginning of 1962 were not the only causes of this drop in tonnage. Had it not been for the disaster wreaked by Hurricane Flora in 1964, there would doubtless have been an increase, though only a slight one. This falling off of sugar tonnage had many reasons behind it. The choice of a policy basically oriented toward self-sufficiency, so that priority was assigned to truck crops, although this was not made as clear as it should have been by those at the top, allowed cooperatives to pull up part of the cane and even to abandon another part, more or less deliberately, at a time when sugar cane, on the contrary, should have been better cared for in order to compensate for losses elsewhere. Drainage and irrigation systems were not well maintained, and weeding in particular was done too carelessly and too late.

Therefore when workers were called upon in the worst cases to cut through a veritable jungle, a mixture of canes and weeds, they set fire to the fields in order to make their work easier. If burned cane is not milled within forty-eight hours—as was often the case—its sugar yield diminishes rapidly. This also makes the new growth much less hardy, and this has a bad effect on the next harvest, especially if this new growth is not immediately fertilized or if the fertilizer is carelessly spread on the surface of the field instead of being carefully worked into the soil.

The work on the sugar plantations was rationally organized; many operations were paid by the piece, and the wages for each job had a solid pragmatic basis and therefore an objective value. In the sugar-cane cooperatives "the new administrators, who had been chosen more for subjective reasons than for their real capabilities, had a way of going about their work that was anarchic, to say the least. Most of the time they did exactly as they pleased," Gutelman writes. As for apprentice cooperative farmers, they had refused to follow the colonialist norms and preferred working for day wages. Assured now of regular work all year round, their effort was often all too modest.

Diversification of crops was thus brought about amid disorder, each cooperative growing the crops that their leaders or their advisers from the INRA wanted them to. The *líder máximo,* the "supreme chief,"[4] Fidel, himself, had set the example in August of 1960. Without any warning, he ordered a vast campaign to sow peanuts, already under way, to be halted, without even explaining why. This was done despite the fact that the major means to effect this campaign had already been assembled at great expense. And the negotiation of a purchase of soya in China, to be paid off in sugar, did not prevent the government from keeping on with the campaign in progress, even if it meant switching over to yet another campaign, if there were sufficient funds, which was not, alas, the case.

3. From underemployment to a lack of manpower and absenteeism

In 1961–1962 the rural scene changed very quickly. Unfamiliar crops, planted amid chaos, with no explanatory pamphlets available and insufficient technical leadership at hand, began to demand too much manpower, while at the same time giving

---

[4] When I first came across this term in print, I hesitated; but I was told that I should take it in the military sense of "commander in chief."

very small yields. In 1962, everyone maintained that there was a lack of manpower, especially in agriculture. A certain exodus from the countryside had taken place: the Domingo Alonso Rodríguez cane cooperative, where there were 220 permanent workers in 1963, had seen 70 workers leave the village since 1960; they had gone into the army, into administration, into labor organizations, into party cadres, to the U.S.S.R. to be trained . . . All this *swelled a tertiary sector that already was hypertrophied,* to the detriment of production. The fact that many fields which had been very neat in 1960—the pineapple plantations to the south of Ciego de Avila, for instance—were overrun with grass in 1963, bore witness to a lack of material means and effort. In reality, it was largely a question of a false shortage of workers, for it was accompanied by persistent unemployment in the cities (where there were 200,000 out of work in 1962), and by a decrease in productivity resulting from an economic policy that was frequently in error.

The depreciation of the currency,[5] which had been poured into the economy in superabundance, increased the demand for products at the very moment when the possibilities of importing goods were being reduced: this was to make people less interested in making the extra effort that would be necessary in order to earn more money. Gutelman cites the case of a family in which at one time only the father was working, and even then only seasonally employed; later the father and three sons were employed full time, thus multiplying the total income of this family by a factor of fifteen. Though this is an extreme case, there was a large rise in income. *Absenteeism,* especially after the year 1962, became a national sore spot; there were posters everywhere denouncing it as "treason to the country." This pillorying of absentees has not done away with the practice, however, for there are objective reasons for it; in 1963 there was a decided drop in absenteeism.

Many agricultural workers were city-dwellers who had to be

---

[5] No revolution has ever taken place without a depreciation of the country's currency.

transported long distances to their work, and the means of transportation were becoming more and more inadequate. The disorganization of production, and even more of distribution and the flow of supplies, often obliged people to go long distances in search of food—or shoes. Thus there were fewer people on the job in the afternoon than in the morning. Along with this there was a decline in discipline on the job; how many groups of workers I have seen lounging about and talking or standing with their arms crossed!

The workers were often told that they had been exploited—which was true. But for many of them, because of a genuine cultural underdevelopment,[6] Revolution meant a relaxation of effort. The fine houses were now the property of the people, and the people did not always realize that once these riches had been acquired they had to be maintained and replaced, and above all new riches had to be created. The increase in salaries seemed normal, or even indispensable, since the Revolution was triumphing.

Very few people were willing to admit that a real rise in the standard of living, especially when it was accompanied by a need for additional investments for development, demanded more work. Fidel was certainly beginning to say this. He should have struck while the iron was hot in 1960, but he did not do so then as explicitly as he did in 1963, when his education in economics had taken him much farther into the subject. In the meantime, this lesson cost Cuba dearly.[7]

Because of the disorderly atmosphere created by an economy that the leaders tried to administer entirely from the capital, the

---

[6] The Spanish aristocracy looked down upon the people and the American influence led to a certain scorn for culture, to the point that some Cubans said: "It's no use having libraries, there are machines for that now." As in the United States, dollars brought more prestige than learning, even if the origin of the dollars was suspect.

[7] Advice to future revolutions: prepare those who will be your leaders tomorrow not only to wage guerrilla warfare but also *to efficiently manage a developing economy,* so as not to have to pay such a high price for it.

on-the-job discipline of the period just before slackened—when there was every need for it to be enforced more vigorously. A happy medium between Stalinian authoritarianism and a certain insouciance could have been found. The result was that there was a gap between the effort that had been made, on the one hand, and revolutionary enthusiasm, which was sometimes merely verbal, plus devotion to the father-land, which was unquestionable, on the other.

4. *The first and second wave of "people's farms"*

In May 1961, a series of cattle ranches, which up to this point had been directly administered, and of "cooperative" farms on land not dominated by sugar cane cultivation, had already been transformed into 266 *granjas del pueblo* (people's farms). These varied in size from 4,000 to 67,000 hectares, and averaged 9,000 hectares. Later there were to be several as large as 130,000 hectares! Work on them was done exclusively for wages and the workers tended to consider themselves as civil servants of a State whose master they were—as they were told often enough. The weakness, both qualitative and quantitative, of the local administrative cadres prevented a rational organization and efficient control of the work done, and it often made for late payment of salaries, which was not very encouraging either.

At the beginning, the administrators had only twice or just barely three times the salary of a manual laborer, though they had the crushing responsibility for a gigantic enterprise on their shoulders. The term "administrator" seems to me to be a real catastrophe: it emphasizes that his work is largely administrative. (At the head of the Russian sovkhoz there is a director, a technical job.) In the beginning, he was not generally a technician, and the quality of his management suffered immediately thereby. The technical training of new administrative aides represents an effort to remedy this situation; I fear that this is still not enough, but it is a step in the right direction.

An administrator of a *granja* in Las Villas who had the best possible sort of reputation and was very devoted to the regime and to his work, made serious arithmetical errors. Confusing the number of litres of milk with its value in *pesos,* he told me that it paid for all his manpower; for this to have been true, it would have had to be a sum twelve times larger. On the subject of how far apart the banana trees were planted, he misplaced a zero, taking a 10 for a 1. If he had had better economic training, full responsibility, and *a salary tied to the profits he made,* he would most probably have paid more attention to these basic facts. He didn't go out to the peanut field with me, though I had many things to show him there. But he was not proud of it, because sometimes one had to walk several yards in order to find a single peanut plant. *Insufficient density is a very common cause of present low Cuban yields.* Because Cubans have long been accustomed to large plots of ground, the traditional spacing of the plants has been kept, even after the application of much fertilizer and the installation of irrigation: *this often causes underutilization of these costly production factors.*

These shortcomings of the *granjas* were easy to predict because of their scanty knowledge, their lack of autonomy, and the fact that they had to turn all their receipts over to the Treasury. *No one had any direct material interest in whether they were profitable; as a matter of fact, none of them has been.* But this was not realized for a long time: everyone emphasized how much land had been cleared or brought under cultivation, with no special mention of the low yields or the costs.

In 1960, as I analyzed the account book of a cattle latifundium in Camaguey, it was easy for me to extract all the elements necessary to understand the situation in the space of half an hour. It was easy to see how things stood: in it were the inventory of cattle at the beginning and the end of a particular fiscal period, the quantity of cattle (weight and value) bought and sold, subsidiary receipts (milk, poultry), and expenses itemized under general headings (manpower, materiel, products). In 1963, what with the clutter of thousands of figures and mountains of documents on the *granjas,* it would have been almost impossible to have any precise idea of such details unless I were willing to work much harder at digging them out.

Because they had not yet analyzed the growing abyss of debts of the *granjas* very clearly in 1962, the Cuban leaders considered it their personal victory to have decided to transform the remaining cooperatives, the sugar plantations, into *granjas*—a decision inspired by these leaders and concurred in by ninety-eight per cent of the members of the cooperatives. Gutelman explains the reasons why this was so readily accepted. "Weekly salaries *were much lower* than those paid on the 'people's farms' and the shared profits at the end of the fiscal year were nil or ridiculously small (forty to fifty *pesos,* in the best of cases); in short, the cooperatives were not glowingly prosperous. In addition, *all the government's efforts were being concentrated on the people's farms:* the workers on them earned *relatively high wages* and enjoyed *generous fringe benefits,* [and] very important priorities for the construction of *housing facilities.*"

Though the workers should have been "exploited" less than they were on the Soviet kolkhoz, their wages should have been made to depend more closely on their real production. But this was not possible so long as on neighboring *granjas,* according to one remarkable Soviet economist, "every time the worker produces a *peso*'s worth of goods, he receives at least two *pesos*' salary." Certainly the sugar-cane cooperatives were no model, especially since the members of such cooperatives had their salary guaranteed from the very start. This encouraged them to *keep the mentality of wage earners,* to care nothing about the relationship between their effort and their remuneration—and admittedly the two things were not in fact related. On the whole, I have the impression that people worked harder in Cuba in 1963 than in 1962; fewer abuses were tolerated, and this improvement seemed to me to be more marked on the sugar-cane *granjas* than on the so-called *granjas del pueblo.* These plantations, which in the old days had often been directed from the refinery, *seem, moreover, to suit the State farm pattern* better than the first *granjas del pueblo,* which were based on the cultivation of several crops.

5. Scattered parcels of land, plans drawn up by surface area, three different administrative systems: nothing is "finished"

These *granjas* did not lead, as might have been hoped, to a logical geographic regrouping of the cooperatives and the lands exploited directly. Getting land was more or less a game of grab, with the most dynamic units seeking to incorporate the largest number of farms possible, even if they were a long distance away. Thus a map of a *granja del pueblo* in the Havana district, such as Lidiel Hernández with its sixteen different farms, or Julio Trigo with its sixty, covered a large part of the province. It was often thirty-five to fifty miles from one end of a *granja* to the other. These parcels of land had very few roads, and more often only trails in poor condition, linking them together; transportation over them quickly became a great burden.

The situation was aggravated by the fact that the *granjas* were created in two successive waves, and because up to 1964 a part of the lands that had been taken over by the State but had not yet been regrouped in *granjas* belonged to the board in charge of farms administered directly. Thus the State sector was directed from the capital by three distinct administrative units, the board just mentioned, that of the *granjas del pueblo,* and that of the sugar-cane *granjas.* Each of them had its own provincial and regional board which often paid no attention to its neighbors, and their lands in large part overlapped each other. The inclusion of the private sector was not the only reason for this; the State sector was widely scattered for no good reason at all. Maps showing the boundaries of each parcel of land, which were drawn up so that this situation could be studied and remedied, were reminiscent of those of our [French] villages before different parcels of land were grouped together, although the area of each parcel was much larger on the Cuban map. A field lying right near the middle of a *granja* might very well belong to another unit a long way away. A pasture bounded on all sides by a larger field might belong to a different *granja* than the field surrounding it, etc. Demolishing a system of production was easier than constructing another one that would be more efficient, and they set to work doing so with a will.

The situation was aggravated by the fixing of production goals in terms of *areas* to be devoted to each crop, and often these were disproportionate to the real possibilities of reaching them. In view of the general disorganization, the insufficient amount of work people were willing to put in, and the lack of spare parts, these exaggerated goals led to the clearing of a larger area than could easily be cultivated. The work of plowing was badly done, but more land was plowed than could be sowed, and often more land was sowed than could be weeded. Too many crops were thus planted without the soil having been properly prepared, even though such preparation is the most important factor in getting a good yield; moreover, the fields were often invaded by weeds. When harvest time came, the combine often broke down, just as in the Soviet Union; rice and sorghum were left standing too long, and this resulted in losses and decreases in quality. Housewives held back from buying "national rice" with its broken grains and its "yellow bellies" that were due to poor harvesting conditions.

"To produce rapidly and abundantly with an inexperienced labor force and yields that are inevitably low, the only solution was to extend the areas under cultivation just as far as they could possibly be extended," Gutelman writes. I do not agree on this point at all. Following this line of reasoning, they have often been extended beyond what is reasonable; people have not been willing to envisage the slightest difficulty, inclined as they are to being ultra-optimistic and unrealistic. Subsequently a number of simple ways to increase yield, such as the creation of artificial pangola pastures, fell within the province of administrators who were not very competent and had reduced means at their disposal. The prime objective should not have been extending the area under cultivation but rather increasing production and reducing costs of production.

But in order to accomplish this, it was often necessary to aim at securing greater yields, intensifying cultivation, and passing from quantity to quality of work put in. This would have been less difficult if these units had been better organized, *leaving a minimum of initiative and responsibility at the base.* Gutelman quite rightly stresses the underutilization of the few rare technicians that were available. Dispersed over too large a number of units, assigned far too large a geographical area to cover, and too narrowly specialized, they wasted most of their time on the road, and often there was a shortage of vehicles. If they had had a more restricted radius of action plus a little wider range of activities, they could have been much more useful.

The excessive diversification of the crops grown as experiments, some twenty-five to thirty-five crops on each *granja,* made the situation much worse. If there had been three or four per farm as I recommended, there would have been fewer technical specialties required in any one restricted radius; the specialist would have found himself employed full time without having to move about a great deal. Moreover, too many agronomists were assigned nontechnical tasks, such as agricultural credit. They were overburdened with paperwork from the three separate provincial administrative divisions in the State sector, without employees to take on all the work that a simple clerk could have handled for them. As soon as there are a sufficient number of agronomists it will be necessary to put them at the head of *granjas* and free them of paperwork, as has been done in the Soviet Union. The lack of technicians is not the only difficulty; people do not have enough confidence in the few that are on the job. It is necessary, certainly, to be mistrustful of technocracy, but the party could control them when it is better organized. We noted in the U.S.S.R., and it was even more noticeable in Cuba, that they were too strictly subordinated to the politician or "rebel" who had been made an administrator without always having the qualities required to perform this function. The agronomist then would go back in his shell, maintain his habit of indolence, work without any plan, and hand in no reports on his activity.

Certain of them even went so far as to visit *granjas* without warning the local authorities, the administrators, or the heads of farms. They then sent very severe reports—that, alas, were justified!—to the INRA or even to the Party. They should never have visited a farm in the absence of one of the farm's heads, and never have left this latter without giving him a sort of prescription, a series of simple written pieces of advice, *which could be carried out with the means at hand;* when technical perfection is not possible to attain, it should not be aimed at as a goal. To remedy this situation quickly, the lesson that facts had to offer should have been followed with even more humility.

6. *The defective structure lowers production*

After a clear increase from 1959 to 1961 *agricultural* production had a slight setback in 1962 and 1963, especially as regarded sugar cane; and this was despite the fact that means of production were imported in even larger quantities than before the Revolution. At the beginning of 1963, a report from the agricultural production board on the 1962 campaign clearly outlined the problems and the gravity of the situation. On a national average, the plan calling for a certain number of acres of sugar cane to be replanted fell 17.3% short, but on people's farms it fell 30% short. In two years the harvest of raw rice fell from 308,000 tons to 207,000, and the yield per hectare from 17 to 14 quintals.

Corn had previously varied in yield from 9 to 11 quintals per hectare, and the yield in the State sector fell to 6.7 quintals per full hectare sowed in 1962, an average year. Since 1959 this production of corn had been maintained only at the price of a vast increase in the number of hectares under cultivation, which went from 175,000 to 231,000 hectares, with therefore a high rise in the cost of production per quintal of corn. The quantity of sorghum fell by half in 1962, and the yield of beans on State farms did not reach 400 kilograms per hectare. Private farmers had a yield of 880 kilograms of peanuts per hectare, less than in central and southern Senegal, where the natural conditions are far worse. But in the State sector the yield fell to 540 kilograms (people's farms) and as low as 320 kilograms (sugar-cane plantations). And in the province of Oriente the yield tumbled to 240 kilograms, which Mestre rightly called "a real scandal."

Tubercules (taro,[8] manioc, sweet potatoes, yams) are almost never in short supply in Africa, where the soil is much poorer, the climate less favorable, and the cultivation done entirely by hand. Yet they were rationed in fertile Cuba, where counter-revolutionary speculation played its role but does not explain everything. And cultivation in Cuba was largely mechanized. The ordinary little peasants of Rancho Mundito (Pinar del Río), without irrigation, without tractors, with poor soil on eroded hillsides, even so harvested almost 7 tons of taro per hectare. On richer soil, with tractors and irrigation, the State farms obtained only a third of this, 2.4 tons per hectare. For lack of manpower and effort, a quarter of the cotton was not harvested; however, tens of thousands of unemployed continued to strut about in the cities, fed by their families who had too much money at their disposal. The technical shortcomings were important: bad preparation of the soil, late sowing, neglected weeding. But we must go back even farther to find the underlying causes: bad diffusion of techniques of cultivation, insufficient effort, unsound organization of the work, faulty pickup of produce, all of these on top of the harm done by the blockade. And the prime cause is the very structure of the *granjas*.

The cattle-raising situation was no better. At the end of 1961 an attempt was made to nationalize almost all the units raising pigs, and the peasants' young pigs were bought up in great quantities. Many of them died on pig farms that were too crowded, though we had pointed out the dangers of such farms more than a year before, along with Julien Coléou. Though there were great plans for developing poultry farms, the results were rather scanty; thus when housewives talked of "a socialist chicken," they meant one that was on the scrawny side. At that it took them too long to reach even this insufficient weight, for the mixed feed given them was often badly balanced, as much on account of internal disorder as on account of the blockade.

---

[8] *Colocasia antiquorum*, a Polynesian plant.

Thousands of choice Friesian cows were imported from Canada in 1961, and their daily production on the dairy farms around Havana where they were taken had fallen almost by one-half three months later. In 1963, it had scarcely gone up at all—a fact that underlines the lack of knowledge, which in turn brought on careless feeding, careless veterinary care, and sometimes careless milking. On the whole, work productivity in the State sector in 1963 was perhaps *no more than half that of the private sector.* This was due in particular to the adoption of an overcentralized State formula for the units of production, which were not left enough autonomy to be able to overcome the difficulties of the situation rapidly; we shall come back to this point.

7. Over-centralized industries, and Soviet aid partly wasted

The U.S.S.R. did not get around to drawing up its first plan for the future until 1927. In Cuba the essential data are still missing; thus in 1963 the outline of a prospective plan for industry based on political directives for a choice of what to produce first had not yet been drawn up. Nor had there been preliminary studies of how and where to do so under the best possible conditions, so that work priorities could be set up. Since people were impatient, they tried to do a little bit of everything, and acquire immediately equipment or seeds that happened to be offered them: it was enough if the enterprise seemed interesting. A large amount of materiel was bought, without the purchasers having the information that is indispensable for a reasoned choice. Serious study of projects, complete with economic statistics, the only basis allowing rational priorities to be established, was never carried far enough. Snowed under by the Center's excessive insistence on handling everything down to the last detail, administrators no longer had at their disposal the time necessary for carrying out the tasks involved in basic planning, which require a great deal of thought. Thanks to a large amount of foreign aid from the U.S.S.R., and to a lesser degree from the other socialist countries,[9] there was too much buying power and therefore much waste. The contribution from these countries was estimated to be 570 million dollars in 1961 and 1962, whereas the rest of Indo-America received barely half a billion dollars net from the United States in 1962.[10] Such "aid" was without precedent, for it was forthcoming because of the fear that the ideology propagated by Cuba would spread. It amounted, however, to just a little over two dollars per capita per year, as against forty dollars going to Cuba, *that is to say almost twenty times more.*

These forty dollars are equal to *the average annual income of the poorest regions of Africa,* such as southern Morocco, the Aurès in Algeria, the north of Nigeria, part of Kenya, Tanganyka, Ethiopia, etc. This sum has allowed many factories to be built without proper study of where they should be situated, and often they have been set up in the wrong place. Some of them are too far from their sources of agricultural raw materials, and therefore transportation is as costly as it is inefficient, especially in the midst of present difficulties. Some of them have trouble finding the volume of water that is indispensable to them; others have difficulty getting rid of waste water . . .

Industrialization was carried out in the same spirit as the diversification of agriculture: the spirit of the Sierra, of guerrilla warfare, which cannot recognize the requirements, the objective laws of the economy (because they have never been studied and understood, a task that is not accomplished easily or rapidly). Nationalization must quickly lead to a formulation of the economic problems corresponding to the new situation, accompanied by an intense effort at organization and administration. Cuba's economic errors do not stand alone: Europe, which is more highly developed culturally, has made a great many, both in the East and in the West.

American countermoves, especially the blockade, put the

---

[9] When China helps Cuba it is those who are by far the poorest giving to those who are richer. This seems curious.

[10] See Chapter 5, 1.

crowning touch on the disorganization of the industrial economy. In order for the Revolution not to grind to a halt, factories had to be kept going despite the blockade, a task that was even more difficult[11] in industry than it was in agriculture. That is why it would have been better not to nationalize the whole non-Yankee sector, at least not in the very beginning; difficulties in securing supplies have been compounded by difficulties in management. The economic action of the Revolutionary government is summed up somewhat severely by Marc Balin: "A wish to develop autonomously without a sound economic base, without the proper financial institutions . . . The planning apparatus mechanically records results, adapting itself to the existing situation instead of seeking to transform it. The plans scarcely reflect the great preoccupations of the present." Serious thought about economics began in 1963, and quickly came of age because of the difficulties encountered.

In order to direct this industrial sector, fifty-three "consolidated enterprises," grouping numerous factories together, both those already existing and later new ones, varying considerably in size, were set up. Here again administration of them was highly centralized, being in the hands of the Ministry of Industry. This latter was composed of vice-ministers (of basic industries, of light industry, of technical development, etc.) and various boards (coordination, statistics, production, supplies, "plans for the future" . . .), which in turn were subdivided into departments. In principle this imposing structure could have fulfilled the logical task of directing, coordinating, and controlling industrial *development*. But despite his unquestioned authority and prestige, Che Guevara never really defined even the broad outlines of an industrial policy.

His Ministry did not seem to be concentrating on its real

---

11 Within the framework of capitalism, too, branches set up in underdeveloped countries are generally run at a loss, as with Nestlé in India and American plastics and machinery companies in Brazil, for lack of rural purchasing power. We shall come back to the importance of underdevelopment, which here is closely linked to that of the building of socialism.

work and busied itself with problems that should not have been its concern; it was therefore snowed under by day-to-day concerns. He tried to run the factories by himself, for the lack of power and raw materials threatened to paralyze these factories at any moment. The first difficulty was solved by the arrival of quite regular supplies of Soviet petroleum (organization in the U.S.S.R. is ponderous, but has some play in the mechanism), but raw materials came almost entirely from the dollar zone. The scarcity of hard currency forced Cuba to limit imports from this source, and ersatz products were sought in the socialist countries. But rationing of a number of raw materials had to be resorted to. This contributed to *an underutilization of the capacities for production already set up, which made the disorganization even more severe.*

Factories erected long before the Revolution represent a given factor, a sort of heritage. But much of the new equipment that was ordered could not be put to work for lack of buildings or qualified administrative personnel. Extremely delicate machines therefore piled up on the docks, and then in temporary warehouses and hangars. A special term was even jokingly applied to them: people talked of machines as being "in raw accumulation." In the warm tropical climate, with its salty fogs, these machines were threatened with rapid deteriorization, for the more modern they were the more fragile they were.[12]

The rate at which factory buildings could be constructed was much lower than the rate of arrival of machines, even though the overly ambitious housing programs (100,000 units were planned for 1962!)[13] were cut down. Production costs increased because of a frequent excess of manpower both in the workshops and to an even greater degree in administrative

---

[12] All the "young" countries, from the U.S.S.R. to India, have been no better at estimating the rate at which the equipment they have ordered can be put to use, and the need that this equipment creates for administrative personnel, engineers, buildings, and an infrastructure: this is yet another problem of underdevelopment.

[13] As against 10,000 built before the war, and 19,000 per year from 1959 to 1961.

bodies. Fidel bitterly criticized one workshop that had been assigned two hundred workers where there were only thirty jobs. It is not enough to stress these particular cases; it is necessary to return to the source and analyze the causes of the difficulties so as to be able to remedy them, without too abstract an ideology, which from now on will be most inopportune, for it has caused Cuba more damage than Hurricane Flora did.

The lack of spare parts often interfered with the proper functioning of machines; more parts could have been made domestically. These spare parts ought to be the very first thing imported, for they do away with bottlenecks at less cost than other measures. The raw materials necessary to use existing equipment are a more pressing demand than building new factories, especially if there is no assurance that these can be used. Charles Bettelheim has stated that the purchase of certain consumer goods capable of making people more interested in earning money, and therefore more interested in their jobs, ought to have priority over any purchase of materiel that runs the risk of being underemployed. Backward countries in general invest *too little*. As was the case with China, Cuba has shown us that *good* investments must also be made, and this requires study and trained administrators. Cuba's present difficulties have been aggravated by the absence of a clear industrial policy, drawn up by a single center having to answer to the political authorities, the Revolutionary leaders, for its decisions. It is urgently necessary to separate the planning of objectives from their execution, in all fields. This requires enterprises to be autonomous as regards all day-by-day decisions concerning work, supplies, and output. On the other hand, coordination is necessary in order to solve major problems that go beyond the local management level: the underemployment of factories, replacement materials, new installations . . .

In areas where centralization would be of benefit to a well-conceived, rational policy of development, such centralization is rarely encountered. There was justification for the unification of the branches of production in a single national enterprise in the case of electric power, which is centralized, even at the scale on which the U.S.S.R. operates. But lumping together dozens of little food stores scattered all over the country into one "business" with a single budget has already made it difficult to single out those stores that are getting along all right, and here again conditions call for autonomy in all day-to-day operations.

The glass industry lacks molds, and above all no one has clearly indicated what it ought to produce. In order to run full time, the match industry ought to collaborate more closely with its paper and cardboard suppliers. Cuban matches in 1963 were as bad as those of the Soviets in 1928. Cubans readily laugh at themselves, and they jokingly say that it took them only four years to do what the Soviets took eleven years to do! Factories manufacturing pharmaceutical products belong to the Ministry of Industry, but come under the control of the Ministry of Public Health: a duality that scarcely favors proper functioning; orders often are late in arriving. The plastics industry buys its raw materials only in the dollar zone when it could procure them in Europe. Wines and liquors are not doing badly, but they have not explored all the possibilities for export. The same is true of Cuban cigarettes, which are much in demand in socialist countries and could be sent to these countries in much larger quantities.

In 1963 we visited the Ecuador sugar plantation, formerly called Baragua, south of Ciego de Avila, which also has a refinery that once belonged to Americans. The head mechanic had had squabbles with his workmen and had had to be replaced; the new man was not familiar with his machines. The head of the refinery was a former assistant head who was promoted very quickly and was not up to the job; the laboratory had not yet secured good quality control. Raw sugar is brown because of the remains of molasses in it, and the color should not go past 8 on the color scale. In 1963 it now and again reached 19; thus it required 114 kilograms of raw sugar instead of 108 to obtain 100 kilograms of refined sugar.

On September 22, 1963, the newspaper *Hoy* stressed the serious shortcomings of the 1963 *zafra* in Oriente. At the end of the season, 85% of the cane that had been milled was burned, for it had been left cut too long, and dried out. This cane could not be mixed with green cane, and the juice obtained, which was too viscous, sometimes yielded more molasses than sugar. "The factory soon saw itself reduced from a sugar refinery to a simple cane-grinding mill," the newspaper concludes.

The Minister claimed that he was administering things, but he was not carrying out his task of setting policy. Consumption and immediate distribution were obviously matters of great concern, and thus the future of production was sometimes neglected. The key sectors that could set off a whole chain of progress were not receiving the priorities of attention that they deserved.

8. A State monopoly on distribution, the absurdity of a number of agricultural prices, a scorn for quality . . .

The pickup of agricultural products destined for consumption was taken care of by Acopio, a body under the direction of the INRA. It had been given *an absolute monopoly on this pickup,* but not the material means to carry out the job completely. For lack of trucks in 1961–1962 (the blockade was partly responsible, but also there was insufficient maintenance and inadequate organization) only half (approximately) of the fruits and vegetables available in the island was picked up. In the provinces of Pinar del Río and Havana, the owners of orange groves often sold their fruit on the trees and the buyer sent his team of pickers over. This commercial network was destroyed before the organization necessary to replace it was fully set up. And the administrators of the INRA, to whom the groves were entrusted, managed them "as before," without worrying about the harvest ahead of time. Since a pseudo-shortage of manpower had succeeded underemployment, and since packing materials and trucks were also in short supply, a fairly large share of the fruit was not picked. Pineapples were scarce at Ciego de Avila when they were rotting twelve miles away, for the factories could not process them all.

The little peasant and the average farmer *had* to sell their harvests to Acopio, but this latter was not organized to pick them up in all parts of the country. Though it exploited the peasant, the private network of peddlers and trucker-buyers was at least ubiquitous, even at the ends of the mountain trails where itinerant peddlers showed up with their loaded mules. Direct sales between producer and consumer were allowed; this gave an advantage to the proprietor or those entitled to use a car, who could feed themselves well and even sell on the black market. On a trip south of Ciego de Avila in 1963 we had great difficulty persuading the peasants we spoke to that we had not come to buy taro but to study the agricultural situation. Since August 1963, the quantity that can be transported by car has been limited to 11.5 kilograms (25.3 pounds).

The Soviet experience demonstrated the practical impossibility of trading goods only through the State network. When I brought up this question at a meeting of INRA leaders, a Soviet expert told me that *60% of perishable goods in the U.S.S.R. were still being distributed in 1963 through cooperatives and kolkhoz markets. In all fields,* Cuba soon ceased its efforts *in favor of cooperatives* and chose to adhere to the State formula, both as regards production units and simple stores to distribute goods. The administrative boards in Havana had special supply centers, which were often badly managed and run at a loss: the budget paid for them, and Cuba's possibilities of economic development were reduced thereby.

The buying prices fixed by Acopio were in a chaos that was impossible to disentangle. First of all they generally *took no account of quality;*[14] this did not encourage efforts to increase it and risked compromising the possibilities of exporting goods.

As regarded tobacco, the lowering of the quality was immediate and catastrophic, compromising the reputation of the famous Cuban tobacco; it was very soon necessary to re-establish a scale of prices depending on quality. In the case of other

---

[14] The sugar refineries did not pay for the cane on the basis of its sugar content, so no one had any interest in raising it. The price of cane has just been tied to its sugar yield.

goods, quality still is seldom taken into account. There are, however, minimum "floors" of quality for goods purchased, below which these products are simply *refused,* and there are almost no other possibilities of sale. Certain of these norms were inspired by the United States, where they were purposely kept severe for the Malthusian purpose of eliminating a part of production from the market and thus "supporting" prices. But this was not a policy appropriate to the famine conditions of Cuba or to a socialist state.

There was good reason to ask producers to cultivate varieties of tomatoes for canning that were rich in pulp, but Acopio refused to buy the other varieties, and the producer was obliged to throw them away—and meanwhile tomatoes were almost impossible to come by in Havana! It should have accepted them and paid a substandard price for them. The government employees of Acopio did not always have the ability to judge the quality of goods correctly. Moreover, prices *generally remained unchanged all year long,* when they should have logically gone down in price when they were in season and gone up in price in periods of underproduction. Not everything in traditional economics is a vice; the traditional variations of prices are not all due to speculation. It is necessary to compensate for the extra effort required to produce certain crops either earlier or later than the ordinary season for them, which is always costly; otherwise everybody would produce these crops in the season when it is easiest to grow them, and the markets would thus be flooded or completely empty, depending on the time of year.

When Fidel almost doubled the price per gallon of gas (from 33¢ to 60¢ per gallon), he was right to put a brake such as this on unproductive outings, as well as on the excessive profits made by taxis. But in the face of the (necessary) rise in price of industrial products, the maintenance of agricultural prices at the same level discouraged agricultural production. This was very obvious at the end of 1961, but was even more particularly the result of defects in the pickup system. The peasants were not even sure whether what they had produced would be bought during the early chaos at Acopio; this made the famine of the spring and summer of 1962 even worse.

Finally the *relations of prices* to each other were often irrational. An effort was made to encourage new industrial crops such as cotton or peanuts, to the detriment of traditional crops, such as corn, sugar cane, and beef, whose prices remained too low. When in addition the retail price of meat enjoys a subsidy (!), consumption increases so fast that soon even more severe rationing is necessary. A partial brake on consumption, which could be brought about by a limited rise in price, was clearly indicated: it would have stimulated production. If the *centavo* of 1963 is estimated[15] to have been worth around 3.3 French centimes,[16] a liter of milk whose production cost was assessed at 8 *centavos* or 26 *centimes,* was much less expensive than in Holland and France! In a tropical climate this was not enough of an encouragement for the development of a product so important to the health of Cuban children. The price of potatoes also discouraged the producer . . .

North of Ciego de Avila, the producer of oranges was being paid 2.5 *pesos* per Spanish quintal of 46 kilograms, or 18 *centimes* per kilogram. But papayas, whose production cost was perhaps half as much, and the yield per hectare more than double, were bringing the producer 6 *pesos.* And watermelons, which yielded five to eight times as much per hectare, after only a few months of simple cultivation that did not require the enormous investments and the high expenditures that orange groves did, brought the producer 4.5 *pesos.*[17] Mangoes, which can be grown much more easily, without burdensome cultivation, "simply picking them off the trees," sell at 2.5 to 5.5 *pesos,* this time depending on which of three qualities they are.

---

[15] By Charles Bettelheim.

[16] Approximately .66 of a U.S. cent.

[17] A great deal of watermelon juice is therefore bought at refreshment counters, sometimes as a replacement for coffee with cream. When the East Germans showed me their breakfast jam, they would say "This is Cuban butter," and make a wry face. They were hardly pleased that they had been deprived of butter so long at home, and that there was still a shortage of it in Cuba. But the privations of certain groups of Cuban workers is even more of a matter for concern.

The Acopio monopoly turned its products over to the administrators of Mincin[18] and did not take care of anything but the supplying of the cities, so that the food situation was not always what it should have been in the villages and farms that specialized (as often was desirable) in industrial crops. There was, however, a great hue and cry about the nutritional shortcomings of the diets of sugar workers, and rightfully so. Better organization from top to bottom would have allowed this state of affairs to have been remedied faster, even with the blockade.

If supplies of a certain food finally managed to reach a rural town, they had to pass through the central warehouse of the region, even if the product had been harvested two or three miles away from the place where it was to be consumed and the warehouse was thirty miles away. Instead of two or three miles, the product had to travel more than sixty miles; this raised the cost and wilted the produce. By trying to develop administrative machinery to collect all produce—even perishable goods—from a private sector of production consisting mostly of peasants with tiny farms, by setting prices that were often absurd, by doing nothing about a lack of trucks and over-all organization, Cuban administrators acted as if they wanted to deliberately provoke the development of a black market—which was not long at all in coming. In September 1963, a Spanish quintal of 46 kilograms of corn brought 15 *pesos* on the black market, compared to the official price of 4.50; beans brought 30 *pesos* instead of 11.50, rice 150 *pesos* instead of 15 (for average quality). A pound of meat—beef or pork—sold at 2 to 2.2 *pesos* instead of 43 *centavos,* a pound of coffee 3 *pesos* instead of 0.2, an egg 20 *centavos* instead of 6.

On certain *granjas* even the consumption of those workers who grew tubercules was rationed, and this hardly helped raise their spirits. For lack of milk cans[19]—and as usual for lack of reflection about the work being done—not all the milk could be

---

[18] The Ministry of Domestic Commerce.
[19] These should have had high import priority, coming before unused factories.

picked up; at times it was fed to calves and pigs, which under-utilized it. Chaos reigned in the supplying of means of production, which were very poorly distributed. An important cause of the late harvest of 1963 was the lack of files to sharpen the blades of the machetes used to cut the cane.

The bureaucrats of Havana had forgotten about them; this forgetfulness might have been less important *if each unit of production had the right to supply itself directly* instead of being obliged to predict in its budget so small an item as the number of nails to be used the following year. Gloves were needed for the cane-cutters, and the number of hours devoted by agronomists to the procurement of such things was wasted as far as their proper activity as technicians was concerned. The establishment of *direct commercial ties* by the various units, both as regards procuring supplies and having their produce picked up, would be a factor in increasing their efficiency, and a logical consequence of the financial autonomy they need so badly.

9. *Waste, rejection of the NEP, and volunteer work*

Prices in State restaurants up until 1962 were much too low, and this encouraged the wasting of food. There was so much excess money that the large increase in prices in 1963 did little to slow down this waste. My driver ordered four courses and ate only half of them, leaving on his plate large chunks of meat, which at that time was very limited on workers' tables, though there was more of it for workers who ate in the *comedores populares* (workers' canteens). Since I was paying for the meal, he was quickly warned that I was quite willing to pay for what he ate, but not for what he threw away—a statement he must have thought was most impolite.

Moreover, he can present the INRA with an unlimited bill for meals, to reimburse him for his expenses while traveling. If he had a daily lump sum for expenses, he might try to save some of it. He *might*—for the double heritage of feudal Spanish colonialism and the wasteful habits of the Yankee *nouveau riche* have not instilled in him the same respect for daily bread practiced so stringently by the European peasant when he had the same standard of living as today's Cuban *guajiro*.

In 1962, Cuba nationalized certain retail stores—hardware stores, dry goods stores, and clothing stores—despite the urgent warnings of experts.[20] Did the control necessary to impose strict rationing imply nationalization, and did it exclude the cooperative? Leaders responsible for the Cuban economy, though warned of the dangers of State management of this sort, risked drowning the rare qualified administrative personnel in a sea of details by replying: *"The Revolution cannot go backward."*

This attitude is reminiscent of that of the majority of Soviet leaders at the beginning of 1921. They were less aware than the popular masses of the true dimensions of the economic catastrophe which was then half under way, and which, if the leaders insisted on turning everything over to the State and denying those economic laws that are most valid for a socialist regime, would soon have meant the end of the Revolution and of the power of the Soviets. Lenin was the only one to see this clearly, and ordered, just in time, the application of the New Economic Plan, the famous NEP, which saved a revolution in mortal danger after an absurd application of poorly understood ideology.

The Cuban situation from March to November of 1962, was not, certainly, at the edge of an abyss comparable to the one that the U.S.S.R. confronted in 1921. Up until the hurricane, this was, however, the most difficult period with regard to the food situation. Counterrevolutionary store-owners delighted in putting a large portrait of Fidel in their completely empty shops, or one of the regime's slogans that circumstances had given an ironic twist to, such as "Socialism is Abundance." Many house-

---

[20] It is amusing to read the new signs along the street in Havana with the most stores: The Nationalized Paradise, The Nationalized Three Kings, Nationalized Philosophy.

wives were bitter about the situation, especially those who worked during the day and in the evening found little more than "garbage" at their grocer's, as I was told by a secretary at the INRA.[21] This encouraged families to have one unemployed person among their number, who would take care of getting food and keep on the lookout for every good chance that came along. Those who lived through the Second World War in Europe will understand this situation better.

Ania Francos' *La Fête Cubaine* described the Cubans' panache with a great deal of youthful and sympathetic enthusiasm. It is a revolution with an atmosphere of a socialist carnival—with *pachanga,* as Che Guevara liked to say. "The tropical rhythm of the dance and music accompanies the life of the Cuban people," G. Fournial emphasizes.[22] But I would hesitate to concur when he adds: "Work loses nothing thereby; quite the contrary." When he speaks enthusiastically about the battalions of volunteers going out to cut cane in the strong sunlight, he forgets the other side of the coin.

These Sunday volunteers were not paid, but their travel expenses were often estimated to be larger than the salaries normally paid for an equivalent job. When they failed to cut the cane right down to the ground, out of a lack of experience, the cane did not grow back right. And the sugar contained in the stub uselessly and harmfully left standing was lost. As for those who stayed longer, they continued to receive their city salaries, which were much higher than those of their new-found comrades on the job, though these latter worked much harder. They were also sent off too early in the season, in January and February, whereas it is in March and April, the period when the sugar content is the highest, that a great number of them are needed.

---

[21] She had a break of a quarter of an hour to go to the cafeteria, but on days when there was a lot of pressing work, her break lasted thirty-five minutes. Multiply this detail by the number of workers, add to it their negligence and indifference, and you will see *that socialism cannot put an end to underdevelopment by a purely political transformation.*
[22] *Cuba, éveil aux Amériques.*

This was certainly preferable to losing the cane, but it would have been better to remedy the economic errors and the lack of organization that caused this situation.

The 41,300 volunteer coffee harvesters from the province of Oriente, many of them scholarship students,[23] gathered only 7.8 per cent of the total harvest in 1962, Mestre emphasizes. And they picked an average of 1.06 boxes of coffee berries per day, as against an average of seven boxes for the other pickers, and twelve boxes for a large group of good workers. Since they managed to pick only one-twelfth of what a good harvester picks, and one-seventh of what a very average worker picks, they did not even pay back the amount spent for their food, lodging, and transportation. Moreover, such a slow pace provokes various reactions, and uncomplimentary remarks, on the part of workers used to such jobs.

There was then an attempt to justify this volunteer work, the unprofitable nature of which was admitted, by saying that it was of educational value. Because of their laziness, which cancels out this educational value, not enough strong arms could be sent elsewhere; 920 tons of coffee were lost in the Escambray zone, 90 tons at Pinar del Río. At certain times of day in 1963, the little corner cafés serving the *cafécito* so dear to the hearts of the little people in Havana had to put up signs saying: "No coffee."

A small cup of excellent, very strong coffee with lots of sugar was still being sold too cheaply, at three *centavos* (ten *centimes*)[24] per cup. The waitress poured it so fast that ten to twenty-five per cent of the liquid spilled over onto the saucers or the counter and was wasted: this was shocking only to Europeans raised in a peasant milieu. If the plantations had been better cared for, there would have been stocks of coffee on hand when the hurricane came, and it would not have been necessary to ask for Soviet cash to buy capitalist coffee in Brazil.

---

[23] The sons of workers and peasants, spoiled by the regime by being placed in the fine villas of Miramar—these students behave like social parasites, and this is accepted.

[24] About six and a half U.S. cents.

10. The middle-sized farmer is nationalized on October 4, 1963

In September 1963, Cuban leaders said that middle-sized farmers with property from 5 to 30 *caballerías,* or 67 to 402 hectares (those farmers whose future the regime did not guarantee) were leaving their farms half-abandoned. This was partially correct, especially with regard to the natural grazing lands, where the struggle against bushes that have grown back and other harmful growth, which must be kept up relentlessly, was often neglected. But this was not universally true, and we have seen several average-size farms near the Ecuador Refinery (in the west of the province of Camaguey) that were well kept.

Even with the owners absent, the two brothers at Varadero, a combined sugar cane and cattle-raising farm of 360 hectares that was easy to run, was getting on well, thanks in small part to the momentum it had acquired. Its 160 hectares of Pangola pastures fed 400 head of cattle of all ages, among them 30 draft oxen and 61 milch cows, allowing the farm to sell 60 tons of milk and 31 tons of meat per year. The cattle-raising was done by two permanent workers, and in addition workers put in about 500 workdays cleaning up the pastures and 100 work days mending fences; this manpower was equivalent to just a bit more than what would have been supplied by four permanent workers. In very round numbers, the work productivity on this *finca* appeared to us to be *four times higher* than on the milk *granja* Lidiel Hernández, near Havana. And this latter unit used more concentrated feed and represented a costly investment on the part of the Cuban State!

Absenteeism of the owner was also frequent on the cane plantations, where a very simple monoculture persisted, since everyone was familiar with the system and it was easier to control than it would have been after diversification. Several operations in particular needed close supervision: harvesting, replanting—this latter being behind schedule—weeding, and fertilizing. But the owners of farms with diversified crops, especially those with plantations (citrus trees, banana trees, papaya trees) participated more effectively in the running of the farm, some of them being on the spot every day, in which case they played a technical role that clearly was useful, indeed indispensable. On the *fincas* studied (which was too small a sampling), the workers spontaneously praised their bosses, in a climate of opinion where it was risky to do so. We thus feel justified in saying that relations were not universally bad.

This extreme variety of conditions should have brought about a more flexible sort of nationalization to solve the problem, with only useless absentee owners and those whose negligence was really obvious being driven off their lands. The other farmers might well have been allowed, at least temporarily, to remain at the head of their *fincas*.[25] In 1962, the private sector had, as a matter of fact, *fulfilled its obligation to deliver its products to the State much better* than the nationalized sector. And if Stalin's collectivization was harsh and cruel, Lenin for his part always advised the greatest prudence in this area. What with the disorder, the lack of discipline, and the correlative fall in productivity, the State sector could in no way be considered exemplary in 1963, as C. R. Rodríguez admits in *Cuba socialista.*

The social classification of agricultural units was decided *on the basis of their size,* which does not mean very much. Certain farms made up of 400 hectares of pasture lands, too poor to be worth cultivating, and therefore judiciously exploited as extensive cattle ranches, could be managed by a single family of three or four workers, without wage-earning employees, whereas farms of 67 hectares producing outer leaves for cigars under canvas, near Pinar del Río, required a whole battalion of workers representing the equivalent of a factory.

---

[25] This policy has been adopted in principle, but it may not always be observed: in order to reach such a point, a classification of owners must be drawn up, based on a thorough survey. Near Manzanillo, the local JUCEI insisted, in the summer of 1963, that an important cane grower be allowed to stay on despite having been absent for more than the month that is allowable, because he had the highest yield in the region.

After two days of rapid opinion polls around Havana, enough to reveal the gravity of the situation, I asked the Prime Minister to hear me out before making public "serious decisions" which hinted at the nationalization of middle-sized farmers. I had announced to him in August of 1960 that he was headed for trouble with his formula for the *granjas,* but since he had already made up his mind to nationalize his kulaks, he was ill disposed to hearing other warnings, for they always turned out to be unpleasant.

On October 4, 1963, he therefore nationalized farms of from 5 to 30 *caballerías,* or 67 to 402 hectares. The proportion of land nationalized thus passed from 49% to 70%. A group of eight thousand young people had been trained for this purpose in special schools, and on the morning of October 4th each of them took over a farm, which he was to manage in the state in which he found it, with the means at hand—which seemed reasonable enough. I had also proposed that the owners of farms who were still playing a useful role as technicians or work organizers be kept on as technical directors, with a share in the profits.[26] As for farms with absentee owners, plans might have been made to create combined crop-growing and cattle-raising units, or little production cooperatives out of them.

11. Enlisting the little peasant, who sometimes hangs back

In 1960 a national association of small farmers,[27] the ANAP, was set up, with a role which was too complex. It was, first of all, a mass organization, in charge of stirring up political support for the Revolution, of "maintaining the alliance of the working class and the peasants." But its functions also included offering technical assistance, advancing credit, and supplying various means of production and various services. At the end of 1963, plans were fortunately being made to separate these two

---

[26] Even if the State got only 50% of the profits, that would be better for it than the deficit incurred by the State farms.

[27] Those with less than 67 hectares (5 *caballerías*).

functions which were so different; the second of these was to come directly under the supervision of INRA.

With its 1,500 tractors (out of 14,000 in service on the island) and the machines at its stations, the SMAPS, the machinery service, performed large-scale agricultural operations such as plowing, harrowing, and in certain cases harvesting, for the peasants. This service was done on credit, and in 1962 the rate of non-reimbursement in certain districts was said to be as high as 90%.[28] It was a question, according to certain responsible officials, of not displeasing a peasantry that on occasion was less than enthusiastic. Even under these conditions, if gifts were going to be given the peasants, it would have been better to go about it openly and declare, for instance, that no one would have to pay for the first block of work done. It is a bad practice to accustom peasants to not settling their debts to a socialist state, as they already had a tendency to do with the preceding regime.

The prices charged for the work done were too low; working within a budget, each SMAP was aware only of money that had come in and was not aware of its real balance, of the amount of its deficit. This prevented it from studying the possibilities of wiping out this deficit. Because there were no mobile machine shops, tractors had to go fifty or sixty miles even for a minor repair, and line up at the door of a central machine shop that had more work than it could handle.

The tractor drivers in the SMAP at Ciego often did not work for nine to eleven days out of each month; if a tractor broke down, its driver continued to earn the average salary[29] that he

---

[28] The Ciego de Avila district was singled out as a good credit risk, for out of the 160,000 pesos of work done for it in 1962, 60,000 had been paid back by September 1963.

[29] This varied from 23 to 113 *pesos* every two weeks at Ciego. And this was largely due to the fact that the uniform rate of 21 *centavos* per 4 *ares* plowed took no account of the widely variable difficulties of plowing: in fact, in hardened clay it becomes impossible. The tractor drivers also would rather plow the large fields of the *granjas* than the peasants' little holdings, because the price per unit is the same. For this reason fields of less than one hectare are no longer plowed by the

had earned the week before without lifting a finger. In these conditions, he could hardly be expected to do his best to see that the tractor was repaired immediately so that he could get back to work as soon as possible; it was as if he had been put on half-pay while his tractor was broken down. And it would have been better still if he had been assigned manual labor meanwhile. In Cuba there is a sort of workers' aristocracy enjoying "special jobs," which on occasion goes so far as to look down on ordinary workers. In September 1963, the labor union representing drivers of heavy vehicles naturally protested against a decree that allowed these drivers to be assigned a more modest vehicle and receive a correspondingly lower salary in case their original vehicle broke down. The union officials called another meeting and the decision was then passed by unanimous vote. Communists are trained to organize unanimous votes such as this, but a decision of this sort is quite in the national interest, and it was the right move to try to convince the workers of this.[30]

Despite this aid, these credits,[31] and help in the technical field (that is not nearly enough), the number of little peasants withholding their support from the regime seemed to be much higher in 1961–1962 than in 1960. This holding back by the peasants had many causes: the absurdity of their relationships with the regime and of price levels, as well as the chaos in the pickup system, have played an important role.

SMAP. In 1963, they no longer laughed in my face in Cuba, as had happened to me in 1960, when I insisted on the need to promote the use of draft animals among the peasantry for a fairly long transitional period, since when all was said and done it was more efficient than a hand hoe.

[30] Certain people who come to the defense of the "free" world after having protested against these maneuvers in Cuba do not hesitate to call labor demands in their own country demagogic. The more imperfect a man is, the more possible it is—and this incident proves it—to appeal to his good will and his comprehension. He is therefore perfectible, but it is not possible to ask too much of him, and above all he must not be asked too precipitously. For his *day-to-day* level of enthusiasm is no longer that of the Sierra.

[31] The credits to private peasants, in particular for cane, have just been increased.

The peasants have often been reproached for selling an orange on the black market at 15 *centavos;* taro at 30 to 45 *centavos* a pound, instead of 7; chicken at 2 or 2.5 *pesos* a pound, instead of 43 *centavos,* and ham for as high as 7 *pesos* a pound.

This, C. R. Rodríguez states, exasperated comrades busy setting up a commercial system, local political directors, and the directors of the revolutionary armed forces. And certain of them "had an incorrect attitude toward the peasants, attempting to force them to sell their products to the INRA." As the counter-revolutionaries found accomplices, in the south of Matanzas and the southeast of Las Villas,[32] it was decided that all those who lent direct aid, and all the "middle-sized" landowners (200 to 400 hectares) who lent them even indirect aid, were to be expropriated.

In March 1962, at the national meeting of the joint revolutionary organizations, Fidel denounced the way in which these measures had been indiscriminately applied to everyone, rich and poor alike, by a sort of popular jury composed of agricultural workers; instinctively hostile to the peasants, these latter always took the drastic step of expropriating their lands. Therefore a certain number of pieces of property thus confiscated were later restored to their owners; those who were half-compromised, with a "weak" political consciousness, were sent back home. But peasant confidence in the regime had been shaken, and the peasantry withdrew somewhat within itself, thus contributing to the famine of 1962.

There was a tendency to ignore the fact that Acopio was not always in a position to officially buy everything that was produced, or that its prices did not always allow farm projects which in certain conditions were being carried on at a large loss to be continued. Farmers too must buy certain means of production, such as corn for their cattle on the parallel market, or even

---

[32] Ania Francos pointed out the existence of "an underground of five hundred insurgents" in the Escambray Mountains in March of 1961, and stated that "most of them were *small farmers* who were going underground with their sons."

such an item as shoes, which wear out faster in the fields than in offices.

Certain expulsions for nothing but trading on the black market resulted in transforming partisans or those who were hanging back into active enemies. In the summer of 1963 the militia engaged in vast encirclement maneuvers in order to capture counterrevolutionary underground fighters. These latter sometimes imprudently (or perhaps on purpose in order to increase repression?) kept lists of those who had helped them, but the names were always those of small peasants, never of important farmers; the strictest secrecy was kept with regard to the latter.[33]

Country-dwellers held back even more on account of the fear *of some day being deprived of free disposition of their little farms,* despite public assurances solemnly given by Fidel to the ANAP in July 1963.[34] Leaders claimed that small peasants were most hostile in districts where there was still a large proportion of middle-sized farmers who incited them to resist the regime. But things do not appear to be that simple; I was told that the nationalization of farms of from 5 to 30 *caballerías* increased people's fears for those that were from 2 to 5 *caballerías* (27 to 67 hectares). This is quite possible, for with farms this size in Eastern Europe farmers are classed as kulaks. In the face of the fear "that they will take our land" nothing will prevail, despite the fact that these little peasants willingly admit that they are earning more and living better than before the Revolution.

---

[33] In 1963 counterrevolutionaries often disembarked in groups of ten to twenty; once their barges had sunk, they fought with their backs to the wall, "like lions," according to the militiamen, for they knew that once they were captured they would immediately be shot. This was doubtless the lot of sixty of them who disembarked at the end of August, 1963, on the northern coast of Camaguey and were captured almost immediately. In Escambray, a militiaman told me, almost all the isolated peasants helped the underground. They were therefore "regrouped" in villages.

[34] After the nationalization of middle-sized farmers, Fidel confirmed that this measure represented the final step in agrarian reform.

12. *A little "cattle and crop-growing unit" is run correctly*

The idea of a cooperative grouping agricultural proletarians together was thus rejected in the end, in my opinion wrongly, as a way of administering the expropriated latifundia. The co-operative had to be provided with an authoritarian administrative body which would see to it that technical demands were met; this distinguished it from the democratic Scandinavian formula. But this framework permitted autonomy as regarded the day-to-day conduct of affairs, and each collective supposedly received only the value of the work that it put in. The ANAP, on the other hand, whose essential task it was to arouse the peasant's desire for large-scale collective exploitation of the land, was passing through the stage of little cooperatives, which were called "cattle and crop units" in Cuba. Gutelman has shown that very few of these units, of which there were 220 in 1962, were set up outside of Las Villas and Oriente. Out of more than 2,000 members, *less than 400 had contributed land,* which amounted to less than 7,000 hectares in all; but they had received from the State more than 10,000 additional hectares of land.

Unlike the majority of the other socialist countries, *no* political, moral, administrative, or even tax pressure has been applied to oblige the peasants to join cooperatives against their will. This forced collectivization would have a disastrous effect on propaganda in Indo-America on the part of a country that considers itself to be an example of socialism. But even more than the granting of credits for getting started, the State's donation of land is surely a much-appreciated advantage.

In a study entitled, "Four years of agrarian reform,"[35] the president of the INRA, C. R. Rodríguez, is of the opinion that "conditions necessary for developing close cooperation between

---

[35] *Cuba socialista,* May 1963. For those wishing information on the policies of those responsible for the Revolution, this theoretical publication is the most interesting one in Cuba.

peasants do not exist yet in Cuba . . . first of all because of the shortcomings of State agriculture, which do not incline private farmers toward socialist forms of production." Another reason is that the size of small peasant landholdings is larger in Cuba than it was in Eastern Europe; and because the present famine "instead favors the centuries-old inclinations of the peasant toward individualism."

There were only two of these units in the Ciego de Avila region. And one of these two, formed by little peasants who contributed land, was not doing well, and the project was about to be abandoned: "To go slowly but surely seems preferable," the local president of the ANAP said, paraphrasing Fidel. We visited the second unit, Adalberto Jiménez, which was located some seven miles from Ciego on the road to Morón. It was set up in December, 1961 (and officially recognized in March of 1963) by fourteen *agricultural workers* whose ages ranged from sixteen to fifty-six. Their case falls within the most general category: they contributed no land at all, and at their request received sixty-seven hectares. This almost "illegal" conception of the unit is just barely tolerated; but it is significant that in practice it is the most widespread: those who have nothing willingly share their lot. Here the whole fourteen of them contributed nothing but two small cows!

They nonetheless earned their sixty-seven hectares by the sweat of their brow, for their labor had to be expanded on a partially abandoned piece of uncleared land covered with brush. They cleared, leveled, and irrigated it, and constructed very simple houses without a single luxury for themselves. They would, of course, not have been able to do so without a credit of 10,000 *pesos* to get them started, but the potatoes and melons they grew allowed them to pay this back a few months later; they therefore had no trouble getting a second loan of 17,000 *pesos*. Let us stress, however, that their choice was not at all a bad one: the soil is fertile and irrigated, and the nearby village furnishes a good market. Conditions as good as this are not found all over the island.

The new rule governing these cattle and crop units provides

that once the members have been paid back what their contributions were worth, half of the *profits* will be distributed among the members, 30% will be put into investments for production, and 20% will be put into the fund for fringe benefits. This represents progress as compared to the 1960 project, since there are provisions for securing the means for development. These units are still quite far removed from the rules governing kolkhozes, which set aside money for taxes and amortization in proportion to the *profits* (which may be nonexistent, or the unit may even be running at a deficit) but rather in proportion to the *gross production*. The cane cooperatives have almost never shown a profit; there would not have been a single one that showed a profit if these units had had to pay ground rent and interest on the money advanced by the State. These units pay out advances on the members' customary wages, 2.75 *pesos* for an eight-hour work day all through the year, whereas the Soviet *troudoden* is a once-a-year residual balance, which often amounts to much less than the minimum legal wage.

These reservations aside, the unit we visited made a good impression; nothing there seemed to have been put on for show, prearranged for visitors, "à la Potemkin." The very simple account book, kept by a volunteer in addition to his regular work, seemed to be understood by everyone, despite a certain disorder. But it was their money, they kept an eye on it and knew where it went; this would not have been the case had it been the State's money. And above all the management of the unit was made easier by the modest size of the enterprise, which suited the possibilities of the moment very well. The crop plan is decided upon by the board of directors, consisting of four members, which meets every month. The president, who is elected for one year, does not have the superior attitude toward the simple "kolkhoz member" that I had noticed eleven months before in the U.S.S.R.

It would not be easy to duplicate these results elsewhere, obviously; a spirit of solidarity is necessary, which is more apt to be found at the beginning of a movement. Though in 1963 these members of the cooperative were paid by the day, standards will soon have to be adopted, so as to give to each according to the amount of work he performs. If one compares the enormous sums of money wasted on the *granjas* to the very modest credits that were granted here, with a strong likelihood that they would be paid back, *one cannot help but regret that such a formula, which is simpler to keep track of, did not come into general use on the land that was expropriated.* Had the available technical personnel been given authority, had cooperative leaders, future presidents, been more quickly trained, had enough educational pamphlets been provided—all measures that would have been less onerous than the errors made on the *granjas*—the necessary intensification of Cuban agriculture could have been prudently gotten under way in such a framework without overturning the systems of cultivation and radically changing the size of farms too rapidly.

This was not to prevent making the cooperatives subservient to the national interest, by making them play their part in the fulfillment of the Plan as it gradually came into being. In 1962, Gutelman, like the Cuban leaders, saw in these units "an intermediary step between private farming and the State farm." To this end "they will have to be much larger in the future." I believe that the difficulties involved in managing larger units make it advisable to be prudent. At the Congress of the ANAP on May 17, 1962, Regalado wanted "the members to have large profits, and as a result enjoy a standard of living *much higher* than that of other peasants."

13. A first tentative conclusion

Yes, that is something to be hoped for. However, this over-fervent desire, the *haste* with which the Cubans tried to fulfill it, while at the same time adopting so-called "superior" forms of property which lead to communism faster, are, along with underdevelopment, the essential causes of the present Cuban difficulties. The wish to quickly pass to social structures defined *a priori* in European books of the last century without seeing whether they suited either the Cuban situation or the Cuban mentality[36] has not thus far produced brilliant results. After making some progress in 1959–1960, due largely to a better distribution of wealth, the standard of living in Cuba remained stationary in 1961, and with strict rationing it went down perhaps 15% to 20% in 1962. The very slight rise in 1963, up until the hurricane, did not bring the country back to the 1960 level, despite considerable foreign aid, which was largely under-utilized.

The essential source that financed Soviet development, agri-culture, despite natural conditions that were much more favor-able, constituted *a dead weight to drag about at the beginning of the Cuban Revolution.* The State had to be the source of all the investments in the public sector, and on top of this pay enormous deficits which piled up one after the other.[37] In the

---

[36] Young Chinese and Cuban communists met in Havana in October, 1960. The former were greatly shocked by the latter's generous consumption of alcohol and cigars, and above all by their attitude toward women. Despite the "Chinese" orientation of a number of Cubans, their "moral" conception, let us say, of communism remains quite different, and life along the Vedado in Havana in 1963 was the polar opposite of the puritanism of Hanoi or Peking. The prostitutes have, it is true, been given other employment and been sent to school, but certain dancers at the Capri often take in money on the side: with so many men with too much money, it is very tempting. The "stars," who often eat in restaurants, and thus do not use their ration coupons, often trade these tickets to poor families in exchange for coupons for shoes or clothing. Former wealthy people who are hostile to the regime and high dignitaries among the revolutionaries make no bones about rubbing elbows in certain fashionable cabarets, without incidents, "in the Cuban way." But even though nationalized hotels to which prosti-tutes take their customers still welcome prostitutes making money on the side, it cannot be too highly stressed that the Revolution greatly raised moral standards. If morals are freer than in the other com-munist countries, prostitution is no longer the social abcess that it was when the Yankees came on junkets to Cuba. In this respect it would be difficult to do much better in such a short time.

[37] The *granjas* producing corn are operating in the red. Acopio buys their grain at 4.5 *pesos* but then sells it to a factory producing cattle feed for 3.7 *pesos*. This factory buys peanut oil cakes at the oil factory for below what they cost to produce, and still operates at a deficit. Deficits are quite common on cattle farms as well.

U.S.S.R. and in the popular democracies, farms generally are not as advanced as they should be, but this lag has been compensated for by rapid industrial development. But industrial development is not going forward as it should in Cuba, where too much unused equipment is piling up. The blockade is not the only cause of this. But the U.S.S.R. in 1928 was worse off than Cuba in 1963, despite the fact that before the Revolution it depended much less on the outside than Cuba did.

During this period Cuban political developments seemed less disappointing. The dangers of Stalinism, in its most negative form, were avoided by the exclusion, in March of 1962, of Annibal Escalante. Fidel was particularly shocked to see his most valiant comrades pushed aside on the pretext that they lacked Marxist-Leninist training. This training often seems to be done in a most unintelligent way. And Ania Francos notes: "certain comrades detached from the rebel army to form the national revolutionary police are beginning to take on a police mentality . . ."

Let us admit forthwith that contact with the Cuban policeman is a pleasanter experience than in most other countries, socialist or otherwise. And Cuba gives its artists and its writers much more latitude than Khrushchev, Graham Greene recently confirmed.[38]

On the occasion of the recent anniversary[39] of the attack against Batista's palace led by a handful of young people under the command of José Antonio Echeverría, the president read the political testament of this dead leader, leaving out one sentence: "We are convinced that the purity of our intentions will bring us God's favor, so that justice may reign in our country." Castro seized upon this omission and used it as the basic theme of his whole speech: "Can we be so cowardly, so morally crippled as to have the moral weakness to leave out these three lines? What sort of a concept of history is that? Can such cowardice be called 'the dialectical concept of history'? Can this way of thinking be

---

[38] *Le Figaro littéraire,* 26 October, 1963.
[39] March 13, 1962.

called Marxism? We know that one can be a revolutionary and have religious beliefs. The Revolution does not do violence to men, it does not tamper with their personal convictions. It excludes no one . . . Let us speak of the comrade who received the order to skip this sentence. He is a poet. He wrote a little collection of poems and among them was one entitled 'A Prayer to the Anonymous God.' At the beginning he spoke to me of his religious convictions and later he confessed to me that he had gotten a complex! How could he help having a complex when on the way here he receives an order forbidding him to read this sentence? What is the Revolution becoming? A school for domestic animals. And that is not a revolution." And Graham Greene judiciously concludes: *"A new voice has been heard in the communist world."*

I would have liked so much to be able to stress Cuba's economic accomplishments with similar enthusiasm. In this field innovations are beneficial only if they profit as much as possible from the experience of others, whether these others are socialists or not. But repeating and prolonging the same cycle of errors as the U.S.S.R., errors based on theories that have been abandoned in the country in which they originated when the first results of these theories proved how dangerous they were, cannot be approved. To a lesser degree than elsewhere, one nonetheless still encounters in Cuba a certain *lack of humility in the face of the facts, in the name of very questionable interpretations of a doctrine that was never intended to be rigid; this is the greatest threat hovering over the future of socialism.* The classic co-operative formula was harder to fulfill at the beginning, but the State structure has given too poor results. It is no longer possible to state outright that a cooperative formula reconciling technical authority with autonomous management and a wage structure depending on production would clearly be worse.

Let us repeat that criticism is comparatively easy, that the Cuban leaders have had to face difficult situations and have been obliged to resort to certain improvisations. Those who are most pragmatic cannot change course too abruptly, for they must first thoroughly study the effects of the measures adopted. But all this aside, we still must try to describe exactly how this sort of "bureaucratization" of units of production that were too large and managed from too far away, following the "centralized budget" formula, got the Cuban economy into the difficult situation that we were witness to on the eve of the hurricane of October 6–10, 1963.

4

Management Through a Centralized Budget, or "Bureaucratization" of the Cuban Economy

1. The situation improves before the hurricane, but too slowly

The low point of disorder, if not of privations, seems to have been reached in 1962. At the time of my last visit, late in the summer of 1963, a number of signs were encouraging, most importantly the positions taken and the speeches given by those leaders most aware of the possibilities and the limits of the Cuban economy, such as Carlos Rafael Rodríguez, the president of the INRA, and the president of the republic Osvaldo Dorticos, who is also president of the Economic Council.

Fidel's speeches during the summer of 1963 revealed a greater awareness of the gravity of the situation, and forthrightly stressed certain economic difficulties. Largely under the influence of Charles Bettelheim's studies, in mid-August and then again at the beginning of November 1963, he proclaimed publicly that "for the next ten years agriculture ought to be the basis of the Cuban economy." This more concrete vision of the realities represents a turning point that in some respects is comparable to that of the Chinese "readjustment" of 1962–1963, another probable source of inspiration for Fidel and his supporters. The need for importing equipment would thus be reduced, and so would Cuba's debts, and as a consequence the country would be less dependent on the U.S.S.R.

The primacy of agriculture took the concrete form of *giving absolute priority to the production of sugar cane,* which was considered to be the country's prime source of cash, and therefore of the possibility of buying goods. Despite the Yankee blockade, this was not a "besieged fortress," as was the case with the Russians from 1920 to 1940. Giving priority to heavy industry would be meaningless strategically, especially when the country was confronted with the greatest industrial colossus in the world, the United States. Fortunately, the overautarchic conception of the economy of 1959–1961 was abandoned, and because of its situation Cuba was proclaimed to be wide open to foreign commerce. Technicians were once again given better posts, and the data needed for planning were less sketchy. And finally, great priority was given to scientific and technical research, which had been neglected at the beginning of the Revolution. And above all, solid progress was made as regarded organization, discipline, and work.

In numerous fields such as agricultural education, however, this climb upward seemed to be too slow. Despite useful press campaigns, especially on the part of the Communist daily *Hoy,* an effort to organize work or to lower costs was still not the prime concern of all those responsible for production units: their awareness of economics was still not as great as it should have been. The militiaman's devotion to the Revolution did not make up for his general lack of professional qualifications, which deprived him of the technical knowledge he would need to prove himself a capable, alert professional.

This lack of technical training was often accompanied by a lack of political maturity in minds which were less rational, less well trained to analyze than ours, and therefore tempers were liable to flare up very quickly. Following the political campaigns without always understanding them perfectly, local leaders lived amid an atmosphere of faith and devotion such that they were not always aware of the difficulties and thus found it hard to recognize their errors in time, even though this was indispensable. If people repeat often enough that everything is going well, they end up believing it; this was true even of the Chinese leaders at the time of the "Great Leap Forward."

A political mechanism cannot function as smoothly if this mentality comes into play too frequently. Mass organizations, copied on the Soviet model, functioning too exclusively as "transmission belts" for power, do not do a proper job of communicating the principal desires of the popular masses to those in power. These organizations did not protest as much as they should have against the many local absurdities which were the end product of the rigid monopoly of collection and distribution and which played their part in jeopardizing the supplying of goods to the population. If labor unions seemed a little too subservient to the former leaders of the Communist Party, the Committees in Defense of the Revolution, the famous CDR, gave the appearance of working better. And the rebel army had always been better organized because it was better disciplined amid disorder that was all too widespread.[1]

It was thus not by chance that the most inspired step toward decentralization, the creation of provincial and local juntas to control projects and execute them, the JUCEI, was taken on the initiative of Raúl Castro. Arriving in Oriente to organize militia there, he found everything in a mess and immediately sought to remedy the situation, for he was not one to allow disorder to creep into his bailiwick. These JUCEI will be completely effective only if local units of production are turned over to them entirely; this is being tried out at present, but not on a large enough scale. The term "local" should be taken in a very broad sense, and bring about the dissolution of the "consolidated enterprises" directed from Havana in cases where they group together only small and middlesized units of production that are too widely scattered. In turn, the provincial JUCEI should let these units enjoy a very broad autonomy; otherwise getting out from under the thumb of the bureaucrats in the capital only to fall into the clutches of certain little local tyrants will hardly constitute progress. But the local leader in Santiago can realize what is going on much more easily than one in Havana, which is six hundred miles away.

---

[1] The author is an anti-militarist, but he has never seen such a look of goodness as that in the eyes of the major building the immense boarding school (which, with 20,000 pupils, is too big) in Oriente at the foot of the Sierra Maestre.

The Woman's Federation[2] seems to be playing a useful role in educating Cuban women and finding them a place in the country's economic and social life. It is trying to get them out of the over-rigid, futile, and oppressive roles they played before 1960–that of a middle-class helpmeet, of a working-class housewife, if not a prostitute. If three-quarters of the 1962–1963 cotton crop was successfully harvested despite difficulties, it was thanks to the mobilization of these women by their federation: the harvest cost more than it would have ordinarily, but the work had to be done. At the level that the Cuban economy has reached, putting women to work could, with better organization, be less taxing for them and require less arduous toil than the jobs assigned Soviet and Chinese women. For in the final analysis these latter bear a large share of the burden of the insufficient and sometimes mediocre organization of the socialist economy.

2. Haste leads to errors: palm and coconut trees

The influence of Nuñez Jiménez, who was not replaced as the head of INRA until the end of 1961, eighteen months after the havoc he had wrought already seemed quite obvious, continues to prevail in that organization because of the consequences of his errors, which have not always been recognized in time. A large shipment of Para rubber-plant seeds of unknown origin that he ordered arrived in Cuba at the beginning of 1963. Since this typically "equatorial" plant is too marginal to grow in the Cuban climate (though North Vietnam with its exaggerated tendency toward self-sufficiency grows it), a technician succeeded in preventing the seed from being heedlessly sown.

Also ordered in 1960 or 1961, 810,000 oil-palm seeds (Guinean *Elaeis*) arrived, their place of origin again unknown because of the negligence with which orders such as this were

---

[2] I asked one leader what the Federation was doing to remedy the serious agricultural situation. Disconcerted by such an unusual question, she told me that only the board of directors was qualified to give an answer; I was promised a reply to my question, but it never came.

put in. Put in charge of cultivating them in the summer of 1963, Gutelman suggested to Fidel, who took this matter in hand personally, that instead of planting the 2,500 hectares possible with these seeds, only the 400 acres necessary to supply a profitable little refinery be planted, as an experiment. Cuba does not have enough rainfall for oil palms, and it is therefore necessary to irrigate it; it also has temperatures that may drop as low as 43 degrees Fahrenheit, which made Gutelman hesitate even more.

With seeds of unknown origin, it was not reasonable to think of making the enormous expenditures demanded by a modern plantation. The moment the seedlings were put in beds, the Cuban press went into ecstasies about the quick growth of the little plants. Fidel wanted to forge ahead; he was pressed for time. At the Paris IRHO[3] these seeds were identified as being of the *Dura* variety. It was finally learned in Africa that these seeds had simply been picked up on the ground underneath perfectly ordinary trees!

Though they had tried to hurry things along, the Cubans did not manage to cut down the time required to get production started, for unselected trees produce at a later age. These Dura trees, even if they are in good condition, will not yield as much as 8 tons at 14% oil per hectare, whereas the latest varieties of the IRHO yield 13 tons at 20% oil; thus the gap in yield is on the order of 1,120 kilograms at the maximum for the unselected seeds, as against 2,600 kilograms for selected seeds. The purchase of selected seeds would cost $40,000 and in less than twelve years' time the difference in value at harvest time as compared to unselected seeds would reach the sum of $11 million. It is hard to find a more profitable investment than the purchase of quality seed if it is a question of costly crops that take a long time to mature; the price of seeds is absolutely negligible as compared to the other expenses, and it is a decisive factor as regards volume of production, and therefore cost of production.

---

[3] The Institute for Research on Palm Oil and Other Oils, whose activity was described succinctly in my *L'Afrique noire est mal partie*.

In an even more careless fashion, 10 million coconuts were ordered from Colombo, Ceylon: enough to fill the holds of several ships. Luckily the shipments could be stopped after the arrival of the first boat, which was about to bring in 1.4 million coconuts. Snakes and rats were also found in the hold, several of them species thus far unknown on the island that might have multiplied dangerously. A cryptogamic disease that attacked both banana trees and palm trees was raging in Ceylon and might also have been brought in by these coconuts.

When the cargo arrived, it was thoroughly disinfected, but this did not do away with the parasite fungus; instead it killed, along with the snakes and the rats, all the young shoots from the coconuts that had germinated during the voyage. The first coconuts of a lot to germinate are the best, the earliest, and the most productive; this is even a means of selection. It was not even known whether these coconuts would resist a virus that periodically decimated the coconut trees of the Caribbean, nor whether they had been specially selected: it seemed likely that they had not been, in view of the large number of them. I advised shipping the remaining coconuts to a refinery to extract the oil from them; they were instead set out in seedbeds, with a few quarantine precautions, without it being known whether these measures will be adequate. And the plants obtained will not be any more profitable than the palm trees we have just spoken about.

The decision to grow more coconut trees and oil palms in Cuba will probably result in their being a more important source of oil than the annual crops of peanuts and sesame, which are so burdensome to grow. And they will doubtless be more important than sunflower seeds, which are not really suited to Cuban conditions and were carelessly recommended by Moldavian and Ukrainian experts homesick for the plants of their homeland. But to carry out an operation that continues to be risky (for palm trees have many enemies in the Caribbean, among them hurricanes), the operation must have as many chances of success as possible in its favor. *Audacity* and *haste* are often necessary in guerrilla warfare. But when it is a question of any sort of technical innovation, the prudence of a Sioux becomes absolutely indispensable; and even so, it is hard to predict the many difficulties that will arise. A revolutionary geographer ought to know better than anyone else that bringing in new crops is not an easy task, or else know his limits and call on agronomists for information.

A specialist in the particular crop they had in mind should have been called in, so as to ask him whether the Cuban environment was suitable, and then he should have been asked in which microregion the chances of success were greatest. Then the varieties and hybrids that were the best adapted, the most resistant, the earliest, and the most productive should have been acquired.[4] Then Cuban technicians should have had practical training in growing this crop, in Africa if nearby Colombia didn't want to have them there. Meanwhile the new crop should have been entrusted to a qualified foreigner, who would also educate his assistants on the spot. Like Khrushchev with his corn-beets-peas trilogy (which was to be a success all over the U.S.S.R., from Moscow to Alma-Ata), *Fidel is the only one who makes decisions, in technical fields that he cannot be sufficiently familiar with to make the right decisions:* to each his own métier. The necessity of doing things fast must not make leaders unmindful of the dangers of precipitate haste. Cuba's present difficulties are partially due to this *underestimation of a basic concept in modern economics, the primordial importance of technique.* However, *the general conception of managing the economy,* such as it is defended by certain leaders, still represents *the greatest obstacle to Cuban development.*

3. Unrealistic, ultra-optimistic planning

Socialist planning thus replaces "the invisible hand of profit" which in a capitalist regime corrected many errors through management that had definite pre-established goals. Substituting his reasoned will for automatic mechanisms, man must be better informed than he is by the "law of the market place" if he is to be able to intervene in the proper way.

---

[4] This has just been done.

A few hours spent in gathering information in the department of statistics of the INRA showed me that, apart from the figures dealing with the pickup of products by the State commercial system, there was little information available, and what was more serious still, the people involved did not always realize this. After having shown the lady in charge of animal production that most of her figures were false, for the facts (which she had tried in no way to check) did not jibe, I said approximately this: "A capitalist regime can function with information-gatherers as bad as this, for the law of supply and demand tends to re-establish the balance, but socialist planning can't work well."

This was all the more true in that from the beginning this planning tried to regulate too much, attempting as it did to decide even small details. With such imperfect knowledge, it would have been reasonable to be content with a general policy, fixing only the desired *quantities of the principal products,* but not the way of reaching such a goal. Because it tried to regulate the surface area that should be devoted to each crop by each *granja,* this goal was not achieved straightway: as late as September, the plans for 1963 had not yet reached the people concerned. These *granjas* were therefore allowed to carry out their own projected plans, which allowed for too much diversification.

Sometimes there was repeated outside intervention in order to set things right. There were thus areas that were replowed every time a new crop was decided on, and in the end they were never sown. The plans depended on means of production that were not forthcoming; thus an enormous amount of effort was wasted, what with so many unfinished jobs, so many fields not cleared, or harvested too late, so many orchards where the fruit was not picked: this was due in large part to the unrealistic nature of most of these plans.[5] It is not enough to describe

---

[5] See in *Revolución,* October 1963, the article entitled "Errors and success of the Cuban experience," in which Che Guevara mentions the plan for shoe production in 1962, which called for the production of 22 million pairs when Cuba had never manufactured more than 10 million. He underlines the excessive importance given to the satisfaction of

them as optimistic, for churning out a series of hypotheses that were extremely favorable, always accepting the rosiest, never foreseeing any breakdown of materiel, nor any shortage of raw material, nor any break in supply lines, nor any unpredictable expense is ultra-optimism.

The most serious side of all this is that those responsible for the economy, perhaps to mask their first failures from Fidel's eyes, announced, immediately after their plans had not been fulfilled, extravagantly optimistic results for the following year. Thus *for a long time the gravity of the situation was not fully grasped by the leaders of the Revolution.* They would perhaps have hesitated to take measures as bold as the nationalization of farms from 67 to 400 hectares if they had really realized that the productivity of agricultural work in the State agricultural sector was often not even half of that of the private sector.

To each his own responsibilities: the directives put out by these revolutionary leaders for the execution of the plans did not go into enough detail about the political policy behind them. This obliged the officials carrying out the plan (Juceplan) to adopt trial-and-error measures from day to day, trying to plug up the principal holes: this is the opposite of a planned economy, which must see far ahead. In order to make these directives more precise, the leaders should have made a more thorough analysis of the situation, seeking out not only the errors, but "their theoretical causes, their circumstances, and their details, so as to be able to rectify them," in the precise words of President Mao. In order to do this, *the major reasons for the present difficulties* should have been sought out.

First of all, as Che recognizes: "One cannot plan down to the very last detail, since economic conditions do not permit this." However, he adds shortly thereafter: "Once underway, it is dangerous to stop, and even more dangerous to retreat, for that is the death of Revolution . . . so we proceed in depth, *vio-*

---

social needs, the tendency of the first plans to be too self-sufficient, "the fundamental error of underestimating the importance of sugar cane," and "the inrealizable ambition to increase the national revenue by 15 or even 20% per year."

lently." Had Lenin reasoned in this fashion, he never would have embarked on the New Economic Plan, the Soviet Revolution would perhaps not have survived, and this would have compromised the chances of the Chinese, and more particularly the Cuban, Revolution. But Lenin had long prepared himself for his tasks as a statesman, and circumstances forced him to be one, which was not the case for the Cuban guerrillas, who arrived in power faster than they had foreseen.

The editorial in *Revolución* prefacing Che's article states more accurately: "The leadership of the Revolution has occasionally tried to go too fast. Measures taken at the wrong moment or with excessive haste . . . lead to enormous waste of human and material resources, to bureaucratic delays, and in the end they will slow down the forward movement of the Revolution." This appears to apply just as well to the Chinese "Great Leap Forward" and the corollary "madnesses" of 1959, the little foundries in the countryside and the rural popular communes, which slowed Chinese progress. In Cuba the socialization of restaurants and hotels, even little ones, of artisans, and of a large section of retail trade seems to be of dubious value: it is certain that a cooperative formula would have been much more suitable here.

Another pitfall, which we have already alluded to, was the lack of diagnostic analysis and basic statistics, which led to the establishment of impossible or contradictory objectives. This often was the result of the habit, already too deep-rooted, of making *the essential decisions at the top,* without really consulting the base, whose only duty was to confirm the decisions made in advance in congresses composed of comrades who were often more fervent than they were aware of their responsibilities.

4. The fundamental error: administration, a "perfect clock mechanism"

In his article written in Algiers in July 1963, and printed in *Revolución,* Che begins by placing the blame on the Soviet experience: "We automatically copied the experiences of our brother countries and that was an error." At first there was no copying, but rather original measures, "a certain mixture of de facto anarchy and gigantic formal 'organizationism' that was not entirely unknown to the Russian Revolution," Mazoyer says. And it never was a question of *copying;* but it would be exaggerating matters to deduce from this that it is no longer necessary now *to take other socialist experiences into account.* Che compares self-management, the financial autonomy granted to Soviet enterprises, to the system applied in his Ministry of Industry, called *budgetary calculation.* The enterprise has no capital; *it is only a specialist* that must deliver the product of all its activity to the Ministry of Finances, which in turn furnishes the money necessary for managing it. He takes an objective tack when he says that "the comparison of these two tendencies [i.e., budgetary calculation and self-management] . . . favors the development of a less rigid system of planning." In reality, only the first tendency continues to be defended and applied by his administration.

In the house organ of his Ministry, in March of 1963, Che justified his system of financial control, which was more centralized than it had been at the beginning, showing not the slightest trace of the autonomy that long experience led the U.S.S.R. to give to units of production. "We are a small country, with good communications overland and in the air, by telephone, and by radio, which makes continuous daily control possible. The bank gives the units the amount of money their budget requires, without interest . . . the product remains a process of internal flow which becomes merchandise only when it changes owners or passes to consumers . . . The unit has no money of its own, and all its receipts go into the national budget."

He believed he could improve this "central control of the economy, with great centralization of decisions" by a "more and more perfect system of economic analysis, an analysis of costs with standards for the consumption of raw material, the indirect costs, the products being produced, and the inventory of raw materials and finished products. The control of inventories must be systematized and all its indices must be made the object of economic study . . . cost control must be established." And he concludes: "We must get to the point where management becomes a perfect clock mechanism." From management by radio from an air-conditioned office to the "perfect" mechanism, we are surrounded by the "clouds" that Fidel referred to.[6] Around 1920 Bukharin denied that there was such a thing as laws of economics; this was more excusable then, since the socialist experience had not yet taken place. Only an armchair economist, with *no practical notion* of how to run an enterprise, either an industrial one or an agricultural one, could imagine that it might one day attain the "perfection" of a chronometer, above all when it is managed by telephone. Several months' training at the head of a *granja* or a factory would give Cuban leaders a useful contact with reality. As Chinese wisdom dictates, "the leaders and managers of enterprises partially participate in the work of production, while the workers partially participate in the daily management of production . . . Participation in work allows administrative personnel to maintain their status as ordinary workers, [and] prevents them from enjoying privileges, divorcing themselves from the masses, and degenerating."[7]

5. Management of units through a centralized budget, a major cause of Cuban difficulties

Other arguments are advanced for this ultra-centralization, such as the lack of trained, competent personnel at the management level. This shortcoming should instead be one more reason to give production units maximum autonomy. An untried technician is far less likely to notice defects, and in particular the

---

[6] "[We must] first get a firm footing on realities, make them our point of departure, and not forget them. Not live in the clouds but on the earth, know what our problems are today and solve them, what our problems will be tomorrow and solve them." Speech by Fidel, April 10, 1963, printed in *Cuba Socialista,* May, 1963.

[7] *Pékin-Information,* no. 18, 28 octobre, 1963.

causes of these defects. He therefore transmits incomplete, if not erroneous, information to the top level. There is then an enormous bottleneck of useless information at the Center, such as the files on tobacco at the statistical service of the INRA.[8]

If more responsibility is granted local leaders, they are in a better position to check the information furnished on the spot. And with all the local resources there are for making deals, they are in a much better position to cope with difficulties in getting supplies, spare parts, and manpower. From a distance, people's insufficient knowledge of a situation leads them to make the wrong move. "A centralized management of all units of production would presuppose a specific and almost instantaneous analysis of costs and of all the limiting factors. And the construction of models of operational research that even the largest electronic machines could not handle at present because of the quantity of data that must be processed. No economy in the world, not even the American or the Soviet economy, is sufficiently standardized, analyzed, and statistically researched to allow the construction of such over-all models. Clockwork is still several decades off, for it must wait until the gathering of economic information has become almost perfect and not very expensive. In the meantime, Cuba should attempt to manage one, then two, then three units and determine the right location and the optimum size for its new economic activities . . ." (Mazoyer). This centralization, as Charles Bettelheim stressed in 1962, diminishes the initiative and the powers of imagination of the management personnel in charge on the spot. Only autonomy allows for the rapid training of the only technicians who are worth anything, those who are hammered into shape amid difficulties and daily responsibilities.

Those who have learned what they know of the Soviet economy in the manual translated by P. Nikitine do not know that he is nowadays considered out of date in the U.S.S.R. In

---

[8] These unique documents can be taken out much too easily: thus all the files of any use, if they ever existed, have already been removed by bureaucrats too lazy to have them copied.

October 1963, a much more up-to-date treatise appeared in Moscow, under the aegis of the Academy of Sciences. The only book on agronomy with wide circulation in Cuba is Lysenko's, and for a number of his proposals the term "erroneous" would be more appropriate than the term "out of date." Much better studies appear in the U.S.S.R. but the needs of propaganda, along with the fear of heresy, which still are primary concerns in the department of publication in foreign languages prevent the best of them from being exported.

The leaders of *granjas* who receive contradictory directives from different technical bureaus too often take two different tacks. The first consists of relying on superiors, executing their orders even if they seem stupid. I have seen seeds being sown too late to give a profitable harvest; it would have been better not to have undertaken the sowing of them at all and to have replaced them with another crop better suited to the season. But I was told when I asked that "we are just carrying out orders" —and my informants added that they knew that these orders were wrong! If the workers were "on their own" within *small* units, in cooperatives with technical leaders with authority at the head of them, they would soon stop taking this easy way out.

The second tack consists of deciding that Havana never has any idea of what is going on, and therefore its instructions are ignored and the local leaders do as they please. This turns out all right in the end more often; but *without control this can lead to abuses.* On the island of Turriguano, Major Fajardo had not put enough forage aside for his magnificent pure-bred Santa Gertrudis herd of cattle, and therefore the herd had more deaths in the first half of 1962 than it had births during the whole year. By foreseeing the need for additional feed during each dry season, they could have held out during the great drought.[9] Planting the rich pasture lands in Pangola, and making hay and silage would have allowed such a massacre to be avoided.

---

[9] In 1961, instead of thinking of the immediate future of his herd, he built "Dutch" villages as a popular tourist attraction, and a magnificent hall for exhibiting prize cattle!

In 1962–1963, Fajardo finally got around to planting his artificial pastures. Instead of plowing up his best land for this purpose (under the false pretense that it had already been made into pasture land; so it had been, but it was very run-down) as was done on the western tip of the island in 1960, he attacked the calcareous "dientes de perro" with a bulldozer; but the hardy Pangola managed to grow there anyway! But the cost of clearing land with these outcroppings of rock that should be left forested is much higher and the yield in grass is very small. Moreover the animals will ruin their hoofs as they graze on these hard, pointed rocks. In any case, there is no possibility of cutting the superabundant grass that grows in summer in order to store it, a procedure that is indispensable to intensive methods of utilizing pasture lands.

The result of trying to create a formally centralized organization is more or less a state of anarchy at the base, where anything goes, because there is no control of essentials. If day-to-day management were autonomous, allowing the base to take care of the many details, the top would have the time it needs to efficiently control all basic policy and make all necessary decisions at this level—in particular those required by the large investment projects, those budgeted at more than $100,000 for example. The more important a project is, the more thoroughly it should be studied.

We have already spoken of the serious consequences of errors in locating units, the piling up of costly unused machinery, and factories being run without sufficient raw materials or producing goods at excessive cost.

The essential cause of such mistakes is often the fact that preliminary studies were not adequate, and they have not always been replaced by good sense, for it is often in short supply: there is underdevelopment here, too. Demanding an exhaustive study is never time wasted, as we have seen in the case of the palm trees; it is, rather, the best way of reducing waste. But under the pressure of events, it has often been necessary to act without information and without trained personnel; these are nonetheless indispensable.

A Minister should not be obliged to telephone personally to settle some minor problem having to do with wire,[10] or to intervene when a construction foreman and a worker exchange blows: having been driven out by the former, the latter was taken back into his labor union. The foreman insisted on leaving at that point, for he saw that he was losing all his authority. The intervention of the Party was not enough; the matter had to go as high as the Ministerial level. Under these conditions the Minister no longer has the time to do his real job. His real job ought to be to spend half his time on the *granjas,* accompanied by two assistants, a technician and an economist, so that he can weigh the factors entering into the most important decisions.

A corps of inspectors could likewise examine all proposals at the top and middle level of importance, and thus a stop could be put to the many fantasies of *granja* leaders. These latter, on the other hand, would be allowed all possible leeway (once those who are incapable are removed from their posts, as is already beginning to be done) in day-to-day management, ordering supplies, and even engaging in commercial transactions; they would be treated as real heads of production, with the salary and the consideration that they deserve. This salary ought to be much higher than those now paid high-level functionaries in the capital. Instead of wasting their time drawing up "budgets" that must foresee every last tool that will be required, they would receive bank credits *that would have to be paid back with interest* for all their expenses. Because this is not done, the *granjas* lose a great deal of time exchanging spare hammers for excess nails among themselves.

Charles Bettelheim wisely advises *limiting centralization* to what is necessary for planning by decentralizing those day-to-day decisions that constitute management in the proper sense of

---

[10] Wire is in short supply, and yet *granjas* uselessly fence in uncleared fields of marabou that they do absolutely nothing with. South American landowners whose title deeds were doubtful, if not forged (a Brazilian specialty), felt a need to lay out concrete property lines where land was in dispute. But who today can dispute the rights of the Cuban State?

the word. And he stresses the advantages that China has secured through a more thorough use not only of resources but of *local initiative*. I have shown how the U.S.S.R. benefited from the greater autonomy granted the kolkhozes in the years 1953–1958, for a rapid advance in production took place in those years, and I have also pointed out that the resumption of State management of them in 1958 did not give satisfactory results.

The present need to use rare resources to the fullest is not an argument in favor of centralization. The present conditions of pickup of goods and redistribution are so bad that an effort should be made to find the shortest possible distribution routes. Each unit should be able to get supplies and deliver goods itself, providing it observes the rationing regulations. Rationing, moreover, should be done away with very soon, for it wastes a great deal of time.

We have pointed out other causes of Cuba's economic difficulties, such as price inequities, and above all the lack of balance between wages and prices, leading to a dangerous excess of cash in the pockets of the consumer. The guaranteed daily wage, which is high and is paid no matter how much work has been done, has relaxed work discipline, especially in view of the fact that there is a predominant feeling now that no one is ever fired, however little work he does. All these shortcomings are in large measure *consequences of the absence of financial autonomy*. Were there such autonomy, it would oblige the leaders of production units seeking to balance their budgets to keep a close eye on the salary level and eliminate the shirkers, whose example is disastrous.

6. *Ultra-centralism leads to bureaucracy rather than cooperation*

The Cuban leaders are critical of bureaucratic tendencies. To hear some of them, these tendencies would seem to be a sort of mysterious and contagious disease raging in administrative units and nationalized enterprises through the fault of bureaucrats and employees who have no resistance against this virus. It would be better to analyze the causes of these tendencies, which are essentially linked to centralization. Centralization gets the worker in the habit of looking toward the leader by leaving this latter all the responsibility. With the exception of a few of them, such workers turn into cogs in a machine from the moment that they must refer to their superior even when it is a question of petty details. Other causes of a bureaucratic cast of mind exist in Cuba, such as the rise of a new social level that is often "petit bourgeois" in character.

Those in charge of the Revolution are splendid personalities, whose honesty and courage are unquestionable, since they were on the firing line in April 1961. They therefore have nothing in common with most present African governments. They are men, however, and therefore fallible by essence; for this reason alone, it is not advisable to give them too much power and leave the base, especially the peasants, with too few possibilities of expressing their desires. The Cuban people's patriotism is still magnificent, despite the fact that their enthusiasm for the Revolution is not as fervent in 1968 as it was in 1960; once the intoxication of coming into power was over, people realized that they had inherited many difficulties. However, even opponents of the regime are willing to risk their lives and get killed by Americans in case there is an invasion. Nonetheless this does not prevent them from condemning, sometimes quite rightfully, the incompetence, the overweening ambition, the disorder and the slogans that seem out of place when there is not enough food on the table.

Between leaders and the people there is a very heterogeneous group of people such as minor civil servants, clerks in American companies, office helpers, typists, and salesgirls . . . As an approximate general rule, their insufficient knowledge does not permit them to be teachers, engineers, or technicians; they do have a little education, however. Some of them have left the country, and others have rallied to the regime, often sincerely; and certain of them may think that it is in their interest to mouth the slogans of the day. It is they who fill the revolutionary offices, having been promoted to jobs that sometimes are beyond their capacities.

There are more and more of them each year, and there is not

enough work for all of them. The amount of useful work produced appears to be even less in certain administrative offices than on the *granjas*.[11] Laziness, which is the general rule in some offices, has an influence on the productivity of the other sectors. The cane-cutter no longer is unaware of what happens in the city, where there are now "workers like himself." This does not encourage him to work a great deal harder in the burning sun at much less pay than that received by the majority of bureaucrats more or less lazing about in air-conditioned offices. And these latter can enjoy the city lights and city pleasures, movies, a more intellectual atmosphere, more chances to get interesting jobs, cars, and houses . . .

Successive campaigns at INRA to weed out those who are lukewarm supporters have sometimes replaced those who are competent but neutral by supposed partisans whom it would sometimes be more accurate to call social climbers. The hiring of more employees, a consequence of centralization, increases the proportion of employees who do not put out very much work, and scatters responsibility so that it becomes less and less clearly defined, for lack of organization. What is more serious still, each Minister pays the salary of functionaries on the stand-by list, waiting in the wings, so to speak, for no work is demanded of them, and meanwhile there is a shortage of manpower in the fields. It was thought that the situation could be improved by changing department heads, but the new heads must become familiar with their jobs, and this takes a long time. Improvement was also sought by changing the famous tables of organization, such as the one that provided for 350 jobs for just the Economy section of the INRA, when the U.S.S.R.'s Gosplan long functioned with 150 persons: happily this table of organization was never followed.

This administrative management of an economy that has too many functionaries also corresponds to *a refusal to cooperate effectively* in the fields of agriculture, labor, and distribution.

---

[11] Fortunately there are numerous happy exceptions, such as the Division of Physical Planning.

Within the framework of a socialist economy, it might, however, have rendered the greatest possible service. It would have
taken solid and prolonged education, and from the beginning a
salary scale proportionate to work productivity, a move that
would have constituted an essential element in work discipline,
so long as this discipline were not compromised by the presence
close by of "functionaries" (in the bad sense of the term) on
State farms who were paid more for less work. In the absence of
cooperation, the *autonomy* of each basic production unit would
make the workers conscious of genuine economic problems. If
such units suffered deficits, they would attempt to remedy the
situation more rapidly, and could put their finger more easily on
the fact that raising salaries without proportionately increasing
production can lead only to famine, rationing, and the black
market.

7. *An interesting interview with Régino Boti* [12]

The most realistic leaders, such as President Dorticós and Rodríguez, president of INRA, are trying, at least in the agricultural sector, to impose sounder economic ideas. They see the
need for autonomy and come close to what I have proposed. But
certain leaders are putting the brake on both the concept of self-
management and the possibilities of Cuban development. They
willingly promise extraordinary results—but for the year to
come.

Boti notes that a system of agricultural production which is
functioning despite its shortcomings should not be broken up
without another system being set up in its place. He stresses the
absolute lack of control of work productivity, and the enormous
differences in yield from one *granja* to another, depending on
whether or not they are headed by a real organizer. The prime
task thus should be "re-establishing the authority and outlining
responsibilities on various levels within the production units.
Why should a guy earning four *pesos* a day doing nothing in

---

[12] The head of the Central Planning Board, the *Juceplan.*

the socialist sector want to go into the private sector, where he would have to work?" he adds. Hearing such regrets from a Minister may be something of a surprise, but let us not minimize his difficulties; let us hail instead his spirit of self-criticism.

This argument allows him to minimize the essential problem, that of self-management. "Can it function in an environment where chaos reigns?" he asks. And he maintains that it is possible to establish a more efficient link between work and wages by the simple introduction of a certain degree of discipline. Since this overcentralized economy has been functioning badly for three years, and especially since forty-five years of experience in the other socialist countries have shown the practical impossibility of this, it ought to be a matter of considerably more reflection.

Cuba happily has not been afraid to innovate in the field of socialist politics; it could, in fact, advance more boldly still in this sector. Yugoslavia has shown the possibility of innovating in the economic field as well, and its decentralization has brought unquestionable success. But *it was careful to keep in mind the experience accumulated by the other socialist counries;* both on the practical and the theoretical plane it sought out *the causes of the difficulties encountered.* "Cuba is pointlessly repeating the whole cycle of economic errors made in the socialist countries," a Polish colleague said to me. For the failure of the nonautonomous production unit is no longer a matter of discussion in the Soviet Union. It is precisely the present state of chaos that appears to me to justify self-management; it would immediately make each collective work unit suffer from the consequences of its private little chaos and prompt it to remedy it. And this would soon lead to responsibilities being pinned down more precisely.

Boti claims that simple, comprehensible, automatic self-management does no more than guarantee a more efficient use of existing resources. "This way, the greatest possible amount of milk will be gotten from a bad cow, but there won't be any incentive to change cows." He believes that self-management would force the decentralization of investments, but this is true only in regard to self-financing. At present this latter is not only nonexistent but negative, since the State offsets profits by making up for high deficits. It is quite possible to combine day-to-day self-management with the general orientation of the economy according to a plan, by the granting of conditional, specifically allocated public credits.

If, in addition, the use to which self-financing is put is decided on the spot, it would become possible to carry out both the projects of the base and the views of those at the top; this can lead to good results. The educational side of self-management is not the least important of its benefits, and the revolutionary leaders attach the highest importance to educational problems. "Be educated so as to be free": this slogan, which is everywhere, also dominates the façade of the Colombia barracks, now happily transformed into school buildings.

8. *The campaign against illiteracy and insufficient technical education*

1961 was the "Year of Education"; after 1959—the "Year of Liberation"—and 1960—"Agrarian Reform"—came 1962—the "Year of Planning," and 1963—the "Year of Organization."[13] It would have been preferable to put organization before planning, which was really disordered, and based too much on personal impressions in the absence of sufficient knowledge. Thus, in 1961, it was decided that Cuban illiteracy, affecting two peasants out of five, would be wiped out in one year, *something that had never been done anywhere in the world*. Grade-school students and high-school students from ages twelve to eighteen were mobilized for this purpose, and classes therefore did not start again until January of 1962. The excellent results obtained seemed to be more important quantitatively than qualitatively; it was not possible to go far enough,

---

[13] 1964 was the "Year of Economy." This is a happy choice, for it stresses the growing awareness of the importance of economic problems.

and a certain proportion of those taught to read and write did not go on with their education. Let us hail without reserve this mobilization of a whole nation in order to open the minds of its most disinherited citizens. It is to be regretted, however, that the manuals, after having taught that *r* was pronounced as in *rifle* and *f* as in *Fidel,* did not give more thought to work in the fields and teach *b* as in *banana tree.*

On other educational levels the situation is still not bright, partly because of *haste and generosity.* People boast of the fact that there are 100,000 scholarship students, the *becados,* and it is admirable that they have been given the sumptuous villas of Miramar west of the capital to live in. The U.S.S.R. has also made its students relatively privileged members of society, but it *obliges them to make a very serious effort.* If they had to take Soviet examinations, three-quarters of the Cuban scholarship students would be sent back to work, and the general orientation of students is not very satisfying. Fidel has just spoken out against the three thousand candidates training to be diplomats as compared to the hundred or so candidates training to be agronomists. This latter profession was formerly considered *infra dig* in bourgeois, and therefore urban, circles which scorned work on farms. It is more tempting to travel all over the world, to shine at receptions, and to participate in international politics than it is to splash around in the mud of the rice paddies in Oriente. So long as technicians are not given higher salaries and more consideration than that granted administrators (both those of the Party and those of labor unions), this very useful career will not seem very attractive. If only 22 diplomas in agronomy were given out in 1962, a good third of the number before the war, in 1963 the number had gone up to 40, but there were still 4,000 students in "art education." I would appreciate their decorative plates more if they were better filled, and folklore dances are less pleasing if they are danced in front of a bare cupboard.

Because the examinations are not difficult enough, these *becados* do not work enough—less than the remainder of the students, President Dorticos has recently stated pointedly. It is a very good thing that the sons of peasants and workers have been given access to advanced education; in the West we put a de facto barrier in their way, which prevents us from developing and using very valuable brains to the fullest. But these scholarship students do not have all the intellectual capacities necessary to pursue higher education; a more drastic selection would lead to better use of their capacities. Instead of opening the doors of the University to students incapable of taking the courses, of delivering "bargain" diplomas and thus making them less valuable, it would be better to create certificates on an intermediary level, allowing those who have obtained them to go on with their education later and earn degrees on the university level. Steps are being taken in this direction, but they are still not enough.

"Cram" courses are given in revolutionary schools that claim to give students within the space of a few months courses that took other students in the same educational curriculum several years to complete; this leads in the long run to a "leveling from below" if the goal is for every student to be able to keep up. It would be better to split the students up into groups where all the students have approximately the same fund of knowledge; each of them would thus get the maximum benefit from the course. The revolutionaries' concern for education, finally, must not allow technical education to take a back seat, and that is what I am afraid is happening at the Ranchos Boyeros school for administrative aides. Many students can be sent to the U.S.S.R. for training in the scientific disciplines and industrial technology, in the use of farm machinery, and so forth. But not for tropical agronomy—except for corn and more particularly cotton—with some reservations, for the climatic conditions are very different.

Too many liberal-arts students, jurists, and artists and not enough technicians: in Cuba, too, we find this turn in the wrong direction that is common in the underdeveloped countries, but which has been eliminated in the other socialist countries. There are too few teachers of mathematics and physics to develop technical education fast enough. Hanco von Neyenhoff, a young

Dutch professor trained at the Sorbonne, teaches mathematics at the University of Havana. Out of fifty-eight students, only four want to become professors; the others want to do research, and every one of the forty-one students in the school of physics want to do research. By 1968 these two schools will thus have furnished only four professors, since there is a five-year curriculum.

For this same year, 1968, José Altshuler[14] has set a goal of 13,000 students in the technological schools, a figure established on the basis of the needs of the Plan. In 1960, I had asked that 200 agronomists and zootechnicians and 600 agricultural technicians be enrolled every year, as soon as possible. What these technical schools lack above all else is professors of mathematics and physics: 260 of each (giving a ratio of one professor for each 50 students) will be needed in the year 1968: there will be exactly four of them. That is why, even though it was not part of my mission in the strictest sense of the word, I took the liberty of drawing the President's attention to a note from Hanco, proposing the creation of boarding schools, far from the tumult of the capital, which would allow professors with sufficient qualifications to be trained faster and in sufficient numbers.

This would allow the all too rare good professors available, both Cuban and foreign, to be employed full time. At the school of geology at Santiago de Cuba, where he was the only geologist teaching classes, young Faure had only two students—and often one of them was absent. Their background in mathematics and physics did not permit them to keep up with his course on crystallography. Productive work during the course of study is useful, so long as it does not interfere with teaching. In Santa Clara (Las Villas), a school of zootechnology was opened in 1962 *with two students and five professors!* What underemployment of teachers that were so hard to come by! They might well have been sent to the analogous school in Havana until the school had fifty or so students enrolled, so as not to set

---

[14] *Cuba socialista,* April, 1962.

up anything but useful and profitable establishments. Here again the notion of the cost of education, in much too luxurious establishments (which caused some students to think of themselves as a new privileged caste), does not seem to explain the phenomenon entirely. Everything happens in Cuba as if the country were richer than it is; does the fact that Fidel came from a family that was well off have nothing to do with this aberration? Education is so highly respected that nothing seems too good for it.

If all the students worked as hard as they should, this would be something of a lesser evil, but this is far from being the general rule, and not only when the coffee crop is being harvested: in that case, the scholarship students showed that they were nothing loath *to being supported by the other workers*. Student co-administration (*co-gobierno*)[15] would seem to have been used largely as a weapon. When even mediocre students lay down the law, the best professors leave. Revolutionary students naturally fought against a rectorship that had too many ties to repressive power in the old regime. But they have not yet thoroughly understood that the Revolution implied a total change of attitude on their part, as on the part of the other workers.

The best students do not militate often; those who do become absorbed in political tasks and no longer work very much. "The student goes after the diploma that is easiest to get. Since work groups have been organized, students do too little individual work. Students criticize the content of courses that they don't know the first thing about," Hanco adds.

The concept of class struggle has on occasion been interpreted in a curious way by students who are neophyte Marxists. For them class struggle consists of a battle between student organizations and their professors. One student, a young woman who argued that professors are right, after all, to demand work from students, is said to have been excluded from communist youth groups for "treason" against the clan of students. The interven-

---

[15] Joining the federation of students is obligatory.

tion of the powers that be is not always well-considered—when they decide, for instance, that the teaching of first-year political economics will be restricted to a commentary of Karl Marx's *Kapital*. Students who have not acquired the slightest notion of basic economic concepts can obviously not appreciate the wealth of knowledge in it. And when they are sent out in their turn to teach political economics after only six months, the country is running a certain risk if they are not specially gifted and very hard workers, especially if all they have at hand is Nikitine's manual.

With all these facts well in mind, along with the thought that these students are to be employed as teachers, thereby lowering the level of education, one reads these words of Che Guevara's: "The future lies in the development of chemistry and electronics." He should at least have said "long-term development"; an automated electronic industry will require very highly qualified technicians that today neither the educational system nor the atmosphere "on the job" can supply. This might be a worthwhile proposal, once important progress has been made in the intensification of agriculture, and once the existing factories, even those as modest as the ones in the food and textile industries, are being used to capacity. Thus production would be increased faster than if a premature electronic industry were the goal. And the country could then pass *progressively, as real possibilities permitted,* to more and more complicated industries.[16]

9. Revolutionary "lumpen" morale and Manicheism

The "lumpen," as they are called in Cuba,[17] are those in the cities who lead an idle life—bums, vagrants, pimps, pederasts, petty thieves, black marketeers: they thus make up a very mixed social group. Following one of Fidel's speeches excoriating their

---

[16] The same argument applies to agriculture. See Chapter 5, 6.
[17] In Cuba, Marx's term "lumpen proletariat" is applied to those who refuse to work or to respect the revolutionary laws.

social parasitism, the revolutionary police were given the job of rounding them up, using beer, which was extremely hard to come by, as a handy lure. When they began delivering the beer in the bars, the news soon spread all through the city and the idlers were the first to come running. They were followed by a police van, and those who could not furnish proof that they were regularly employed were sent off to work on the *granjas*. I had lunch with a group of these lumpen in the workers' canteen of a palm plantation in Las Villas, a province where 1,800 had been rounded up, beginning with those who were considered most "compromised."

Those who really buckle down to work thus have a chance to rehabilitate themselves, and it is better to send them to the country where they can be useful—a fact which in itself helps to give them a boost—instead of sending them off to prison. Hardened offenders, on the other hand, are deported to the Cayos, the little islands off the coast, where the work is much harder and where there is no way for them to escape. The policeman, a benevolent-looking sort, was not at all reluctant about telling all this to a Western expert whom Cuba does not fear to consult, revealing all the country's difficulties. Once admitted into the country, the visitor can circulate with much more freedom than is yet the case in the U.S.S.R. and China, and see everything he wants to. The situation in this respect might be compared to that in Poland.

The paternalistic cop was visibly surprised to find fathers, sons, or brothers of rebels, and sometimes real revolutionaries among them. A number of these ne'er-do-wells, he added, are nonetheless quite capable of courageously fighting Americans if need be. This fact left him in a thoughtful mood, and he asked us to help him understand it. Up until then he had always believed in a Manicheist humanity, with the pure and the just, in a word, the rebels on one side, and on the other those who were idlers and therefore traitors to the Revolution, and who were suspected of being agents or accomplices of the CIA.

The unlimited devotion of the best guerrillas gave them too simple an image of man. Therefore the excessive centralization of the economy counts first of all on moral stimulants or professional ethnics and neglects material stimulants more than it should: this seems to constitute a serious cause of error. It is a primitive conception of man, the one dramatized in traditional theater. In the Basque country the actors entered through the door marked Good or that marked Evil: the audience thus knew immediately what sort of person they were dealing with. This is also true of Chinese opera, because of the colored stripes on the actors' faces which classified each character.

To sum up: a magnificent effort to educate the people has been made in Cuba.[18] Since time was short, the most important steps taken were not sufficiently coordinated within the framework of a master plan for education. The educational system is thus still not suited to the needs of tomorrow's economy. It is quite possible to correct Cuba's aim, but here again it is high time for this to be done.[19]

The organizational structure of the economy failed for a long time to be adapted to realities, because of hypercentralization that is now undergoing a setback, especially in agriculture. Attributing excessive importance to the modification of property relations, and believing that collectivization of the means of production represents the *only* really important fact[20] might be a matter for debate hereafter. The experience that has now been acquired shows us that in order to "develop" a socialist economy, which is the principal aim, a country must also know how to *organize* the most efficient utilization of these means (or at

---

[18] See in particular the "Report of the Republic of Cuba at the 12th Meeting of the General Conference of UNESCO," 1962.

[19] Hanco stresses that the lowering of the present level of studies taught by catch-as-catch-can teachers will be felt most strongly in five years. It will take five more years to train really qualified teachers, and five years after that for the first large-sized batch of well-trained technicians to graduate from the University. His proposal would allow this delay to be cut down to ten years, if there was *an immediate awareness of the problem.* And the plans of this first decade must be made with the scarcity and the shortcomings of technicians in mind.

[20] It remains essential nonetheless, in particular because of its irreversible nature.

least a utilization of these means that is better than before), once they are put at the disposal of the collectivity. This brings us around to proposing a series of constructive measures for Cuba,[21] without which our critical remarks run the risk of being described as negative.

---

21 These are interesting to study in other countries as well.

5

The Possibilities
of Righting
the Cuban Economy

Let us make it immediately clear that it is a question here of suggestions, the majority of which have already been submitted to the president of the INRA and the president of the Republic in the form of two more detailed reports. Only the Cuban government and the leaders of the Revolution are in a position to decide on their worth, but we are not going beyond our role when we propose solutions, for it has been requested that we do so.[1]

1. No helpful solution with "the Alliance without Progress"

This series of observations comes from a critic who is known to be severe and must not lead to a "classic" conclusion: that it would be better, after all, to accept the traditional "benefactor," the United States of America, which is still so powerful. For this country began to be philanthropic for its own benefit; and its private investments, which were relatively limited (the sums invested in all of Indo-America being smaller than those invested in Canada alone), were aimed above all at getting raw materials for itself. Thus the copper mines of Chile, the iron mines of Venezuela, and above all, that country's oil, were exploited. As Alain Birou[2] reminds us, fifty-one per cent of

---

[1] Unlike the advice submitted eleven months earlier to the Soviet government, which was not requested at all.
[2] In a very interesting article, "Les déboires de l'Alliance pour le progrès" ("Problems of the Alliance for Progress") in *Développement et Civilisations,* septembre 1963, a study used in the writing of this paragraph.

American capital was invested in petroleum and mines in 1959. Bananas were also grown in conditions that made them a sort of agricultural mining, since the United Fruit Company exploited both the soil and the people (despite progress made recently).

Without these investments, the United States could not mobilize such an unthinkable proportion of the riches of the world, a proportion that is steadily increasing, to assure itself a scandalous standard of living (if it is measured on the scale of world poverty). These investments bring profits to the capitalists first of all, and in the countries in question they have set off almost no general chain of development as would investments aimed at the satisfaction of these countries' domestic needs. Caracas has many oil millionaires, but the *llanero,* the worker on the vast latifundia of the Orinoco, like the *conuco,* who still lives in clearings in the forest within a subsistence economy, has scarcely seen his lot improved by the manna that came in the form of oil.

On December 8, 1961, speaking in Miami to members of the AFL-CIO, President Kennedy declared that "in 1960, we have taken $1,300,000,000 from the underdeveloped world that needs capital, whereas we sent only $200,000,000 of investment capital outside the country." It is therefore a question of exploitation rather than of aid, reinforced by the constant shrinking of the buying power of basic agricultural and mining products from 1953 to 1967. Birou estimates this annual deficit that must be made up at $1,400,000,000, or more than the *total* loans and gifts of the U.S. government through the Alliance for Progress in 1961 and 1962, which he estimates at $700 and $500 million. He also estimates private investments to be $141 million in 1961, and *minus* $18 million (withdrawal of capital) in 1962.[3] And he concludes that there has been "a

---

[3] Confirmed by *The New York Times* in an editorial early in 1963. At the ministerial conference of the Interamerican Economic and Social Committee, which met in São Paulo in November 1963, Averell Harriman maintained that the United ᶜ ᵃtes "granted" $2,300,000,000 to Latin America in 27 months. To attain such a figure, he surely did not take into account either withdrawals of capital nor repatriation of profits, and he must have scraped the bottom of the barrel.

continual and progressive decrease in capitalization in the Latin American countries."

These Americans advise agrarian reform, on condition that an indemnity be paid property owners. In 1961, a Colombian student at the Institut des Hautes Études d'Amerique Latine [Institute of Advanced Latin American Studies] in Paris, reported that a short time after having voted for initial reform in his country, the Treasury began to worry about the sums of money that would be necessary to buy this land back under the terms of the law. The first estimate amounted to *about twenty times the annual budget of this country*. A "reformist" reform thus leads to a blinder and blinder impasse, for speculation continually increases land values.

The constant increase in the value of land often "pays" better than the net profit of the crop grown, which is hardly an incentive for making investments with an eye to increasing production. When Adlai Stevenson spoke of agrarian reform in Chile he was told: "Before we can expropriate the large native estate owners, we will have to dispossess your companies mining copper"—just as in Algeria, foreigners have priority. Our fine Yankees have never gotten any farther than considering a real estate tax "increasing in geometric progression as the surface of the property increases in arithmetic progression"—Thomas Jefferson's proposal would have been very interesting if it had been adopted at the time, at the end of the eighteenth century. But today we find the Yankees "asking for a revolution of 1789 almost a half-century after the 1917 Revolution."

This isolated reform would be all the more ineffective in that it would not stop the constant drain of capital, which is fleeing unstable currencies, and fleeing even more particularly these very prospects of reform. Almost two and a half billion dollars are said to have left Venezuela from 1958 to 1961; the amount of Latin American capital deposited in the United States and Switzerland is estimated at $20 billion. What use is it to pour in more dollars if they too flee? And Moscoso, a Puerto Rican, concludes: "The United States thought it could encourage social reform and private investment simultaneously. In point of fact, these two objectives are incompatible. Our efforts at reform, added to the agitation of forces on the Left, have brought about the flight of private native capital." Let us add, with Birou: "The survival of the 'Free World' depends on the liberation of the Third World, which itself is impossible without putting an end to the freedom of the strongest to do as they please."

The United States still has reason to regret 1959–1960, a moment when, in the words of Claude Julien, "they drove Fidel's Revolution into the arms of the U.S.S.R. . . . . Washington's policy toward Cuba got tougher when the interests of the oil and sugar industries were affected, two years before the installation of Soviet rockets." And farther on: "Not only were grants in aid amputated by Congress, but they gave priority to social investments or the support of weak currencies, and therefore still have no practical effect on economic structures, *which must be overturned* if Latin America wants to escape poverty and hunger."[4] And when Cuba overturned them, it was excommunicated, whereas a military dictatorship that supports oligarchies hostile to any sort of reform often continues to receive aid.

All the difficulties that Europe encountered in Africa might also be placed side by side with those encountered in Cuba. The many aids that have been accorded have their effectiveness lessened by the essential obstacle presented by a barter economy. The most general and the most alarming phenomenon is the African countries' *great difficulty in surmounting underdevelopment*. In this battle for development, Cuba's lack of experience, as it applied a poorly digested theory, made it lose its first economic skirmishes while running the political battle. This country can quickly right its situation, *if its leaders are wise enough to abandon* a priori *thinking in favor of clear thinking*.

---

[4] *Le Monde diplomatique,* novembre 1963. Out of the $4.5 billion dollars in grants in aid requested by Kennedy for 1963–1964, by Christmas of 1963, Congress had granted only $3 billion—much less than this country spends on stupid frivolities.

2. *Righting wages and prices, re-establishing local markets*

Che Guevara underscored the fact that Cuban workers worked much better in times of political crisis—the attack of April 1961, and the tension of October–November 1962. The hurricane of the 6th to the 10th of October 1963, thus gave rise to a sudden genuine increase of national *effort,* which hopefully will continue. This labor would be much more productive if Cuban leaders could quickly overcome the present chaos which is the triple heritage of the capitalist past, of the leaders' lack of experience as regards the conditions of development along socialist lines, and of the necessities of foreign and domestic political struggles. These latter have led those at the top to display a generosity that, along with the overturn of institutions and the blockade, brought on the present difficulties.

It is now necessary for experts free of all responsibility for day-to-day management of the country and free of all concern for everyday problems to calmly study the real situation of the Cuban economy. They should analyze the established production capabilities in industry in order to establish priorities for the procurement of raw materials. Industry has lost the guide once provided by the market, and has not discovered precise enough new guidelines within the framework of a plan that has remained too vague.

A sound currency is the first requirement for recovery. A rise in prices, rather than a nominal reduction in wages, will make this necessary step more readily accepted psychologically. If certain imports permitted partially doing away with rationing at the same time that this rise in prices was imposed, this step would even be welcomed: the population's first thought would be of the substantial lowering of prices that this would represent as compared to black market prices.

This rise in prices should be selective, and its aim should be the re-establishment of prices that bear a closer relationship to realities, to the work-value of each article. Taking market prices before the Revolution as a point of departure (including seasonal and qualitative variations, which bear quite a close relationship to the cost of production), they could be adjusted without throwing them too far off balance, so as to encourage the peasants and the *granjas,* as well as industries to fulfill the Plan. This could be done by raising the price of the most necessary products (milk, tubers) or those most in demand (coffee, meat). Only milk seems to justify a consumer subsidy, to be limited to those families genuinely in need.

This rise in prices would be more acceptable still if it were accompanied by a *smaller* increase that would apply only to the lowest wages, especially those paid for the hardest agricultural labor, such as cutting cane. This rise in wages should be closely tied to the increase in productivity in this sort of work, which as we have seen is too low. Thus there would begin the indispensable adjustment of price and wage scales, whose present disparities discourage workers and peasants. The distribution system would rapidly be improved if *a double price sector* could be instituted, at least as long as there is famine, with the reestablishment of local markets somewhat like the markets of the kolkhozes. This would put an end to the numerous instances of waste brought about by the State's absolute monopoly on trade, would reduce the distance that foodstuffs must travel, and would guarantee that they were fresh.

Once his contracts to supply goods to the State network were honored, the producer—collective or private—would thus have the right to sell the rest freely. This would tend to make him work harder, since his production over and above the contract would be the best paid. Nonetheless, contract prices should not be set too low,[5] but rather should amply cover the costs of production incurred with normal productivity. These "free prices" would give all rural Cubans the means to increase their investments and to take a reasonable social step forward— building more modest but nonetheless comfortable houses, with thatched roofs, wooden partitions, wide windows, a cement

---

[5] As happened with the "obligatory deliveries" in the U.S.S.R. until 1953.

floor, water, and electricity—*without running the national collectivity too heavily in debt.*

Once assured of finding desirable merchandise on these free markets, the workers would be encouraged to make a greater effort in order to acquire them. They would thus find the material stimulus that is indispensable to the increase in work productivity, the essential key to Cuban economic recovery. It is also necessary for the general framework of the economy in turn to favor this greater productivity. We shall examine this problem in the field of agriculture, the only sector that we were able to study. It is now recognized, moreover, that this will be the most important sector in the decade to come. It is in the countryside, on the *granjas,* that the economic, and therefore the political, future of the Cuban Revolution will be at stake, especially in the period from 1964 to 1968, now that a direct military attack seems less probable. It is therefore necessary to devote more attention to this top-priority, decisive production front, even though it may appear to be less exciting.

3. National diversification and regional specialization

It is now an accepted fact that new State farms of the same type, constituting units of exploitation of conveniently grouped sections of land of a reasonable size, must be reorganized so that all of them are under a single board of directors. Studies in view of this reorganization are being carried out under the direction of Soviet experts south of Havana (Guinés) and west of Camaguey (Ciego de Avila). They will require a fair amount of time, more than five years in all, for they will also seek to determine the optimum size of each unit.

I have proposed measures that go both faster and farther. They go faster as regards the first step to be taken, for two neighboring *granjas,* by friendly agreement, might immediately *exchange pieces of land,* thus doing away with the most obvious, the most glaring anomalies, thereby reducing useless expenses and consequently the costs of production. They go farther, for the second step to be taken might profit from the extensive studies thus made not only to regroup farms in sensible and logical units but also to assure a better *placement* of the various production units, cattle farms and crop-growing farms, plantations, and factories treating raw materials.

The diversification of crops, which is certainly necessary on the national scale, has unfortunately been applied down to the smallest region, the smallest unit on the island, a scale on which the need for specialization continues to be obvious. As a general rule each *granja* should not grow more than two to four principal crops, plus those needed to feed the unit. As a general practice, perishables ought to be supplied the workers by their own unit, even if the cost of production is thereby increased, for by so doing much higher freight costs and distribution costs can be avoided. Beginning in 1968, the cane-cutter should no longer be obliged to worry about supplying himself or his family with food. He could easily get more work done with less fatigue if he received a large glass of milk each morning.

Insofar as crops that are to be exploited commercially are concerned, the line of reasoning is quite different. It is absolutely necessary to see that they are grown in the best possible place (since in any case they must be shipped away), so as to increase the yield for a given amount of work, and thus lower costs of production. It is also necessary to reduce the expense of transporting these products to the factory that will process them, especially in the case of heavy or perishable products. This necessity has been understood in the case of sugar cane, which would cause ruinous expense if it grew too far from the refinery. We have seen how this has even led to the takeover of land by refineries.

This encourages the concentration of each new crop in the place where natural conditions are most favorable for it; the factory that processes this or that crop can then be located in the center of the region where it is grown. By thus increasing the density of production, the radius for pickup of milk by the existing factories that process it could be substantially reduced. By so doing, the milk delivered to the factory would be fresher and therefore worth more, and at the same time transportation

expenses could be cut down.[6] It is also necessary that pineapples, citrus fruits, mangoes, tomatoes, and other fruits or
vegetables to be canned or made into juice have only a short
distance to travel. This is also indispensable for kenaff, which
furnishes a fiber used for making bags, because of the heavy
weight of the raw plant that must be shipped to the factory for
extraction of the fiber.

This regional specialization is called for first of all in the case
of perishable foodstuffs for the large cities, and the capital in
particular. We have already advised[7] that it be surrounded by
concentric circles of decreasing intensity of production.[8] Beyond
this zone given over to the supplying of food to the cities, the
problems of the use to which farms should be put require a
previous and *more precise* definition of the agricultural policy
of the nation if they are to be correctly solved.

4. Cuba in 1975: the primacy of sugar and a limited degree of self-sufficiency

The Cuban leaders have now fully recognized the obvious fact
that the island must grow sugar cane and they are according the
highest priority to the re-establishment, and later on the expansion, of this crop.[9] In addition to the difficulties that it would
have in getting the cash necessary to set up industry in the
country in any other way, the change in the price sugar has
brought on the world market since December 1961, constitutes
a second justification of this position. In some eighteen months,
this price has more than quadrupled. For the first time since

---

[6] The pickup trucks of the Bog Walk factory in Jamaica run up more
than 96,000 miles a year to collect less than 11 million liters of milk,
which often is spoiled.

[7] Chapter 2, 7.

[8] The classical pattern of the German agronomist Von Thünen.

[9] This top priority for sugar has been confirmed by the recent commercial agreements set up with Moscow during Fidel Castro's visit to
Moscow, and in speeches by Fidel and by Carlos Rafael Rodríguez
which indicate that cattle will be given second priority.

the past. The integration of agriculture and cattle raising, long considered as an essential form of agricultural progress, thus becomes a matter for discussion economically: *but only under certain specific conditions.*

In the heart of the Corn Belt of the United States, south of the Great Lakes, in Ohio and Iowa, yields of five tons of corn per hectare without fertilizer, at the cost of ten hours of human work in the field, from plowing up to and including harvesting, are still common. Farm machinery, tractors, fuel, herbicides, and insecticides are available locally and are cheap. Highly skilled manpower is very expensive, and it takes much more of it to produce silage.

The average yield of corn in Cuba is not over a ton per hectare under cultivation (as compared to four tons for the whole of the United States)—at the cost of often fifty hours or more of human labor. Progress is certainly possible, but it will take a long time to come close to the costs of present U.S. production. On the other hand, Cuba has in Pangola a cereal grain of exceptional quality, capable of yields that are unknown in the United States, due in particular to there being no winter in Cuba, a distinct advantage. Thus it can produce all year round with irrigation, and this does away with the necessity of reserve forage, which is always burdensome. On farms that are not irrigated, hay and silage with present techniques are much less expensive per forage unit than Cuban corn. This will be true, that is, if Cuban farmers learn how to make them better, and are careful not to transport them unnecessary distances, but instead store them and feed them to the cattle in a corner of the meadow that has produced them, under a light thatch shelter.

At the present stage, the most economically profitable step forward, the one that will most immediately bring money in, is thus *the wider spread of artificial pastures,* especially of Pangola, which yield infinitely more than natural meadows. Moreover this is easily done: a simple plowing covers up cuttings placed a yard apart. Thus Pangola has not recently had the frequently serious failures that new crops, such as peanuts or cotton, have often met with; this Pangola becomes even more profitable with rational fertilization and intensive pasturage, rotating the animals, which remain on the same piece of pasture two days at the most and come back to it three weeks later: these are techniques that are more exacting, but they are already well known. The third important step forward in forage production would be "zero grazing," whereby grass is cut every day where it has reached its maximum lushness and put in the troughs of animals kept permanently in barns.

But this step must not be taken prematurely, for even though this system saves the grass from being trampled or covered with dung, the operation is very costly in materials and buildings and involves high day-to-day costs. Here again a form of mechanical cultivation, or at least of harvesting, is involved; this requires costly expenditures of cash so long as the equipment is not produced within the country. A precise study would allow an impression I have to be proved either true or untrue: it would seem that the country's rare resources at present would be better invested if a larger surface area of artificial pastures were created than if their area were reduced but exploited with zero pasturage. In reality things would not happen in this way, for different factors of production are involved. The zero pasturage technique requires the importation of very costly machines, a level of capital (fixed capital and machines) and of scientific organization of work much more efficient than it is today in Cuba—a level which France has just barely reached. The feed line must function reliably every day of the year, and this is difficult to guarantee under the present conditions of disorganization and poor supply. The spread of Pangola, on the other hand, takes only muscle power and simple cultivation.

This observation applies as well to large-scale hydraulic projects, which are very costly and will take too long a time to be productive to be given first priority at this time. Fidel seems to have been too impressed by the drought of 1961, an exceptional phenomenon: with an average rainfall of 1.35 meters this is not South Morocco. Contrary to a belief that is all too widespread, irrigation is not a magic tool. It represents above all *the last step in agricultural progress,* which pays off *only when all the other factors involved in progress have played their full role.* If you irrigate a pasture with inferior plants, the yield will go from 500 to 1,000 or 1,500 kilograms of equivalent grain per hectare, which will not "pay." But if you irrigate Pangola that is already well cultivated and fertilized, you will go from 6,500 kilograms to 13,000, which will allow you to more than compensate for your outlay.

The full utilization of irrigation equipment already installed is much more urgent, for it yields high profits at little expense. It consists of planting two or even three crops per year, south of Havana, in irrigated fields where often people have been content with a single short-cycle harvest. In an irrigated rice paddy, such as those in South China, it is possible to plant two rice crops, or a rice crop and a dry crop, in the same year. It is only by preparing the soil better, by fertilizing and effectively protecting the plants against all their enemies, *that water can be turned to the best account*.[13] Khrushchev temporarily avoided the necessity of making over-all progress in intensified agriculture by bringing virgin land under cultivation, waiting for the time when he could develop his chemical industry on the necessary scale. Fidel cannot avoid this necessity either, with just the aid of irrigation. People have had the benefit of much less experience in intensifying topical agriculture than they have in intensifying that in temperate countries, and more difficulties are encountered. To overcome them in Puerto Rico, it was necessary to invest an enormous amount of capital and call on numerous competent technical experts. Cuba will have to come to this too, and in a socialist framework this cash outflow *could* be put to more rational uses.

The second step would improve drainage wherever that is necessary; this has already been done with considerable success in the south of the province of Havana. The multiple possibili-

---

[13] An analogous argument would lead to the conclusion that massive applications of fertilizer, so costly in hard currency, often represents the next-to-the-last step in agricultural progress—a fact that Khrushchev should have mulled over.

ties of small-scale hydraulic projects could be investigated next; small-scale projects are much more profitable than large ones, so long as they are preceded by *the necessary preliminary studies.* This would show which projects were the most profitable and allow them to be classed by order of priority, through the establishment of a logical schedule for their completion. These studies, which would also deal with large-scale projects, would generally lead to doing away with such projects in the third stage, for the additional reason that a long period of time is necessary in order to reach the point of full utilization of them. *The hurricane serves as a reminder that it will be necessary to provide the sloping sides of the large dams intended to reduce floods with protection against erosion;* if not, they will soon be filled with silt. In Algeria the dam at Ksob, which filled up in ten years, was of almost no practical use at all, and it had cost a great deal.

7. The "norms for piece work," which are as necessary as they are short of the mark

The difference in the amount of work being done on construction sites in 1963, depending on whether the workers were being paid by the day or by the piece, was striking: as we watched them working there was no need to ask how they were paid.[14] After the rejection of "capitalist" norms, the first socialist norms sometimes were so favorable that a worker in a nursery earned 25 *pesos*[15] (instead of an average of 3 *pesos*) per day without having to work too hard. As late as 1964 a worker could earn 15 *pesos* a day on certain public-works

---

[14] The same is true on the autonomous farms in Algeria: "The principle of self-management escapes them. When I see them lolling about and pass a remark, they reply: 'It doesn't matter; we're only cheating ourselves.' " J. F. Kahn, *Le Monde,* 21 décembre, 1963. But they often borrow the equivalent of a day's wages from the State, which are guaranteed in Algeria also.

[15] An ample meal in a restaurant cost 1.25 *pesos* at that time; a *peso* was worth about 70 U.S. cents.

projects if he worked conscientiously, and this often made them feel they could take off four or five days every week.

Payment for work by the piece is therefore a necessity that is quite widely recognized especially by bureaucrats, who are well aware that it is practically impossible to apply this method of compensation in their case. The norm is easy to estimate for simple jobs such as processing materials. It becomes a more delicate matter to establish such norms for moving earth, for the hardness of the soil and the number of rocks to be removed, which sometimes vary a great deal, must be taken into account. It is even more difficult to set up norms for many agricultural jobs, although it is possible to go back to previous commonly accepted norms (correcting them if necessary). The payment per *arroba* of cane cut would have to vary a great deal, depending on the yield per acre, on how clean the field was, and therefore how difficult the work was, for from now on growers of sugar cane are no longer going to give in to the dangerous temptation to burn off their fields. The rate for clearing cane fields must be established with care, for weeds on the perimeters of the fields and those inside the field vary in thickness; in the latter case it varies a great deal, from "empty spaces" and bare patches in the planted field to areas overgrown with weeds.

Within the quite limited framework of a wage fund, the fixing of these work rates could therefore be turned over by the workers' unions to the oldest and most skilled workers, whose authority is not questioned.[16] Such a decision will be even more delicate with regard to operations having to do with the preparation of the soil, for between a clay soil so hardened and dried up that it is impossible to work, and a light, loose sandy soil, all sorts of intermediaries exist, according to the nature and the degree of inclination of the soil, the amount of humidity, the presence of stones or roots and weeds that choke the soil, for the scale of norms cannot be infinitely variable.

However *necessary* they may be, especially in peak periods, in

---

[16] "Democracy would not be harmful if units were allowed to be self-managing; this would resolve the contradiction" (M. Mazoyer).

order to stimulate effort and allow a *relative* increase in work productivity, norms will never take the place of conscientiousness and professional training. Basically, the one thing that is certain is *the global effect of all the agricultural labor* in any one field, from plowing to harvesting. It is measured, beyond all possible question, by the yield per hectare. But this yield also depends on the play of factors of production other than labor: the fertilizer, the variety of seed, the means at hand to fight the enemies of the crops, the varying depth to which the field has been plowed . . .

One decisive factor that comes into play is the fertility of the piece of land in question, whether there originally or brought about by man, and the influence of the sum of previous investments, in the form of crops planted or buildings of any sort. In order to approach a proper scale of remuneration for work (which is indispensable to a renewal of effort), we have thus been led to re-establish a whole series of economic laws which the Cuban leaders did not properly appreciate.

8. *The optimum size of self-sufficient units of production*

We must first envisage the re-establishment of true units of socialist production, where all day-to-day decisions would be made at the point where they are most effective, that is, at the site where the work is being done. In the reorganization that is now under way in Cuba, each *granja* will have its *plots of land regrouped* and have its size brought down "to the human scale," that is, to a size such that a good director, a real technician (and no longer a mere administrator) will be capable of managing it properly, keeping up with the over-all running of "his" unit, whose head he will be beyond all question. This size will depend in large part, first of all, on personal ability. The agronomist who can organize his management team, assign tasks properly, and provide leadership can easily "manage" a plot of land five to ten times larger than one that someone else "administrates" very badly.

Given the likelihood that the plots of land would be regrouped in a single unit, I nonetheless proposed, as a first estimate of what the maximum size should be given the present state of equipment and labor, units that varied from 150 to 400 hectares for truck gardens and farms that would grow flowers. Orchards (citrus fruits, bananas, papayas) could be as large as a thousand hectares. Units devoted primarily to sugar cane could be around 2,500 hectares in all, with 1,500 hectares devoted to sugar cane, 30 to supplying food for the workers, and the rest to annual replanting and intensive forage crops. The greater number of cattle acquired could be fed a large part of the leafy tops of the cane stalks. The mechanization of harvesting the cane and loading it would provide the free time necessary to take these stalks to the edge of the field, where the cattle would eat them. They can even graze right in the field in the case of stands of old cane that are going to be plowed under and replanted.

Two thousand to twenty-five hundred hectares seems an acceptable size for those mixed farms that have pasture land but have even more land planted with a major crop: alternating a cereal crop with an industrial crop and a forage crop, for example, or growing rice. The optimum surface might later become larger in proportion to the amount of natural pasture land on the envisaged unit, for beef cattle allowed to range relatively freely take very little work. However, since it will soon be necessary to increase the proportion of artificial pasture land and milch cows in all the zones suitable for cultivation, it does not appear to be a good idea to go beyond five or six thousand hectares; this will allow this necessary intensification to take place all the sooner. Later economic analyses will allow the optimum size of units to be determined on the basis of precise figures.

9. Financial autonomy for day-to-day management along with commercial ties: thus ground rent and interest on state investments

The production plan, being adapted to the natural conditions and the equipment of the unit, will reduce speculation to a minimum and will set only the major policies to be followed by the unit, based on tons to be delivered and not on areas to be cultivated. Within this framework, each head of a *granja* should have every latitude so that he can adapt himself day by day to an ever-changing situation. And each collective work group on the various *granjas* should be rewarded for its successes and penalized for its reverses. In order that this measure may be applied with the utmost possible fairness, for the Cuban has a strong sense of justice, each *granja* must be assured that its system of accounting, first of all, and then its finances, will be autonomous.

From 1965 on, deficits should no longer be covered by the State, so as to tie wages obligatorily to the real labor productivity. By 1970, the great majority of investments would thus be taken over by the *granjas* themselves, as is now being done on the kolkhozes. In order to make these collective units responsible for their financial situation, their commercial ties should be made more flexible and the *granjas* should be allowed to meet their own day-to-day needs out of their own resources. Once they have filled their delivery quotas to the State, they should be able to sell their surpluses on the local market.[17]

At the beginning of 1964, plans were being made in Cuba to allow not the *granjas,* but rather "groups" of *granjas,* to be autonomous, as regarded their systems of accounting first of all, and later their finances. We advised against the creation of such groups,[18] which in principle were to be temporary, but which may well seek to perpetuate themselves. Since the island is to be divided into 44 natural regions, there is to be a lower-echelon representative of the INRA in the center of each of them. This representative could be officially in charge of the management of heavy equipment such as bulldozers and steam shovels, for

---

[17] All units should be told that everything that is not forbidden by precise regulations ought to be considered permissible. At present, units demand authorization for the silliest little thing, and get no answer. "A mediocre decision taken at the right time is often preferable to a better decision taken too late."

[18] Too often you are told in Cuba: "You're right, but Fidel doesn't agree." He seems to be a stubborn man, and his opinion remains gospel; this is sometimes costly.

the individual *granjas* cannot ensure that these will be used full time. An accounting office could also be created to go through each *granja's* accounts, establish their balances, and keep them informed of their current situation, so long as these *granjas* could not do this themselves, as would be preferable. It would play the role of French Management Centers and set up basic policy for the *granjas* in accordance with the Plan and on the basis of their economic results.

Finally, the "work collectives" of each State farm should have the possibility of making about the same amount of money for the same amount of work. Certain of these are located on the rich clay land of Matanzas, and others on very poor sandy savannas. The former have ample equipment of all kinds— buildings, fences, irrigation, drainage ditches, roads, and fields of cane or fruit trees. Their land has been cleared, leveled, and fertilized for a long time now. But those on poor soil do not "inherit" very much of anything except more or less run-down natural prairies or even nothing at all, just wasteland still over- run with marabou and other underbrush. Within the framework of financial autonomy, such different initial situations must be compensated for, not only for reasons of social justice, but also in order to further economic development in all the regions of the island.

The logical re-establishment of ground rents to be paid to the State would also take the economic environment into account so as to be more equitable, with special note being taken of the greater or lesser proximity to favorable outlets—large cities, ports, and factories; of the means of transportation, by rail or by road; of central repair shops, etc. We recently pointed out the great injustice being done certain kolkhozes in the U.S.S.R., largely because such rent was not paid, and despite differential regional prices, which were quite insufficient to make up for it, the average income, *for a given amount of work,* probably still varies by a factor of from one to seven or eight, and the de- velopment of the poor collectives is thereby very seriously com- promised.

The *granjas,* like the sovkhozes, as far as their investment credits are concerned, do not pay any interest on the means provided them. Thus the Cuban State unjustly favors those which receive a great many loans, by the very fact alone that the speculative investments decided on by the Plan require a great many such loans. This is done to the detriment, once more, of the poor zones, in the very place—the ranch with natural pasture land—where the continuance of the most extensive speculative investments seems indicated and requires no new factors to come into play. Though perfect justice is beyond reach, interest at the very least would reduce the injustice.

As with ground rents, the most equitable, the most efficient interest rate could be decided on only after trial and error. The amount of interest would allow the State to increase the amount of money accumulated and place its investments better: that is to say, in regions and on operations able to support a normal rate of interest. This does not mean that these investments must be reserved for highly profitable zones. But there is the greatest advantage in being able to invest in exactly the right projects. If a collective must pay interest and pay back loans, it will be less wasteful than if it were receiving budgeted allotments; in the latter case it is careful not to return any excess unused money, since it does not cost anything.

In short, rent ought to be paid for *the use of the rare factors of production,* such as land and development capital, even under a socialist regime. This should be done first of all to equalize the prospects of the workers, since it is impossible to give each of them (and even each collective) work tools of absolutely equal value. This should be done, secondly, to guarantee society that the rare resources will not be wasted, as they are necessarily, automatically, *every time that they are handed over free.* This is already largely the case with irrigation water in Cuba, as we have seen it to be in the U.S.S.R. The price charged for irrigation water should always cover its cost of production (the expense of bringing it to the field); natural water, that of rivers and that underground, should be charged for, since it is both limited and productive.[19]

---

[19] We discussed these ideas at greater length, in connection with Soviet agriculture, in our previous work.

10. Is the production cooperative a step backward?

This is the opinion of most Cuban leaders, who are overly impressed by the "classic" description of two forms of property: "inferior" property, if it is that of the cooperative group; "superior" property, if it is that of the State, of all the people. Unfortunately for the worker, this notion of "all the people" is very abstract and more or less ungraspable. On the job, this worker has not proved to be as completely devoted to this theoretical collectivity as the revolutionaries imagined he would be. Indeed, some of them were not afraid to rob it on occasion—fortunately less frequently than on the sovkhoz, but nonetheless this no longer allows us to believe the theory that imperfections have been inherited *only* from the capitalist past.

The essential vice of the Cuban *granjas* in 1964 was that two *pesos'* worth of wages were paid every time that a worker created one *peso's* worth of wealth. The principal remedy, therefore, was to do away with the *guaranteed* daily wage, not just the lowering of this wage (relative to prices). This could be done by *paying wages that are linked as closely as possible to the amount of work produced,* as measured by norms; but we have seen how difficult it is to set up such norms properly.

Refusing to attribute any "inferior" character to cooperative property (our opinion is exactly the contrary), we were very much inclined to advise the leaders of the Cuban Revolution to return to a formula that closely resembled a "flexible" kolkhoz. We were then told that this would mean getting into politics—I was about to say into forbidden territory. The question is first of all an economic one; and in the case of Cuba, as with any other country, we are morally obliged to carry our thought through to the end. A field trip in 1963 showed us that the *granja* worker doesn't feel at all "at home," as I told Che in 1960. This causes him to feel less loyalty, and consequently to produce less.

If all agricultural workers were placed within a cooperative framework that was adapted to the situation, and given fair warning that the Cuban State would no longer make up deficits due to the laziness of certain workers, or to the lack of foresight of some of those in charge, it might prompt a change in attitude on the part of everyone. Everyone would soon understand the basic economic relationship, the close link between his productivity and his wages. People would be even more aware of it on the level of a *small* work collective, of a small team assigned a certain specific work area that would not change.

In a cooperative made up of a thousand workers, the individual worker does not have the impression that he can have any real influence on production as a whole, on the over-all economic result. But if accounts are kept by small units, of the same size as the majority of the former farms that have been regrouped, the *fincas,* they straightway become much easier to manage. And each worker is able to feel and to see the immediate effect of his own work on the harvest, as well as that of his teammates. Under such conditions, the worker who lolls about interferes with his little team's chances of winning the prize at the end of the campaign, and the team will be quick to criticize him for it. This principle will not be easy to apply in every case.

Modern heavy capitalist industry, however, keeps accounts not only for each company, but for each branch of a factory, workshop, or product. Even before the war, Dubreuilh showed us the advantages that accrued when the giant Bata shoe corporation in Czechoslovakia adopted the principle of autonomous workshops. Each one of them "sold" what it produced to the next unit in the production line. Unlike the "specialist" in administration (the Boti-Guevara conception) whom it is practically impossible to interest in the over-all result obtained by his group, everyone in this case can be aware of the value that has been added, and therefore of the value of his own work. This remuneration proportionate to the work put in does not imply that the ownership of the land should be given back to the group; but it does prompt the group's being given the greatest possible autonomy. The U.S.S.R. is also seeking an intermediate formula between the kolkhoz and the sovkhoz. The workers take better care of the material belonging to the group than of that which is the property of the State. Certainly the peon, the *guajiro,* has no personal experience in managing an agricultural unit that has developed to the point reached by the Danish farmer in 1880. If all the power is given to the Assembly General, this peon will be in no position to handle the management of a collective unit, which will be all the more difficult the larger this unit is. But if this plan had not been systematically disfavored by making much of the contiguous people's farm, it would have been quite possible to develop the first formula of cooperatives of the INRA, which was rather paternalist, on more reasonable plots of land. The director would continue to be in charge of technical matters, for this is indispensable for the adoption of modern practices; he would be aided by an agricultural adviser close at hand, thanks to the plan of regional specialization. He would be in charge of applying the broad guidelines of the Plan, while at the same time keeping his autonomy of management. He would collaborate with an elected workers' council, whose powers would continue to increase. In this way, each person would be paid a wage that would be immediately proportionate to the over-all results of the unit; each worker would thus be personally interested in bettering them, which is not the case on the *granja,* even with work norms.

11. An "agrarian socialism with little work collectives"

Cooperation along these lines leads us toward *small-sized* work collectives. We have seen that the Soviet kolkhoz is tending to increase the autonomy of its production brigades, and we advised them to go farther in this direction. Algeria has tried to do so with its "Yugoslav-type" self-managed farms, but the workers tend to withdraw within themselves and to reduce the number of workers employed, so as to increase the amount of money received by each worker. Moreover, advances from the State are not paid back properly at all.

Socialism must seek to better reconcile the interests of the nation with those of each of these little teams. The Plan would thus be the supreme law of the *granjas,* which must therefore see to it that supplying goods for State commerce is given first priority. The *granjas* would divide up their Plan between their teams, which would thus be in a position to organize their work themselves. Under these conditions, the *granja* would evolve not so much toward a giant cooperative as toward a *federation of small cooperatives,* which could often be the same size as the former farms.

Within this framework, on the technical, ethical, and political scale of the person of our generation, each head of a unit would in the end be freer in his actions, and thereby *more responsible.* A solid cooperative education, and numerous cooperative leaders, preferably devoted ones, would be required in these units. The specialization of these little units so that they produced only two or three crops would allow the time required to train technical cadres to be reduced. Gutelman has indicated the possibility of educating specialized workers, who would be primarily responsible for these little groups, in a period of a few months.

Thus, democratic centralism, which elsewhere has too often been the cover for totalitarianism, would take on its real meaning once again. Within this structure, the top echelon would be responsible for the Plan, for the broad guidelines, for the allotment of State credits. The heads of cooperatives, who would be appointed (until such time as they were elected within a cooperative framework), would acquire experience in day-to-day management, including managing self-financed resources. A dialogue would begin between the two levels, but this time along lines that would be less unequal than those of pure subordination, for the rights and duties of each person would be better defined.

12. Second tentative conclusion: a socialism with autonomy

We have seen how, in addition to the blockade and the upheavals inherent in every revolution, the overadministrated management of the economy led Cuba to very unsatisfactory results.

A more realistic appreciation of human imperfections, the recognition of the fact that a person is certainly perfectible, but only very slowly, leads to exploring the ways in which existing structures can be improved. This implies, first of all, the right to question them, as a consequence of the typically Marxist fact that evolution, therefore constant revision,[20] is the essential law of human societies.

During a study of Soviet agriculture, we recently concluded that it was impossible to reach communism such as it was defined by the Twenty-second Congress of the Communist Party of the U.S.S.R., in October 1961. For communism supposes an almost perfect human being, an unattainable goal within the foreseeable future, the year 1980, that was to see its fulfillment. In more prudent later writings, moreover, the Russians are content to evoke the passage to the "first phase" of communism.

Socialism for its part realizes that people are long imperfect, and perfectible only very slowly, since it gives "to each according to his work." Respecting this formula supposes that it is possible to measure everyone's work. In order for all of the human individual's possibilities of taking the initiative to emerge, socialism must learn to be more respectful of his dignity, and therefore of his autonomy. This must be done politically first of all, and this means that there must continue to be a plurality—I do not say a multiplicity—of political parties. This must next be done economically: the supremacy of the interests of the collectivity over those of private individuals, assured by the Plan, in no sense implies the centralized control of the smallest act. And *it in no way excludes the cooperative formula,* which has not been properly worked out in Cuba. In the area of handwork, distribution, and small-scale industry, and above all in agriculture, it could still be most useful if it were to occupy the place it deserves once again.

---

[20] China allows readjustment and consolidation, but condemns revisionism. The line of demarcation between what is a matter of principles and what a matter of application of these principles is not easy to determine.

Collectivizing the means of production frees "hidden productive forces," but it is not a magic formula; it is still necessary to learn to manage these better than before, which is not always convenient. In the space of a few years, Cuba has provided us with the spectacle of extreme underdevelopment of the land and people within a capitalist framework, followed by a series of wasteful measures, errors in investment, disorder in production, and distribution under a socialist regime, thus canceling out a great many of this latter's advantages.

It is not enough to proclaim the victory of the social revolution and take over the leading posts in the economy. The "hidden productive forces" thus brought to light must be put to better use; this is true of popular enthusiasm as well. The disappearance of Malthusian obstacles, such as the lack of markets, is always beneficial. On the other hand, the suppression of the law of profit becomes a double-edged weapon. On the one hand this law demands that the value of goods be maintained, through scarcity if need be; but on the other hand it stimulates production through the quest for profits. *The primary goal is development,* which will bring about abundant social justice and the distribution of wealth, not the rationing characteristic of a state of poverty, or at least of austerity.

Let us make no mistake on this score, and may the privileged not claim victory too soon. We believe that we have shown *that it is less difficult* (even though the task must not be underestimated) to surmount Cuba's difficulties, by allying frank analysis to pure determination, than it would be to effectively relaunch the Alliance for Progress.[21] Cuba will not be prostrated by the disorganization of her economy, above all if she becomes more aware of it. Even if the Cubans find our criticisms bitter, we believe them to be salutary.

But the problem of Cuba, because of its ramifications, goes

---

[21] "To imagine that the simple injection of capital for technical assistance in structures such as those of the Shah of Iran or the Peru of the generals can set off the chain of positive initiatives that lead to systematic economic development [is folly]." (Tibor Mende, *Un monde possible,* Le Seuil, 1963).

far beyond the limits of this country; it interests, excites, or worries the whole planet. It obliges us to re-examine *the difficult but necessary building of socialism* in the light of this experience. An arduous task; yet this is the direction that leads toward a "possible world."

6

The Construction of Socialism Is the Most Difficult Task of Our Time

1. The role played by underdevelopment is essential

A craftsman who makes wooden shoes, Georges Beaudenon, tells me that I am right to believe that the good worker is never satisfied with his work, and the mediocre worker almost always is. It probably should be the same for good government; unfortunately the political struggle sidetracks it and causes it to indulge in propaganda, which in turn prompts it to congratulate itself,[1] *thus diminishing its awareness.* This is the prime obstacle standing in the way of the rapid correction of socialist errors, which are very costly if they persist for any time at all.

The Cubans, happily, want to "build socialism." But this should in no way mean that they should neglect the experiences of the other socialist countries and begin the cycle of what are now generally recognized economic errors all over again. Most criticism is subject to debate, including that in the present book. But public discussion of some of the points made would at least give the popular masses a chance to collaborate closely in the making of major decisions, such as the choice of structures of production and distribution. In so doing, they would feel more "involved" in the socialist adventure. Fidel makes a great and laudable effort to *explain* his decisions to the people. The essential decisions are not submitted to discussion, and often they are thought to be based on Marxist theory and therefore beyond all

---

[1] Khrushchev's speeches included self-criticism, and Fidel's include even more.

possible question, whereas in reality such a theory provides only a very general guideline.

The difficult situation of the Cuban economy at the end of 1967 was the result of many factors; first of all the blockade, the sabotage, and the attacks of émigrés and the United States. The blockade forced a total change of policy amid difficult conditions, and the sabotage and the attacks made costly precautions necessary. The hurricane of October 6–10, 1963, which ravaged the richest province, certainly did not help the situation. However, three other causes appear to be even more essential. We have just seen the many disorders, only a part of which are inevitable, that have arisen at the beginning of every revolutionary government, especially after 1960: this is no longer 1918. In addition to an economic structure that often did not fit the situation (the possibilities of managing the economy; the Cubans' general cast of mind . . .), there was also a lack of professional experience and often a certain overweening confidence. Future revolutions in Latin America ought therefore to see to it that the leadership of the country, once the rebels are in power, includes a higher proportion of people *having the experience and the maturity that comes from the prolonged practice of a profession,* men such as O. Dorticos and C. R. Rodríguez.

Along with this debatable suitability to local conditions of a socialist ideology that was not always perfectly understood, there is also the historic, ethnic, South American heritage that can often be described as underdevelopment. For Cuba, the terms misdirected, distorted, unbalanced, or disjointed development would seem to be more exact, for the sugar industry was not really behind the times. As for the capital with its deluxe tourist attractions, which once pumped dollars into the economy, its catering to the luxury tourist trade was *overdeveloped* (37 per cent of Cubans in the "tertiary" sector of the economy in 1953 was too high a percentage); this stood in the way of austerity becoming a general practice, even though it is indispensable for socialist development.

The lack of precision and exactitude, both in the way Cubans think and in the way they keep appointments, the absence of any predilection for true facts set down in exact figures, the lack of prestige of technical jobs, the expressions *momento* ("in a while") and *mañana* ("tomorrow") which crop up all too often in conversation are to be classed among the essential characteristics of this underdevelopment. Crossing the island three times in 1960, I found my trips considerably, and point-lessly, lengthened by the often hourly stops insisted on by my Cuban colleagues so they could have their *cafecito*. I never quite got across the idea, despite my ineloquent chiding, that they had a responsibility toward the children of the poor, who risked going hungrier still if they did not get down to work.

The Russian and Chinese revolutionaries matured when they had to go completely underground; they had already had to solve difficult problems (the latter in particular) long before their accession to power. More people belonged to the intelli-gentsia in Russia, which had been trained in universities with more solid traditions. Yet the disorder of the Soviet economy lasted much longer than that in Cuba, for the first signs of "recovery" in this latter country can perhaps be compared to those in the U.S.S.R. in 1935. And the Soviet Union recovered only because of the iron constraint imposed by Stalin; Fidel has been able to avoid this totalitarian phase by eliminating "Han-nibalism." Thus this man turned out to be first the Kerensky and then the Lenin of his budding Revolution, a feat that by itself is unique.

He was able to avoid playing the role of a Stalin, and today he has climbed to the level of the very greatest men: more human, less a Party man than Khrushchev, and less dogmatic than Mao Tse-tung. Many of his economic errors will be forgiven him in the paradise of the history of revolutionaries because of his political success, especially if he can make his regime's "Hundred Flowers" of liberalism bloom.

At the end of 1967, however, expenditures for purposes of prestige, though they were not as large as they once had been, still persisted—the Cuban pavillion erected for the Interna-tional Congress of Architects, for example. And the delegates of Colombian youth groups who came to Cuba just before that were ecstatic about how luxurious the houses of agricultural workers built in 1960 were, by comparison with the more modest buildings erected in their country. Such an opinion, which lacks all critical discrimination, betrayed a total ignorance of the real possibilities of an underdeveloped economy. And they did not notice that many of these badly built buildings will not last very long.

2. When to change to a collectivist economy?

The texts of Marx and Lenin show that social conditions of work in large units of production conflict with private ownership. Corporations already represent a de facto socialization of the economy, which "calls out for" collectivization. Socialism, according to this theory, should thus be built on the foundations of an *industrial, already developed* society. But in actual fact things did not happen that way: the first social revolution took power in a Russia that was just reaching the *take-off point;* it was thus semideveloped and lagged far behind Western Europe, where it had every intention of spreading rapidly. But it failed to do so, thereby putting more obstacles in the way of the advent of socialism, especially in the atmosphere of general hostility prevalent in these more highly developed countries. This helps a great deal to explain Stalinism: *the influence of the birthplace of the first social revolution has continued to permeate those revolutions that followed.*

Development was even less advanced when the Communists took power in Red China. This explains the difficulties of the period from 1958 to 1962, when the leaders of this revolution abandoned the prudence they had shown in the beginning; this coincided with a period of the most severe weather conditions. The errors of the second five-year plan in China stem essentially from the lack of statistical data, and a general lack of economic information on the part of the central power. In an atmosphere that is more oriented toward propaganda than it should be, there soon is a tendency to take one's desires for realities.

The direct passage to socialism of a *less developed* economy therefore risks encountering difficulties so great that it will sometimes have to beat a retreat later, as we shall see in the case of Guinea. Communists put the prime emphasis on the *political* conditions of revolution: the establishment of the Party as the "spearhead and avant-garde of the working class," which will exercise power by means of the "dictatorship of the proletariat." Without wishing to discuss these political premises here, nor the results of their application, the Cuban experience allows us to discern many conditions that must obtain for the efficient, successful passage to a very rapidly collectivized socialist economy.

This latter proposes to put into effect *voluntary* decisions about the use of power, and to put an end to most automatic regulations (which are imperfect, to be sure, but often are useful), such as those of the market. The administration of this "voluntary" economy must be much more precise in the absence of "guardrails" such as these. It is necessary not only to *direct* the economy from day to day, but also *to foresee, and then try to bring about,* the sort of evolution that is considered to be most desirable. These judgments must be based on *extensive knowledge* of the existing economic situation. *The least developed countries of tropical Africa are still very far from having fulfilled these conditions;* this justifies the present prudence of Mali, of Guinea, of Somalia, and of the Brazzaville Congo.

This leads us to a first conclusion: *the nationalization of the dominant positions in the economy cannot be brought about efficiently without discernment, no matter what the stage of development.* Moreover, when development is at the take-off point, there is no heavy industry, or hardly any, to nationalize. But the commercial sector, and above all import-export trade and the banking network, are often quite concentrated, which prompts their being collectivized. This step has the great advantage of making commercial profits, which too often have been exported, aid in the country's own development.

This is true so long as these profits continue to hold up, and so long as these profits are distributed fairly efficiently. This in turn requires that administrative personnel be available, preferably to work on the national level, but in any case sufficiently *competent and honest* to take care of the management of the commercial units that will have taken the place of private companies. The difficulty of finding such honest men seems to have been an essential factor in the lack of success in Guinea, where the return of private trade had to be permitted. It is better not to venture out onto ground that will be impossible to hold later, rather than expose the country to a defeat such as this, which is very costly for the economy, but more serious still for the prestige of socialism in Africa.[2] Mexico, too, had to take a step backward, and in order to attract Yankee investments once more, they had to be granted exorbitant tax privileges this time: up to fifteen years' total exemption.

3. Revolution is also on the way in technical and economic fields

This should in no way lead to revolutionary defeatism. It should lead, rather, to the recognition of the fact that *the building of socialism is the most difficult task of our time.* The experience of the other socialist countries allows fundamental errors to be avoided. It cannot, however, replace profound knowledge of local conditions and casts of mind, for this is indispensable to the success of the revolution. A group of young Brazilian revolutionaries who were taking my course on "The Cuban Experiment in Socialist Economy" at the Latin American Institute of Advanced Studies in the fall of 1963 reproached me for my severity toward recent economic steps taken by the Cuban revolution. This "severity"—the classic reaction of an old professor searching all about for possibilities of improvement, which leads to a certain twisted professional way of looking at things—was expressly for their benefit. It was a question of showing them the dangers of certain policies that were very

---

[2] This prestige today rests in the hands of the Algerians, and I am a bit worried (note written in 1964, and still true in 1968).

likely to fail, and pointing out errors that should not happen a second time. They are thus better forewarned than were the Cuban leaders who took over power so suddenly.

The young Latin American students put *agrarian reform* at the forefront of their program of action; it does in fact appear indispensable, both to arouse the enthusiasm of peasant guerrillas and to further later economic development. However, they must not repeat the mistake of Algerian students, who even though they proclaimed the same priority in 1955, did not embark upon agronomic studies until 1962, and there still are not nearly enough students in this field after [at the time of this writing] seven costly years of lagging behind. Politically, it was nonetheless necessary to nationalize the "colonial" sector, which was the most modern sector and therefore the most difficult to manage, in order to make it self-managing, but this was done without the leaders having at their disposal the native skills necessary to develop it. This state of affairs is now causing an undesirable setback in Algerian agricultural production.

This time my South American revolutionary friends will not be able to say that they were not given warning in time. The great majority of them should begin right now to devote themselves to pedagogical studies (of how to educate teachers) and scientific and *technological* studies: agronomic surveys above all, and then industrial ones. The studies of *economics* also should be particularly penetrating: econometrics and statistics, general economic theory and Marxist theory, the economy of different systems of production—industrial, agricultural, and commercial. As regards this latter category, we must subsume a double education, a technical one and an economic one, under the same head; this is indispensable in order to be really "on top of" the problems.

The education of doctors should be dealt with on the same level. The faculties of letters and law should come last, for they attract too many candidates because they now open up the possibility of a career in politics. The fact that Fidel began his career as a lawyer is regrettable, for he has turned too many young revolutionaries away from pursuing technical studies. It is no longer necessary to defend private property, and it is absolutely necessary that the large majority of future leaders acquire solid technical and economic training. Then the Fidels of tomorrow will no longer plan to plant palm seeds of dubious quality, for they will have at hand a solid basis for their judgments.

Particular mention must be made of the middle level of administrators, those noncommissioned officers of the battle of production who will actually determine whether it will be successful or not. Foremen and qualified workers, "master farmers" and experienced accountants are as indispensable as prestigious planners and engineering "experts" who come out of the graduate schools. The lack of such cadres, and especially of accountants, is being sorely felt in Cuba. The establishment of work "norms" can also begin long before the Revolution: we have seen that it was a basic factor, essential to the success of the State farms or the cooperatives.

In the midst of the struggle for power—I am thinking of Venezuela—the Revolution must take care to preserve the valuable heritage from the past; the artistic patrimony; researchers, their laboratories and their libraries. Mexico took a long time constructing buildings to replace those ruined by the civil war. It is also necessary to protect everything that represents a valuable technical acquisition, such as an estate or a well-equipped factory, along with those valuable members among their staff who are not hostile. As with the new Soviet (or American) position regarding neutrality, the Revolution will find it in its best interest to proclaim from the outset: "All those who are not against us are for us."

In short, socialism, considered at this point in our argument as *a particular form of development,* meets with the same difficulties and has the same general requirements as other forms of development. It is necessary in every case to save in order to invest, in order to accumulate. The need to enlarge people's knowledge and improve their skills is even more urgent: without them the original internal or external capital and costly equipment risk being wasted; after Africa, Cuba has proved to be another example of this. Socialism, however, being a voluntary form of economic leadership, needs these things to an even more marked degree than other economic structures.

A revolution which would thus have a large number of young political, technical, and economic administrators and labor leaders at its disposal, men who were competent and devoted, all of them well up on the concrete problems of production, and not just theories, would have every chance of expanding successfully. The chances would be even greater if these young people were aided technically by at least a part of the older generation in charge of the management of production units at the time of the revolution. This revolution must be considerate of the nation's cadres—the agronomists, the engineers, the statisticians, the economists and accountants, the teachers and researchers of all sorts, the doctors and veterinarians and so on.

And there must be respect for anyone who *has mastered a useful trade,* whatever it may be, whatever the person's political and religious opinion may be, so long as he is not hostile to the socialist experience, even if he does not always share the juvenile enthusiasm of the leaders of the revolution. And above all, these leaders, in Latin America as in Africa, ought *to give second thought to their attitude toward the peasantry*[3] instead of copying the thought of nineteenth-century German intellectuals of bourgeois origin, who were necessarily full of urban prejudices.

4. Instructing the "hundred per cent proletarian" peasants

If the majority of the troops of possible African and South American revolutions will in all likelihood be recruited in the country, agrarian reform will be given top priority over all other revolutionary demands. It is therefore necessary for revolutionaries to play all the aces they have in order to make this reform successful. Illiteracy, which is all too common among the

---

[3] Cuba has treated them better than the other Socialist countries, sometimes "too well."

peasants and which leads to insufficient professional knowledge, is the most dangerous obstacle standing in the way of such reform. The educational pyramid in Latin America is too narrow at the base. For even though there is sometimes a remarkable proportion of students in higher education, grade-school education in remote districts of Alagoas, in the Brazilian northeast, reaches less than one child out of five. Moreover, only twelve to fifteen per cent of the adults in this state[4] have been taught, more or less badly, to read and write.

The disproportion between the education of the rich and that of the poor, and also that between the cities and rural districts, is becoming less and less acceptable, for it represents *the most serious social injustice,* since it determines the children's whole future. In Chile, a fine upstanding Yankee explained to me that primary education made revolutionaries, but secondary education made very respectable people: in his view this latter sort of education should therefore immediately be made a general practice. He had neglected to investigate whether this was possible; he thought he was still in the United States, and did not see that such a step required prior development at a lower stage. He wanted the middle class to forge rapidly ahead in order to consolidate the established order in the face of the rising revolutionary class.

Widespread rural education would allow future middle-level administrators to emerge from the peasant masses: political leaders and labor leaders, certainly, but also the society's movers and shakers, its leaders of cooperatives and its professional people. The *outlook on cooperatives* would thus be much broader than it is in Cuba, where there has been such a lack of competent administrators. On the other hand *devotion and honesty are much more frequently encountered in Cuba than*

---

[4] In December 1963, the senators in this state resolved their family differences right in parliament, killing one of their colleagues who had nothing to do with the dispute: these are Texas ways! These "colonels" from the latifundia are not afraid to kill a worker on their land if they think he is an organizer: the files of the peasant leagues of Francisco Julião—another lawyer—are all too full of documents attesting to this.

they are in Africa. However indispensable these qualities are, they nonetheless cannot replace technical knowledge and a minimum of organizational ability.

Agrarian reform in fact requires not only large numbers of agronomists and technicians who are the products of education on the middle and upper level, but also leaders and managers who have come from the rural base and therefore are well acquainted with the environment they must structure, prompt to act, and organize. They will have to *attack the essential obstacle by first of all bringing about a desire* for change, and the proper frame of mind for development; this would be easier for young country people who had gone to school. Feeling quite at home with rural people in a rural setting, these educated people will then, with the help of technicians, have to put the leadership of at least a part of the economic groups resulting from the agrarian reform *in the hands of the peasants.*

Cooperatives supplying food and trade, credit, and service cooperatives must be able to have *good presidents, who have come from the mass of peasants* these cooperatives have at their disposal, along with their technical advisers. This will be even more necessary in the case of production cooperatives, for the peasants will be more loyal to them if the person at the head is someone like themselves (and not a worker from the city, as happened on the first kolkhozes). But this makes it necessary for the person in charge to have received the fair amount of technical, economic, mechanical, and commercial education the position requires, plus *a keen sense of human relations.*

This *necessary promotion of peasants* above all should not be limited to the field of cooperatives, the professions, and labor organizations. If Marx believed the peasants to be incapable of participating in the leadership of the revolution, it was because the peasants were landholders, ignorant and isolated, and therefore often were selfish and withdrawn. This was quite true on the farms of the Franconian Jura or the Black Forest, though it was not as true on the farms in Baden and the Rhine valley.

The farmer of the last third of the twentieth century, and not only the one in Europe, has closer and closer ties to the modern

authority necessary for the adoption of measures that are indispensable to success within the framework of the available resources.

The outline of an agricultural structure in continual evolution thus becomes visible. In it the family cell would at first be made up of a *little group* of people who know each other and have respect for each other, and therefore are more willing to help each other. A certain number of these groups—whose great flexibility would allow them to take many different forms of association—would be aided by a series of specialized cooperatives. Certain of these would devote themselves to accumulating credits and transforming agricultural raw materials. Instead of nationalizing a sugar-beet refinery, a milk-processing plant, or a winery, why not turn them over, under the control of the State, to the group of farmers whose products these plants use? The representatives of the workers and the consumers ought to be able to have a say in the matter at certain times.

6. A multiplicity of socialist forms and patterns of change

In this way, a country could emerge all the faster from the monolithic pattern it would have come to have by copying Soviet or Chinese models too slavishly, for these models came into being in special circumstances that are quite different from those that prevail today from Caracas to Santiago, Chile, and from Algiers to Conakry and Tanganyka as well. The need *to keep socialist experiences in mind* does not automatically imply *that identical formulas need be adopted.* Moreover, the kolkhoz and the sovkhoz have changed a great deal since taking the first faltering steps in 1919. And they are destined to evolve even faster because of the fact that they have spread out in the same geographical directions and are now tending to bunch together and form larger interkolkhozian Unions.

An agrarian socialism *whose primary aim is development* does not necessarily require sudden collectivization imposed from above as was done in the U.S.S.R. in 1929, or that imposed by the popular democracies around 1949–1953, for such collectives have not yet proved to be economically efficient.

The original principles of Marxist socialism reject private ownership of means of production that are *already practically socialized,* such as banks, mines, railroads, and large factories. Marxist socialism is well able to come to terms with the continued existence of family businesses, whether on farms, in shops, or in craftsmen's studios, even if such businesses have one or two employees on salary (I say this even though it will be held against me as heresy). For with such bases it is not possible for true capitalism to come into being once again, as Stalin seemed to fear. The power being in the hands of the workers, they would have every means—and first of all the means to impose taxes—to prevent such a thing from happening.

As far as craftsmen, little retail shops, services (restaurants, hairdressers), and above all agriculture are concerned, the socialist solution is not necessarily identical with what appears to be best for large-scale enterprises. *A progressive evolution* can take place, based essentially on *cooperation that has been volunteered.* It is not a good idea, therefore, to suppress these prerevolutionary cooperatives, which as we have seen are very useful in the training of management personnel and the making of the first changes after power is taken over. In 1945–1947, Poland wiped the slate clean, and then later had to re-establish such cooperatives, beginning in 1958, in the form of agricultural clubs, with many more difficulties and much more hanging back than if the earlier forms, which had sprung up from the base, had been kept.

In short, socialist evolution, in agriculture and in services, can assume a very flexible form which will have advantages that are not economic alone. Once a certain freedom as regards forms of organization has been restored, *this* sort of socialism can bring man even more dignity. Giving him back the initiative will allow him to flourish; and this would be well worth the possible price of a certain number of provisory economic imperfections. On May 20, 1960, I told Fidel that it would be hard to do worse than capitalism, and that he thus had a wide margin for error. He has somewhat abused this privilege; therefore it is not possible to say that another form of socialism—which would have been planned only in broad outline yet at the same time would have been worked out cooperatively—would have done more harm.

The sugar-cane cooperatives failed, as did the *granjas;* but this failure was because of the guaranteed wages paid on them and because more advantages were given to the nearby *granjas del pueblo.* This in no way allows one to conclude that cooperatives directed by technicians (where economic retribution for the errors committed would be immediately forthcoming, contrary to what happens in centralized State enterprises) are generally inferior. The whole budgetary apparatus dangerously covers up these errors, prevents them from coming to light for too long a time, and thus prevents their being corrected. Accompanied by an excess of authority, these same economic errors would become even less acceptable, for they would be more of a burden and less easy to correct.

This latter form of socialist evolution would be easier to bring about if *increased aid of a more intelligent sort,* a more intellectual sort (teachers and technicians) came from rich countries that were also moving toward a true, more flexible socialism. This could be done either by increasing these countries' political liberation and by recognizing real economic laws in the East, or by more radical socialization in the West; certain labor leaders are finally ceasing to consider the popular democracies as necessarily enemies.

True socialism knows that it is intended for imperfect men, who will always be imperfect, even though they constantly continue to improve. It realizes that it is faced at present with a long-term task that will span many generations. It no longer blinks the fact that the traditional idea of communism seems utopian to these generations, since it presupposes an almost perfect citizen, a goal that is unattainable in the predictable future.

Seen from this angle, how can backward countries that express the desire to develop themselves by following "the road to socialism" (which is not always very clear in their minds) approach that goal without the risk of piling too many failures one on top of the other, while at the same time steadfastly continuing along the path to socialism? This question remains to be examined before we draw the final conclusion.

7. *Nationalizing or administering cooperatively only what can be well managed: the example of Guinea*

I have pointed out that the premature restriction of leadership to Africans in production units brought on many problems in French-speaking Africa. The oil-processing plant at Dibmobari in the Lower Cameroons, that I had pointed out as a particular example of bad management,[8] has since closed its doors, and clusters of palm nuts are rotting on the trees. However desirable nationalization may be theoretically, in practice it demands competent, honest, and devoted administrators to succeed, and these were sorely lacking in Guinea in the period 1959–1968.

Jacques Miandre's article "L'expérience guinéenne" ["The Guinean Experience"][9] is particularly depressing to read:

"Agricultural cooperatives came into being with capital that was so badly managed that it was quickly exhausted, and they were so badly organized that ripe crops were often not even harvested. Despite the enormous sums invested (fifty billion[10] instead of the ten billion originally planned), the three-year Plan did not noticeably improve economic conditions, for lack of competent personnel, thorough studies, and a *minimum of honesty* on the part of the leaders. What few factories there are do not function properly or do not function at all, and their management is so disastrous that they are constantly in debt.

"The training provided is poor, the Russian teachers, who do not know French, are inept . . . Two cement barges disappeared from the wharfs, having been stolen by a ring involving ministers and regional military leaders . . . Sékou Touré, whose honesty no one doubts, enjoyed the use of

---

8 *L'Afrique noire est mal partie*, p. 77.
9 *Esprit*, octobre 1963. See also *Afrique*, décembre 1963, pp. 14–15.
10 CFA francs, worth two French centimes (approximately half a U.S. cent).

several luxurious cars, and many splendid villas. Ministers in office have magnificent houses built for their personal use. Two thieves, the perpetrators of petty larcenies, have been shot by a firing squad. Almost all of the leaders consider certain material advantages as an integral part of power . . . Guinean currency soon was worthless, and a black market came into being . . . slowness, ineffectiveness, underhanded dealings by the administration . . . extortion by leaders on all levels . . ."

Let us stop there, and admit quite readily that in Cuba extortion is far from the general rule and is severely punished. These difficulties that piled up in Guinea can be linked to a take-off point from a degree of underdevelopment that was much more pronounced than was the case in Cuba. The possibilities, and therefore the limits of effectiveness, of socialization and collectivization ought to be recognized from the very outset. *Most underdeveloped countries do not fulfill the conditions necessary for the immediate passage to a collectivized economy* (that is, one with a completely centralized administration with no feedback from the collective) that is fruitful, efficient, and productive. This does not mean that an economy dominated by a persistent barter system and outside purchases of all industrial products should continue to be accepted. Nor should there be neo-colonialism of the type developed along the Ivory Coast, whereby a limited beginning of development allows "new gentlemen" to accumulate handsome fortunes, thanks to fancy deals or their political position, a state of affairs that compromises the subsequent phase of development.

The lesson to be learned from this is that there should be no hurried nationalizations that risk being ruinous, and that the future should be carefully prepared for. The spread of education must be accompanied by a reform that stresses the learning of a trade, and accelerated professional training, in such a way as to allow the whole educational system, which in the beginning is so costly, to become productive more quickly. Education ought also to encourage a *mentality* that will be more favorable to socialist development: devotion to the collective unit, respect for communal property, a pioneer spirit of genuine progress, through an effort on everyone's part . . .

In a country that is still uneducated, the cooperative movement cannot come into being through the initiative of the peasant base, as was the case in Scandinavia in the nineteenth century in a milieu that was already educated. In Africa, therefore, it has been necessary to stimulate such a movement from the top. It would be possible, however, to interest the peasant more directly in such a movement by laying the groundwork for his rapid emancipation from this cooperation that will have begun under guardianship, through the education of peasant leaders. The first thing that would be demanded of the cooperating unit would be *a contribution in the form of money and above all in the form of work,* a *disciplined* sale of its products. Unless there is sacrifice, unless there is real *participation* in the common effort, and real sharing of the equipment in the village, there must be no more talk of cooperation. All this is easier to write about than to put into effect; IRAM[11] is in a good position to realize this. The most delicate task yet to be performed is to set up an economic structure sufficiently adapted to this phase of evolution. Such a structure precedes certain details; nonetheless this structure is meant to prepare the advent of socialism. We shall now study such a structure briefly by citing the case of tropical Africa.

8. *A cooperative structure for an African pre-socialism*[12]

The goal of such a structure would be above all to prepare and protect the future chances of socialism, while at the same time

---

[11] See *L'Afrique noire est mal partie,* pp. 166–170.

[12] For more details on the measures suggested for Africa, I refer the reader to *L'Afrique noire est mal partie.* At this writing, six years later, I would tend to put more emphasis on the necessity of a better-organized cooperative solution, which would appear to be the only basis leading to a socialism that would be genuinely *accepted.* And I would also tend to be less optimistic about the possibility of rapidly emerging from underdevelopment, after so many failures have piled up one atop the other . . .

beginning the economic take-off, in an environment whose technical and economic development would not yet permit fruitful socialization. If the political team in power were as devoted to the cause of all the workers as the one in Cuba and better informed economically and technically, the problem would already be more than half solved.

In a totally different international context, leaders of this caliber would be in a position to bring about a more progressive socialization, adapted to the available means for efficient management. This would be all the more likely the more the leaders are really won over to the popular cause, and the more moderate the rate of socialization they impose, without compromising with the privileged, and thus taking careful thought of what the future might bring.

In accordance with this theory, development of the country could progressively take the positions of power over from capitalism, *yet at the same time not cease to develop production.* Each country will have to have the profoundest possible awareness of its particular conditions, and the choice is up to Africans. Let us try, nonetheless, to be of help to them, by making a few general suggestions, which will necessarily be quite sketchy. We can specify priorities and submit detailed reports on the measures that must be taken only in the case of precise states, situations, and dates, and only after the leaders have themselves decided on the general guidelines, such as the rate of development that they want in the country.

The most urgent measure to be taken would be to modify the structure of foreign commerce, by doing away with luxury imports. At the same time, semi-luxury goods that people can do without quite easily, or that could be manufactured in the country and thus be replaced fairly easily, should be heavily taxed. This would soon allow increased imports of heavy equipment, while at the same time reducing the trade deficit, and therefore the *dependence* of the national economy on foreign trade.

The second step would force wholesale merchants and import-export companies to invest almost all their profits *within the country*.[13] This could be carried out by the creation of the enterprises provided for in the first program of development, which would continue to be quite flexible. At this early stage the creation of new enterprises provided for in the Plan could be prohibited if they were obviously harmful (*e.g.,* breweries) or uneconomical, in which case all that need be done is to refuse to give them government subsidies.

The temporary plans and then the over-all Plans, which would be more and more complex and more and more restrictive, would at best make plans only for developing rare resources. They would assure, first of all, the primacy of *productive investments* (equally divided between agriculture, the infrastructure, and industry) over the administrative apparatus, which has turned out to have gone to extremes in the execution of the first plan in Senegal and in many other places. At the beginning, the only funds that should be granted are those indispensable for certain collective social activities such as a health service and education, once this latter has been thoroughly re-examined. If austerity became a common practice in public life, if the members of parliament were assembled and their modest salaries paid for only three months per year, this would soon change the work atmosphere. Within this framework, once things have been cleaned up and new blood brought in, *the peasant could at last hope* to raise himself to a higher social class without abandoning his profession as a farmer, but instead by modernizing his calling.

In agriculture it would be necessary: "to free the individual from the chains of tradition, pass from itinerant tilling of the soil with a hoe to intensive agriculture using draft animals . . . [and] through the destruction of the great families [proceed to] the development of a sense of prideful individual ownership of land . . . Cooperatives in Guinea are a failure, for

---

[13] At the end of 1963, Ghana gave up its policy of obligatory savings, as well as the provision that sixty per cent of profits be invested within the country. It would be interesting to know the motives underlying such a measure. No serious study of economic progress in Africa can skirt the thorough study of local experiences in Ghana, Guinea, etc.

agricultural production there is either at a standstill or has taken a step backward. In Ghana, where people are more realistic, a way is being sought to free the forces of individualism without allowing "New Farmers" to become a distinct and very different class. The plow, an individual tool, cannot be the material basis for a *premature collectivization.* Mechanization cannot take place until the machines can be produced within the country . . . the cooperative [must be] based on the willing support of dynamic little producers, freed from the traditional chains of family and society, and limit itself to commercialization and credit. It would be a far harder task to be forced to build socialism in these artificial states of West Africa amid the hostility of their neighbors."[14]

Getting rural areas moving ahead would then permit the prudent adoption of a *cooperative sector* which would little by little continue to grow, and this time from the bottom up, with modest aid and periodic financial audits by the State, with a careful eye on economic self-management. The first step would be to set up trade and food cooperatives, which would lead to the establishment of a National Office, as in Senegal, or to Marketing Boards similar to those in English-speaking Africa. Thus the activity of large foreign commercial enterprises would largely be handled by public authorities, and this could prepare the way for the following step, that of groups with a mixed economy. This movement would soon lead to its natural complements, such as collective credit unions, and then to *service cooperatives* oriented toward the most urgent tasks: the bottlenecks of production, and the struggle against the enemies of the farmers' crops.

A similar cooperative movement could lead little by little to disciplining the craftsman and providing him with tools: it is better to make him change than it is to try to wipe him out, especially if this is done prematurely. Certain retail cooperative unions then might cautiously embark upon wholesale trade with the intelligent aid of public officials. These agricultural, craft,

---

[14] An anonymous study, published in *Revolución,* diciembre, 1963.

and trade areas, which are private sectors tending toward progressive and voluntary cooperative development, would remain, at least for quite a long time to come, free to choose what degree of collectivization they prefer. Forced collectivization of farms, restaurants, craft studios, or family-run stores never entered Marx's head, though he wanted to see the great capitalist system collectivized. Such treatment of family businesses would therefore amount to ultra-Marxism, ultra-socialism.

This cooperative development would be the first step and would vastly facilitate the passage to a more thoroughgoing socialism. We continue to believe that in Cuba such development, if it had been thoroughly understood, could have taken a much more efficient form than placing *granjas,* little hotels, and little craft shops under State control. René Gendarme,[15] however, thinks it is superior to capitalist enterprise as regards development; and he gives us a pertinent description of its triple role: renewing the traditional sector, fighting against the economic dependence of the peasant, and providing the means to facilitate the economic dependence of the peasant, and providing the means to facilitate the economic action of the State. He puts great emphasis, finally, on the four essential conditions for the success of cooperatives: the proper size (many of them are too small to pay qualified personnel); the proper budget; the choice of what they will specialize in; and a priority assigned them for getting started. Cooperative education of the population and the support of the State are two conditions *sine qua non.*

9. *The public sector and a mixed economy prudently developed*

This first step would thus allow a large part of the peasantry to organize, perhaps in labor unions. It would thus be in a position to bring sufficient pressure to bear on the government to permit it to resist the pressure of privileged city-dwellers of the tertiary

---

[15] *La pauvreté des nations,* Editions Cujas, 1963.

sector.[16] The second phase of pre-socialism, which could be begun along with the first, but should not swamp it, would be aimed at a progressive build-up of two sectors, which we shall call the socialized sector and the semi-socialized sector.

If they were capable of doing so, the public authorities would take charge of the banking sector and certain large-scale mining activities and new industrial plants, which are indispensable to development but are not very profitable in the beginning, as created within the framework of the Plan. For the Middle East and Venezuela, the Beyrouth conference, in November 1963 clearly demonstrated the possibility of State management of petroleum products, a step that is receiving more and more serious consideration by the Arab States. If E. Mattei[17] had not died before his time, he would have been able to smooth the way for taking the steps leading to semi-emancipation, paving the way for State management, which is exactly what is required in such a sector.

At this stage the possibilities of mixed economic companies, which I advised President Ben Bella of Algeria to adopt in January 1963, seem even broader. It would have been better to have taken a firm half-step that would have allowed production to be expanded than to try to take one whole step toward socialization and then later, in 1964, have their backs to the wall as they faced the Hobsonian choice of either creating a New Economic Plan and allowing a partial return to private ownership, or else suffering a serious setback in production. In Algeria there is still time to go back to mixed-economy enterprises in certain sectors, even though future revolutions would find it much more efficient to go directly to that stage, using the old structure as a point of departure. Let us try to transform the units and systems of production that already exist for the benefit

---

[16] This was what Mamadou Dia was trying to do in Senegal, but the urban lobby practically sent him to prison, much to the delight of the Chamber of Commerce.

[17] The director of the nationalized petroleum and gas industries in Italy.

of society as a whole instead of demolishing them, whenever they are not outright parasites.

China has shown us how profitable this formula can be, for it allowed that country to continue production in factories already set up, and assured continuity of distribution. Within a capitalist framework, it is the State that furnishes financial funds and capital that gets the profits. But if power is really in the hands of the workers, it becomes easier to make these companies with mixed economies go along with the general interest. Such companies can also be established in the new industries, such as those that produce consumer goods or transform local raw materials. In the field of agriculture, such companies would also be a suitable base for *plantations* (Para rubber plants, palm trees, sugar cane . . .), an absolute condition for the success of such units being their *following technical advice to the letter.* Annual crops, on the other hand, even cacao and coffee, can be made to give good yields within a framework where the peasantry has been well supervised.

A certain degree of competition whereby cooperatives run by technically trained, authoritarian leaders and these enterprises with a mixed economy would vie with each other in the same sectors of the economy, can lead to healthy emulation. The State must help the cooperatives without subsidizing them too much. A monopoly that is too authoritarian—whether capitalist, co-operative, or State-run, risks exempting those who take unfair advantage of it from unceasing efforts to get ahead, which will always be indispensable. With such a situation as its point of departure, a State that was no longer subject to authoritarian rule could encourage the structures that seemed to it to be the most advantageous, while at the same time continually reserving to itself the right to determine the optimum speed of socialization compatible with the continuity of development that is required.

But this supposes at the very least a kindly neutrality toward these young socialist experiments on the part of already developed countries: Cuba has not had this neutrality, and the hostility still circumscribing her interesting experiment is *really a crime*—more than a crime, an error, Talleyrand would say—on the part of American imperialism. Fidel Castro nonetheless proved to Jean Daniel that the United States might well have respected him as much as Sékou Touré and Tito.[18] He urged Daniel to repeat this message to President Kennedy; two days later Kennedy was assassinated, in a climate of hatred stirred up by those who wanted to oppose any form of progressive evolution by every possible means. The lesson, however, is beginning to bear fruit, for even Gaullist France has proved this by adopting a much more understanding attitude toward the Algerian revolution, "which she does not want to treat the way the United States treated Cuba," Minister de Broglie explains.

10. *In Latin America, agrarian reform has the first priority*

From Mexico to Chile, we find a very different situation, which in general resembles that of Cuba. Within the framework of the underdeveloped latifundium of the feudal type, it is not simply a question of reorganization, as happened with the *granjas*: it is necessary to energetically overturn a structure which at present is standing in the way of progress, and to cast off the heavy yoke of American monopolies. Certainly a land tax proportionate to the original fertility and the economic environment, which would get larger as the property became larger in size, would be a useful measure if it were really enforced. It would at least prevent owners from leaving enormous acreages fallow and unused as they simply wait for real estate to go up in value. It would encourage at least some small measure of intensification to enable the owner to make a substantial profit on each unit over and above the taxes imposed.

On estates where the miserable wages paid allow the owners to continue to earn a little money, even though their technique is far behind the times and their equipment is very shoddy, as on the centuries-old plantations along the "sugar coast" of North-

---

[18] Two heretics—I was about to say two *other* heretics. See *L'Express,* 5 décembre, 1963.

eastern Brazil, the badly mistreated workers will no longer accept changes that come too slowly.[19] Again in this case agrarian reform is the number one priority, but it will have to take place amid conditions better than those in Cuba if it is to be followed by an immediate *and prolonged* increase in production.

The first condition for success would be the education on a large scale, beginning now, of the tens of thousands of technicians and agronomists necessary to provide better management of the expropriated lands, throughout Latin America. Instead of making anonymous State farms out of them, this reform[20] would instead opt for a cooperative formula, which could come close to the Algerian type of "self-management," but with much better organization and a much better technical staff, with competent directors alongside the presidents, who in this part of the world are sometimes illiterate. The State would furnish the administrative personnel and *part* of the investment credits: it would lay down the broad guidelines for production (the Plan). But it would leave all the responsibilities of day-to-day management to reliable *appointed* technical directors, along with those officers *elected* by the workmen in the collective. In the absence of any sort of wages guaranteed by the State, every individual would be better aware that his lot remains within his own hands, and that he must work hard; otherwise he would be stealing from the comrades he works with every day.

It is not terribly important whether these production cooperatives *possess land or not;* the essential thing is for them to have a certain freedom of action, and a freedom to use the land that would be guaranteed over a long period of time, so that there will be an interest in investing in it. I would strongly suggest,

---

[19] The capitalist plantations of British Guiana (the Bookers group), which are much better equipped and much better managed, can pay wages that are three or four times higher than wages in the Northeast of Brazil.

[20] I take it for granted that this reform will not have paid indemnities; or if really necessary will have paid very partial symbolic indemnities that must be reinvested in the country, if the revolution implied by the first measure could not be carried out.

therefore, that the ownership of the land be left in the hands of the local municipalities if they have gotten out of the clutches of the large estate-owners. For they are in a better position to take care of them rationally than they would be if this land were national property managed from much too great a distance away. I would prefer, however, that the other means of work and development capital be owned collectively, with the whole group of workers owning them; there would thus be a tendency to take better care of them than if they were still something that belonged to the "administration" in the workers' eyes.

Such cooperative workshops, which would at the same time be under the Plan and autonomous so that this Plan can be carried out, would be aided as soon as possible in their task by a whole network of service cooperatives (for heavy work, for protection of crops against their enemies), credit cooperatives, and cooperatives that would supply food and sell farm produce. Better still, this network, which should include farms run by peasants, should be established even before these production cooperatives, for they will make it much easier to set them up. Thus these different cooperatives could group both cooperative enterprises and private farms together in the same unit.

All these intercooperative ties should have a sound monetary basis. Each collective could thus exert an influence on its client, and more particularly on its supplier, and defend its ideas; and the consumer could have an important effect on the direction that production should take; demand would find a way to express itself. The remuneration of each of them would thus be directly linked to the amount of work done. The State would never supply all the investment capital, for it is impossible to imagine a true cooperative that would not entail a very large contribution from its members, in the beginning in the form of the work they do. Their share of the equipment that is bought would be likely to constantly increase, as is the case on the kolkhoz.

If this path were to be followed, the building of socialism would be seen to be not a hasty decision, a sort of decree by the political power seeking to hurry development along, but as work that will go on and on, and always be perfectible. It will therefore have room for a whole series of transitional stages, in which collective forms and private forms of ownership of the means of production will coexist (each of these two categories being essentially different). The return of capitalism can be avoided if the power of the State, held in firm hands, does not encourage it. It will require great effort on the part of interested parties, and a *great deal of austerity and physical labor.*

The workers can do all this willingly if they are not faced, in their own country, first of all, with those who flaunt their privileges and insolently display their wealth. The North Vietnamese peasant and the Yugoslavian worker are quite willing to make sacrifices that they know are shared by a great many other people, unlike their neighbors in South Vietnam and Greece, who make no effort to share in this sacrifice. The abyss of privileges ought not to yawn wider still between nations, and the gap between rich and poor ought not to continue to dangerously increase. *In view of the misery of the poor, the spectacle of waste is a scandal,* even though it takes place in a far-off country. If it is believed that those who are starving will continue to accept this spectacle when they are better informed each year, such a belief would be yet another instance of ultra-optimism. We in Europe must be aware of this sooner than the Yankees, and this is going to lead us far afield. Will the mentality of semi-primitives (that we in Western Europe have as regards the real needs of our era) be capable of accepting the new needs of international development? The whole future of our civilization depends on how this question is answered.

11. A take-off now impossible under the system of free enterprise: agriculture as an absolute priority at the beginning

Infatuated with their success, which many hands helped them obtain, Yankees are often content to repeat, from Latin America and Africa to Southeast Asia: "Do as we do, look how successful capitalism has been for us." Paul Bairoch[21] shows us that

---

[21] *Révolution industrielle et sous-développement,* SEDES, 1963.

except for Australasia, Canada, and a small number of pre-dominantly "white" zones of Latin America (the north of Argentina, the south of Brazil, the center of Chile, and part of Mexico), no underdeveloped country has been able to achieve an economic take-off since the end of the nineteenth century. He puts forward a very interesting explanation for this. The industrial revolution in England and Western Europe, in his opinion, was not fundamentally determined, as has often been claimed, by progress in the technical field, the impact of the population explosion, or the role of the financial system. Rather, it was *"the previous increase in agricultural productivity* [that was] the determining factor that brought about the beginning of development . . . [and] favored and made possible a general and cumulative development of the economy." And he demonstrates this by tracing the history of Franco-English development. The high cost of shipping, the relative simplicity of the first techniques of this revolution, and therefore the small investments that were necessary at the time, accompanied by high profits, favored the spread of this industrial revolution (to its neighbors) and its self-financing. Anyone in Western Europe, and then in the United States, could build a steam engine, for it was both simple and heavy, and shipping one was very expensive.

At the dawn of the last third of the twentieth century *the situation of the underdeveloped countries is totally different.* The population of Western Europe was increasing barely .5% per year before its development and often only .7% during the first phase of this development. The underdeveloped countries have an average population increase of 2.2%, Bairoch tells us; but more recent estimates place the figure much higher. The rate of population increase is now 2.5% in India, 3% in Morocco, 3.6% in Mexico, 3.8% in the Philippines. In isolated provinces (such as the high plateaus of Madagascar, or the southwest of Dahomey) the rate goes as high as 4%. At a rate of just 2.2%, the population of a country triples in fifty years. At 3.1% it multiplies by a factor of 20 in a century, and reaches 64 million (20 to the 6th power) in six centuries.

Let us not brood on the apocalyptic long-term prospect. On the average, if an increase of 2% per year in the standard of living is desired[22] for a population increasing at the rate of 3%, the gross national income ought to increase by at least 5%. This would mean *investing 22.5% of this latter sum,* if an average of 4.5% of capital is required to furnish 1% of gross income. But the countries that today are developed invested only 5 to 6% of their income at the beginning of their economic take-off. It was not until the second half of the nineteenth century that an investment rate of 12% of investments was reached in Western Europe, and not until the twentieth century did the figure reach 15%. During the first century of European development, over-all agricultural progress over a long term only once went higher than 1.5% per year: this was in Russia from 1860 to 1915 (1.7%), stemming largely from the previous blockages to expansion brought about by slavery and insufficient shipping facilities, and the cost of farming new land.

Within the framework of a liberal economy the other fundamental obstacles to an economic take-off in the backward countries are the social laws, which often forbid child labor and too low wages. This is quite justifiable, but such laws take away from these economies two of the essential factors in European capitalist development in the nineteenth century. And the hypertrophied tertiary sector, according to Bairoch, often occupies 25% of the active population and corners 40% of the national product; it also tends to become inflated all by itself, through self-financing. Industrial capital brings in much less than in the days of the Manchester mills, often 10% per year instead of 30 to 40%; but the capital devoted to trade still brings in profits such as were described by Balzac.

The modern techniques of the twentieth century, finally, are not at all what they were in the nineteenth century, when they were within the grasp of the traditional craftsman. French boilermakers could copy the English locomotive imported by

[22] A rate that is not nearly high enough, for it is less than that of the developed countries (3 to 8%), and will never allow it to catch up.

Marc Séguin. A diesel or electric locomotive, a truck or a tractor, a modern textile machine can no longer be manufactured by an African or Indian smith.

Technology having become much more complex, with a base that is no longer empirical but rather scientific; this calls for a thoroughgoing general and technological education, as we have shown for agriculture. In India in 1960, industrialization takes *thirty years* of a worker's wages, of investment credits put to work, instead of the four months of wages it took in the case of England in 1912. Pieces of heavy equipment were almost all made in the countries that were industrializing in the nineteenth century. They are almost all imported in the case of those who are trying to develop their countries in the second half of the twentieth century. Their manufacture outside the country thus no longer leads to "general and cumulative development of the economy."

This development is also blocked by the regression of traditional craftsmen ruined by imported objects manufactured by industry in the developed countries. Shipping costs went down from a factor of 10 to a factor of 1 between 1800 and 1900, thus doing away with the de facto protective wall that was erected in the nineteenth century, to the profit of budding industries. This led to the excessive specialization of tropical agriculture with its crops grown for export cash, allowed minerals and crude petroleum to be exported without transforming them before they left the country, and sharpened everyone's desire to reach a modern standard of living before development.

Bairoch's demonstration seems particularly impressive. Within the framework of free enterprise, of capitalism, a certain type of development was able to flower in the nineteenth century, from Western Europe to the United States. In Japan, a stronger impetus on the part of the central power would have been necessary. In places where it is well under way (Mexico, southern Brazil), it is possible that this capitalist development will continue, despite certain difficulties. But in countries where such development has not yet begun, it has become practically impossible within a liberal framework. The Alliance for Progress is thus not only doomed to failure; Africa will follow close behind if it prefers liberalism.

Within a socialist framework, Cuba has shown us the diffi-*culties* inherent in development; it will demand more effort than in the already advanced capitalist countries. And we have shown, with regard to Soviet agriculture, that after a certain stage this development called for more self-management, and required that everyone be given more initiative and responsibility in order for it to expand in an economy that had already become a complex one. But *the possibility of an economic take-off remains open* within this framework, on condition that the country does not rush into economic adventures and emerges from the liberal system prudently and progressively, but also resolutely.

To achieve this take-off, a minimum of authority, both technical and economic, if not downright constraint at times, appears to be indispensable if everyone is to be put to work, even in the slack season on the farms and plantations. These workers would be given only their food, or very modest wages so as to increase the amount of money available for investments and fight the population explosion. Children should soon all be attending a good school. But when more than a third of the population does not reach the age of ten, and if one adds to them the elderly, the sick (who are more numerous in the tropics, especially where there is so little medicine), and the mothers of families with a dangerous number of children, this is quite a high proportion of inactive people to be included in plans to accelerate development.

From this point of view, the country is faced with having to combine the general education of children and their professional training, which would be begun earlier than in Europe. This might be done by requiring that children put in two hours of educational and productive work from the age of ten to twelve, and four hours after they have reached the age of twelve—providing that the dominant class of this backward society, which wants to copy the colonizer, accords manual effort the prestige that too often it refuses to give it.

Peasants and workers in Europe in the eighteenth and nineteenth centuries put in such effort and accepted such austerity, both of these being factors that are indispensable for economic take-off, amid conditions that at times were very painful, and at the same time they gave "their" privileged class a life of luxury. At the end of the twentieth century, the sacrifices indispensable for economic take-off are going to become too painful to be acceptable to those who will have had too close a look at the easy life of the few privileged people among them, and also of the more numerous class of those whom development has already come to, another group of privileged people, even though part of them claim to be proletarians.

A change of social climate and cast of mind is now an essential preliminary to development. And it would appear that such a development is now *easier to carry on than it is to set in motion,* in particular because of the fact that too highly developed forms of exploitation are being done away with. For the young industries of new countries are now subject to rough competition. It is certain that such competition must be made less severe, *so as to give each nation a more equal footing in the beginning.*

Hard work in the hot sun will continue to be bearable only if each worker has the feeling that he is working not for the benefit of others, but for himself and his children. This will require that a minimum of social justice be available to the peasants, who are exploited by the privileged class in the towns. On the world scale, all so-called attempts to aid these countries or cooperate with them, including the efforts of the Russians in Cuba, have thus far proved to be absolutely inadequate. This problem of development must therefore be the object of new reflections on the part of people no longer afraid to attack the taboos of privilege or sclerosed attitudes.

"The change in the basic facts," Alfred Sauvy writes after having studied Bairoch, "demands on the contrary a new mechanism of development, which this time cannot do without rather thorough planning and substantial foreign aid." To Sauvy's list let us add a progressive socialization, closely dependent upon the possibility of administering it effectively. With development, agriculture will see its relative role in the economy diminished. But we have seen that bettering agricultural productivity was the essential condition for a take-off in this field. Thus the absolute priority of agriculture, which Cuba[23] and China now recognize.

12. Re-examining the structure of the world economy

The world's outlay for military purposes, according to a memorandum submitted to the Council in November 1963, by a group of French atomic scientists, is around 80% of the *total* income of the underdeveloped countries. Though this proportion seems high, these outlays have nonetheless become less and less acceptable in the face of the misery of poor people, of whom there are more each year, and in particular in the face of the risk of worsening this state of misery, which is the consequence of a *phenomenon that we are more and more losing control of, the population explosion.* Mexico had a fair start, despite its sabotaged agricultural reform. Its rate of progress even approached 7% per year, but the 1962–1964 plan foresaw a reduction to 5.4%. Meanwhile, its population increase in 1962 reached the frightening, intolerable figure of 3.6%, the only large nation to have such a rate. And meanwhile the conquest of new lands, through irrigation or the development of coastal regions, is becoming more and more onerous, as in China and India.

In this latter country the increase in farm production, which hovers around the stagnant figure of 2% per year, is more than canceled out by the rise in population, which has now reached the figure of more than 2.5%. The Indian situation, which is more difficult, has become even worse with the poor harvests of 1965–1966.[24] All the projects *that we have embarked on up to*

---

[23] The recent trade agreement with Moscow also confirms this order of priority.

[24] There is starvation in a number of villages; our major newspapers that were so zealous about reporting famine in China have had nothing to say in this case.

now in order to fight against underdevelopment are absolutely, dangerously, and ridiculously inadequate: since the gap in income per head continues to widen, we must seek other solutions that this time will be effective. They will be recognized as such only if the gap in standards of living becomes narrower, and only if the real situation of haves and have-nots becomes more or less comparable. The gap between the group of rich nations and poor ones was on the order of 8 to 1 in the nineteenth century; it reached 14 to 1 in 1962, and statisticians predict that it will be 17 to 1 in 1970, and perhaps even 25 to 1 around 1990.

This obliges us to re-examine our policy, our attitude toward the underdeveloped countries. We must abandon the mentality that involves charity, begging, assistance, and aid which has thus far prevailed, and envisage a real cooperation on everyone's part, built on new bases which must be discussed by all the parties concerned, rich and poor, on a plane where all are recognized as citizens of the world, and therefore not such unequal partners. The very structure of the world economy, which is not adapted to the new situation marked by the increasingly severe distortions brought about by development, ought to be reorganized. This could be undertaken by a body (yet to be defined) to direct this economy, a body that must little by little be given increased powers which one day will be supranational and therefore binding on all parties.

We are not unaware of the weight of the geographic, historical, and ethnological facts, nor of the weight of resistance to a world economic power, which would not be restricted to the capitalist countries alone. It is only when the first attempts to establish a world mentality are taken that the best ways to go about taking this preliminary political step will become clear. A handful of speculators will rise up in protest, for they are the classical profiteers when there is famine, but once they are seen to be harmful to the collectivity, it will be easier to isolate them. World production could thus be progressively controlled, and then planned in advance, a step that would allow it to develop in such a way as to satisfy the needs of all peoples, *whether they were solvent or not.* This aid, or rather this cooperation, would allow the volume of possible markets to be constantly increased.

Thus the various countries could avoid the latent defects of capitalism, such as the lack of buying power, which leads to Malthusian setbacks and aggravates cyclical crises instead of correcting them.

All this may be considered a utopia today. But it is really only a long-term perspective that will soon become a necessity if leaders of the various countries really want to confront the enormous difficulties resulting from the population explosion (until such a time as it can be effectively held in check) by making use of any and every available resource. Such a mobilization of the "hidden productive forces" requires a new framework, which will be difficult to create. It will encounter resistance on the part of some, and a lack of understanding on the part of a great many more. World development thus requires a preliminary step, even in the countries that believe that they are very well-educated: a concerted effort to provide an education free of the chains of nationalism so as to be able to face the new demands of international solidarity.

If this long-term prospect, which grants the necessity of profound changes, were to be more generally accepted—and securing this acceptance is the essential task for those of our generation who believe it to be useful—it would serve as a guideline for short-term and middle-term action, which would allow this ideal to be approached by successive empirical trial-and-error experiments, without dogmatism. In the first stage, let us seek to increase the volume of cooperation everywhere, whatever its origin, by every possible means: there is too much to do to refuse to compete. Let us channel it into the field of industrial equipment, as soon as it is possible to make it profitable, thanks to a better-educated population able to use complicated machines. At the same time, an effort should be made, insofar as this is possible, to progressively replace bilateral aids with multilateral cooperation, which one day will tend to become universal. While awaiting such cooperation, it would be mad to refuse such bilateral aid.

This initial step would also include an effort to reorganize world commerce on new bases. In his *Un monde possible* [A possible world] Tibor Mende furnished an interesting plan for such a reorganization. If the stabilization of the market for raw materials is the most important objective, it must be sought in a constant and rapid expansion of consumption, thus allowing an expansion of production to be envisaged without the risk of making the market collapse. For if international agreements for the restriction of production, on the order of the one that has just been concluded for coffee, were to become the general rule, they would soon lead to universal poverty.

The necessities of development do not require this or that level of prices for this or that product, for such a level can be defined only in an arbitrary way. These necessities require a fierce defense of the purchasing power of these raw materials, expressed in manufactured products, especially in equipment goods. International accords could be discussed more practically on this basis. It is also necessary *to open the doors of the most highly developed countries wider* so as to let in productions of the backward countries, especially manufactured products.

This would correspond to a constant evolution of the advanced countries toward activities that require more skill and are more difficult, but at present more within reach than they would be in the young countries: complex machine tools, electronic equipment, very involved synthetic chemistry. Naturally, an effort should be made to close this gap in development, but it is impossible to do away with it through arbitrary decisions and a mere stroke of the pen. It can only be a long-term project. This, however, should not lead to the neglecting of such a project today; quite the contrary.

This plan is no more than a search for a rational international division of labor which would progressively eliminate all trace of domination and unequal exchange. At a later stage, the progressive constitution of an efficient supranational political and economic power would reduce all these tendencies toward domination, which keep cropping up again and again among the great powers that have already been developed. Cuba is the first country to have escaped Yankee domination, but the attempts to ruin it persist, with the complicity, if not the all too widespread servility, of the so-called free world.[25] This obliges Cuba to pay a high price as it makes its important contribution to the economic liberation of all (army, militia, sabotage, millions of hours on guard duty . . .).

Within this worldwide perspective, regional communities, such as the Six in Europe and other common markets, would be managed in view of their becoming the solid bases of the future world pyramid, which will be attainable only if there is an international solidarity that is truly accepted and constantly increases. Thus a certain number of present efforts, whose divergence is sometimes more apparent than real, could be reconciled. An international tax of 1% on the national income of the developed countries, which was proposed some time ago, represents only a small fraction of the annual increase in income of these rich countries; it is not nearly enough, and already France has reached a rate of 1.5% to 2%. Before asking for more, it is necessary for the backward countries to put themselves in a position to be able to utilize a much larger amount of aid more effectively than has been the case in South Vietnam (and even in Cuba).

13. New juridical and international conceptions

A new conception of the relationships between the developed countries and the underdeveloped would have a better theoretical foundation if juridical structures were overhauled, especially if these structures were adopted by a growing number of nations and thus were to go beyond the limits of our small national territories.

Roman law in its essence was oriented toward the protection of property. The basis of the security of the rural family at the beginning, it has sometimes become a dynamic factor in the development of capitalism, but it is something quite different

---

[25] The recent English decision to sell buses to Cuba and the Spanish decision to build boats for Cuba show that this servility is becoming less pronounced.

when it takes the collective form of a corporation. The decline of this juridical principle, especially in Latin America, the homeland of so many jurists, is coming more and more to be a fearful obstacle to social justice, especially in the case of the latifundia, as well as to the rapid development of production. The relatively few profiteers in this regime would not have been able to uphold it without the more or less conscious aid of the monopolies and the powerful neighbor to the north and without the lack of understanding of a large proportion of the population, who were political illiterates.

Tomorrow's law must grant priority to *everything that facilitates and contributes to the full employment of the factors of production.* Land, first of all; thus it is justifiable to dispossess those who do not use it enough. On the individual level, this leads to agrarian reform. But this concept must be extended to the international level. When vast regions of Australia, Siberia, Africa, and South America cannot be put to use in the near future because of their underpopulation, and when western and southern Asia are about to literally smother to death because of their overpopulation, we must go beyond the selfish concept that would reserve the whole of a national territory for the use of its native citizens. The nineteenth century, despite its faults, nonetheless allowed men and capital, two essential factors in production, more mobility than they have today, and this is an important condition for their being better utilized.

At the same time the full employment of the labor factor would take the form of granting every individual *the right to work,* which would put a definite end to unemployment. As a corollary of this principle, every individual fit for work would have *the obligation to work* for the collectivity and social parasitism would be forbidden: he who doesn't work[26] doesn't eat. If it became an essential base of the New Law, the full employ-

---

[26] If clipping coupons, receiving farm rents, and speculating on the market or on real-estate developments is not accompanied by some technical or organizational role, it cannot be considered a productive activity.

ment of existing capital would make it necessary to find the best possible uses for it. These would be determined by the people as a whole, within the framework of a Plan, which would be very flexible in the beginning and progressively become more binding. If an American steel mill does not find enough markets at the list price, it would be better for it to keep producing at full capacity and put the supplementary steel thus produced on the market at the marginal cost of running the plant, a cost that would not include amortization and general expenses.

This might well lead to compensations on the part of various national and regional collectivities, and then later collectivities on the worldwide scale, and bring about the institution of double price sectors, which would be lower for the nondeveloped countries than for the others. Do not protest too quickly: this double sector already exists, but it works in the opposite direction. "World" prices for agricultural products can legitimately be considered to be abnormally low; they are bargain prices, the fruit of reciprocal dumping and a prolonged shortage of orders from nations that are solvent. But poor sellers must accept such prices as are offered by rich buyers such as England, Germany, or the United States, who thus rob them, though their consciences may remain perfectly clear.[27]

The New Law would extend this notion of protected agricultural prices to farmers all over the World, not just to those of them that are richest—and even these latter have great need of protected prices, for they are the poorest people in their wealthy countries. Our administrative unit directing the international economy would buy these foodstuffs at the world price and give them to the poor, so long as this aberration lasted, or it would give them to the most backward countries in exchange for investments of labor in projects that would help these countries along. For these countries will never get out of trouble unless the socialist countries collectively put in an enormous amount of labor inside these countries and give a helping hand financially,

---

[27] The first shepherd we met in rural Pennsylvania, in August 1946, explained that our host, the owner of the farm, was a pious soul. The best proof of this was the fact that the Good Lord had rewarded him by making him rich.

faster. Let us hope that theirs will be a peaceful victory, despite the obstacles and the difficulties that they will encounter. On reflection, obstacles and difficulties are really the only things of interest in a life where self-mastery is sought—and without such a life we would all be under a suspended death sentence. Within this perspective, our destiny lies in our own hands: only cowards will give up.

The Cuban Revolution, waged "in the lion's mouth," as Claude Julien put it, would have found it extremely difficult to resist the blockade and American attacks without the military and economic support of the U.S.S.R.[30] Perón's downfall, the difficulties in Guatemala in 1954, and those in Bolivia show that another South American revolution, which like the Cuban one would suddenly cut through the umbilical cord that links its economy to the United States, would have an acute need of even more support than that received by Cuba. But the Soviet possibilities[31] of extending foreign aid will be rather limited for long years to come. A number of South American revolutionaries, and often the most ardent of them, do not want the U.S.S.R. to have too tight a hold on their movement. This would force them, from the very beginning, to organize a more efficient economy.

Cuba, moreover, represents an original element, whose totalitarian nature within the communist group is not as marked as that of Peking or Moscow. A certain political liberalization of this Revolution is still a possibility, if the United States could only understand this Revolution and not demand a return to capitalism or impossible indemnities that fly in the face of the new principles of international aid. Nonetheless, the Yankees would still be able to carry out a decolonization in South America that would be acceptable to them, if only they could get their extremists and their monopolies into line. Only one question need be raised, but it is a crucial one: will they be

---

[30] And the courage, the resolute decisiveness of the revolutionary leaders.

[31] And even more the Chinese possibilities.

aware in time that their Organization of American States is compromising their whole future as is their involvement in Vietnam?

Within the Cuban framework, once the principal errors have been corrected, it will be quite possible for the country to develop rapidly. By contrast, the Alliance for Progress seems to be leading to an impasse, except in those countries which have already had an economic take-off. If these lessons to be derived from the Cuban socialist experience are studied without complacency and without hostility, they can be very useful to all backward countries. *They will be more aware that it will be hard for them to emerge from underdevelopment* without redoubled effort and solid organization of their economy, which is better adapted to real possibilities than to a dangerous reliance on *a priori* principles, especially in the case of those who are neophytes where socialism is concerned. But they will also know that this take-off is within their reach, *if they do not underestimate the difficulties,* if they realize what these difficulties demand, listen to the lesson that facts have to offer, and study all previous experience without prejudice. It has been in order to help them better that we have been hard on our Cuban friends, in order that they may become an even more convincing example for future revolutions.

1968 Afterword

Since this book was published in 1964, the situation in Latin America has grown no better. Brazil, now that it too has undergone a military dictatorship, continues to expand demographically at an insane rate, and seems to be incapable of making progress in agriculture. Hunger is even more severe, from Guatemala to Honduras and El Salvador, from Bolivia to Peru. *Un cri* [A Cry] by Armand Chartier, a film that stresses the hardships in the mountains of Peru, no longer mentions the name of this country, as a consequence of pressure brought to bear by representatives of that country; nonetheless the name of the country where it originated can be mentioned when it is shown.[1] The Green Berets of the United States are everywhere, and have cloaked their actions under the mask of "the defense of democracy," for instance in imposing a regime in Santo Domingo that was favorable to them in the beginning.

Unsatisfied with the results of his attempts to transform the Cuban people totally and rapidly, Che Guevara has gone to join the Bolivian guerrillas, along with Régis Debray, amid conditions so difficult that the question arises of whether he has not, voluntarily or involuntarily, chosen the supreme sacrifice, the better to serve the revolutionary cause. The building of socialism has continued in Cuba during these four years, in an atmosphere that is still fraught with difficulties. Fidel Castro has eliminated the pro-Soviet "micro-fraction" of Annibal Esca-

---

[1] Cinémathèque of the Ministry of Agriculture, 78 rue de Varenne, Paris 7e.

lante, has refused the advice of the Chinese, and is attempting to establish an original and very interesting "Cuban path" to socialism, while reinforcing his ties outside the country. The reigning atmosphere in Havana is not totalitarian, and Michel Gutelman,[2] who sympathizes with the revolutionary cause, is no longer afraid to publish a detailed criticism of the dangers of too centralized a management of the economy for agricultural development.

Nonetheless Gutelman does not dare to embark upon discussions of such essential points as the deliberate rejection of production cooperatives and the decision to go along with only State farms, the rejection of ground rents to raise revenue for the State, the problem of interest, etc. Though Cuba is more tolerant of dissension than the U.S.S.R. and China, this study nonetheless could not be distributed in Cuba. At the beginning of 1964 I stressed the fact that the goal of ten million tons of sugar, which at that time was set for 1970, could not be reached before 1975, if then. And the 1968 harvest will perhaps not be even six million tons, or a return to what it was in 1958. In *Le Monde* of January 30, 1968,[3] Henri Denis recalls that Castro "seems to believe that the fight against poverty must be carried out the way the revolutionary war was, and that enthusiasm for the building of socialism must be the factor that will lead to victory . . . and one trembles at the thought of the failures that so lofty a scorn for the laws of economics may lead to."

Fidel Castro was a magnificent fighter, and he is a born educator, but he continues to underestimate the technical and economic difficulties. He believes himself to be more capable than other people of finding the very best solutions, and always reasons like a guerrilla. His economic errors have cost Cuba dearly, however, and the Soviet Union is beginning to tire of paying the bill; this has made the rationing of gas necessary too. It would nonetheless be sad to see the pride of one man doing its share to compromise the economic success of such an exciting

---

[2] *L'agriculture socialisée à Cuba,* Maspéro, 1967.
[3] "Le socialisme cubain à la recherche d'un modèle économique."

revolution. Fidel should acquire a little of the humility of men who are truly great; then Gutelman could write with good reason: "Without a doubt, Cuban agriculture will be the most modern in Latin America around 1975–1980." Certainly the general failure of the Alliance for Progress and the new dignity conferred upon the Cuban worker compensate for many weaknesses, though they by no means justify them.

1969 Afterword
for the American Edition

The first edition of this volume was written at the beginning of 1964 following three research trips to Cuba (May and August 1960; September 1963); it was partially revised in 1968. Many things have happened since 1964 in this little country. It has dared to make a revolution "in the lion's mouth," close to the shores of Florida. Its political situation, which was more dramatic from 1959 to the missile crisis in 1962 and even up until 1963, has since tended to be relatively stable. Thanks to Soviet aid and the relative independence of certain European countries, Cuba has been able to resist a blockade that has sought—and still seeks—to make it give up its Revolution.

Rationing goes on, however, agricultural progress is still slow, and exchanges with other countries are still fraught with difficulties. We shall study two essential aspects of the Cuban agrarian economy: its economic policy, first of all, which seems to us to be dominated by its relations with other countries, and then its original system of planning, of managing the agrarian economy, whose excessive centralization was an essential cause of the difficulties that we have studied at length in the remainder of this book. And we shall conclude with a discussion of the principal features of the most recent changes.

1. Cuban political economy, dominated by its needs

In the first phase of the Cuban Revolution, up to the beginning of 1964, this country took steps to industrialize that were as gigantic as they were disordered. Industry was given top prior-

216

ity, and Cuba attempted to produce everything at once, steel and shovels, nickel and antibiotics. We have already seen the disastrous effects of an autarchic tendency as far as agriculture is concerned, which took the form of excessive diversification, a veritable atomization of all the crops grown throughout the island. The *granjas del pueblo* set up at the beginning were not able to cultivate their land properly, due to insufficient means, defective organization, and the large number of crops. Around the end of 1963 this led Cuba to the edge of economic catastrophe: this was due above all to an insufficient flow of supplies and an excessive shortage of cash. The production of sugar had fallen to 3,800,000 tons and the Soviet Union no longer was willing to make very large unsecured loans, which Cubans had fallen into the facile habit of making.

At the beginning of 1964, therefore, Cuba decided to make an agonizing reappraisal of this policy, putting off its plans for industrialization and agricultural diversification until after 1970. This policy was still held to be correct and was maintained as a long-term objective, but for the moment it was recognized that it was premature. Cuba therefore decided to again concentrate on agriculture, and in particular on the production of sugar, for which this country has unique climatic and historical advantages. An enormous investment had already been made, there were factories with railroad sidings, and Cuba had greater technical knowledge in this field than in any other.

The plan for sugar, however, that was adopted at this time, setting a goal of ten million tons for 1970, was extremely ambitious.[1] Given the low prices on the world sugar market in a normal period, it could be justified only by long-term contracts concluded with the socialist countries. By the terms of the agreements of February 1964, these countries contracted to buy larger and larger amounts of sugar: beginning in 1970, the U.S.S.R. was to take as much as five million tons per year,

---

[1] In a report to the Cuban government in 1963, I indicated that it was more reasonable to set 1975 as the date for the realization of such a goal.

China a million, and the rest of the popular democracies around a million. The only agreements of their sort in economic history, they specified, long years in advance, not only quantities but prices. The sudden withdrawal of Cuba from the United States market after 1960 had brought on an unusual rise in the price of sugar on the free market, which went as high as 13 U.S. cents per English pound for a few days.[2]

Thus Castro could contract to sell sugar at 6 cents per pound to China and the U.S.S.R., and 5.5 cents to the popular democracies, certain of which accepted this political sacrifice with more or less bad grace: Hungary, Poland, and Czechoslovakia produce sufficient sugar for their needs with their sugar beet crops. Even this latter price was advantageous if it is true, as was being said in Cuba in 1967, that the cost per pound to produce it was 4 cents. In reality, this price seems to vary a great deal; on an average it is probably a little higher than that. But it costs the U.S.S.R. much more to produce sugar, perhaps around 13 to 15 cents with Ukrainian sugar beets, which are still grown under rather poor conditions. In the event that it were to make very large purchases on the free market, instead of getting it from Cuba, the slightest break in the market might cost the U.S.S.R. dearly in hard currency, whereas it pays for Cuban sugar in petroleum, equipment, and so on . . .

The 1970 goal, however, goes far beyond the outlets at an advantageous price provided by the socialist countries. Castro was not afraid to explain why in a published speech made on July 7, 1965: "Many bourgeois sugar producers are ruining themselves . . . When sugar goes down, it brings social problems, ruin, work stoppages . . . We for our part will hold out at 2 cents a pound. A large part of our sugar is bought by the socialist countries at higher prices."[3]

---

[2] The only time that the world wholesale price went higher than the French retail price.

[3] Cited by Gutelman in his remarkable study: *L'agriculture socialisée à Cuba,* Maspéro, 1968. In addition to this book, we have used notes taken during a lecture given by Gutelman on March 21, 1969 at the Institute of Advanced Latin American Studies in Paris, sponsored by

Thus Castro, on the basis of these agreements, wanted to use the Cuban sugar economy *as a political arm in the international class struggle.* Those who were unemployed on the Dominican plantations because of the collapse of the market were definitely behind the Santo Domingo rebellion, which brought about the intervention of United States Marines: a heavy blow to the prestige of this latter country, comparable to that of Budapest and Prague to Soviet prestige. In Argentina that same year, only a part of the cane in the Tucumán region was harvested, and because of this there were bloody strikes. In both cases, however, the result was *a strengthening of fascist positions.*

The possibility of pursuing such a political line, however, was in the end in the hands of the Soviet Union. With its infrastructure of American origin, its materiel pool that came from the United States, and certain consumer goods that the socialist countries could not furnish, Cuba needed a minimum of 300 million dollars a year, or its equivalent in free currency. This sum could be obtained only by excessive quantities of sugar on a free market whose prices had collapsed;[4] other exports would not bring in enough. Thus Cuba demanded that 15% of the sugar it delivered to the U.S.S.R. be paid for in dollars; but this country has very few dollars, and the popular democracies fewer still; there were lively discussions on this point in 1966–1967. Cuba reminded the Soviet Union that Ukrainian sugar cost much more and that Cuban sugar necessarily entailed the use of dollars (to purchase spare parts).

In January 1968, the Soviet Union decided to put a ceiling on its deliveries of petroleum to Cuba, holding them to the 1967 level, even though that country's consumption was continually increasing. But Cuba was unable to furnish the quantities of sugar specified in the 1964 agreements, since its harvests had

the economic commission of the France–Cuba Association, plus the afterword that he wrote to the Italian translation of his book, which was published in the first 1969 number of *Etudes rurales.*

[4] At 2 U.S. cents per English pound, this comes to around $44 a ton, or 6,800,000 tons of sugar to get 300 million dollars! More than the 1955–1959 exports, which were just over 5 million tons.

not increased at the rate that had been foreseen; the Soviet Union also wanted to limit its aid: Cartierism is not unknown there. It must support the Cuban Revolution, of course, but since Cuba has proved to be very independent politically, it was thought in Moscow that the moment had come to make it more aware of its dependence: petroleum is the U.S.S.R.'s most powerful means of putting the pressure on.

In the socialist countries, as in the so-called "free world," *it is always the strongest who continue to make things go their way;* proletarian internationalism has forgotten its Leninist principles, which are called to mind only insofar as they justify the policy of whoever is most powerful. As for the underdeveloped countries that depend on France, Europe, and the United States, Cuba's economic decisions cannot be absolutely autonomous. Its room to maneuver remains fairly large, however: if the U.S.S.R. let the Cuban Revolution go down the drain by stopping deliveries of petroleum, which could be done quickly and easily, it would at the same time undermine its whole reputation, which is already quite compromised, in the eyes of the more or less revolutionary elements of the Third World. Politically, the U.S.S.R. could not allow itself to do this unless it openly admitted that it needed the support of the United States, against China for example.

In order to reduce its degree of dependency, Cuba is buying more and more fertilizer, transmitters, locomotives, and other equipment in France and Great Britain, countries which happily have not given in to American blackmail. When it could not obtain Soviet dollars in July of 1968, Cuba had to give up an aggressive dumping operation that it could not sustain all by itself. It decided to participate in the international conference on sugar, within the framework of the United Nations Commission on Commerce and Development. The agreement of October 24, 1968, indeed, granted it an export quota of 2.1 million tons, the total amount of the quotas being set at this time with the aim of keeping the price of sugar above 3.5 cents per pound, a price that only a very small minority of extremely efficient cane producers can hold up under. Without Napoleon's blockade, France would probably never have made the acquaintance of sugar beets which in free competition within a truly liberal economy on an international scale could never have fought it out with cane.

The affluent countries call themselves the defenders of the Third World, and boast of the aid they give it, though this aid is quite limited, but say less about the profits they take out of it. In *L'empire américaine* [The American Empire],[5] Claude Julien shows us that from 1959 to 1965 the United States took out of Latin America and Asia nine billion dollars more than it put into these areas as "aid" or new investments. It should not be too surprising, therefore, that the United States and the European Economic Community, the two big producers of sugar beets, did not ratify the sugar agreement, and thereby made it worth almost nothing. The E.E.C. demanded an export quota of 1,100,000 tons, and got only 300,000!

Let us take France as an example. Now that this crop is mechanized, who can prevent it from increasing the area planted in sugar beets to a million hectares, each producing five tons, or five million tons of sugar? The obstacle to that large a crop is no longer technical; it is merely an economic question. Large investments in equipment, means of transportation, and new factories would be required, and therefore a guarantee that the very high present market prices would hold up over a prolonged period. If the Europe of the Six demands to export sugar, it can only do so by dumping, at great loss, and thus only under pressure from its powerful sugar-beet lobbyists.

2. *Projects that were too grandiose, with more modest results*

Let us go back to the subject of Cuba: in the spring of 1969, the year of decisive effort, the whole country bustled about trying to reach the goal of ten million tons of sugar, which Castro keeps reminding his compatriots is a "matter of honor," that must be held to come hell or high water. Sugar was planted every-

[5] Grasset, 1968.

where, in some places after hastily clearing land. The amount of effort put into irrigation has been enormous: 340,000 hectares of cane fields will be irrigated in 1970, as against 80,000 in 1965; but the question was whether the enormous amount of cane thus obtained, even if it did not reach the goal that had been fixed, could be harvested. In February and March 1969, Cuban newspapers emphasized how difficult it would be to finish harvesting the cane in the province of Camaguey even with the enormous amount of work contributed by volunteers from Havana. Despite the re-establishment of "sugar secrecy," which forbade the publication of the figures, the expected 1969 harvest was often estimated to be closer to 6 than to 7 million tons.

Cuba is very proud of its mechanical loaders and harvesting combines, but there are still a limited number of them, and they do not seem to work properly under any and all conditions. Plans are now being made to harvest cane only once every two years, though there is little mention of the large loss in sugar that such a technique would represent by comparison with the traditional harvest once a year: in the second year the growth of the cane is substantially reduced. In the face of probable difficulties in finding sufficient foreign outlets at a profitable price, there is much talk of sugar chemistry, of paper made out of bagasse,[6] wax, medicine. But the stem of the cane must not be squeezed too tightly if a good quality of paper is to be made of it, and this leads to losses of sugar. And the cost of transporting the large amounts of necessary bagasse to one place, as must be done for a modern paper factory, may very well be prohibitive . . .

Fidel Castro often mentions cane as a very important source of cattle feed in the future. In 1960 I pointed out to him how profitable it would be to use the tops of the leafy stalks as forage. With irrigation these "white tips," as they are called in the Antilles, will stay greener and keep more of their protein.

---

[6] Crushed, juiceless sugar cane as it comes from the mill. [Translator's note.]

But when Fidel speaks of putting millions of tons of molasses to use, he forgets to supply economic statistics to support his proposal. As he wishes—rightly—to develop greater milk production, he must first see that his Frisian cows[7] or those that are a cross between Zebu and Frisian cattle, have a great many proteins. Molasses has no protein at all and the added urea cannot supply more than a very small amount of the necessary nitrogen. It would be better to develop Pangola grass (abundantly treated with fertilizer rich in nitrogen and irrigated), bersim clover, or alfalfa if they prove successful, for these do not need to go through a factory. The sugar plan is going to absorb investments of more than a billion dollars, to the detriment of expenditures that more careful study would surely have proved to be more profitable. An economy cannot be run like a guerrilla operation, with reactions where sentiment plays an important role.

Castro has of course paid a great deal of serious attention to agricultural and economic problems. He has learned a great deal in this area, but he still has a great deal to learn, and always will have—a fact that in large measure he is unwilling to recognize. He therefore decides things a bit too quickly, and his entourage does not always have the chance—or the courage—to point out his weaknesses to him, though Che Guevara was not at all afraid to do so. It is said that he was soon put in his place by British researchers when he visited a station for research in animal genetics and tried to teach them their job. They spoke of going back home, and he backed off.

Fidel's visit to the Niña Bonita cattle center, shown on television and described in the newspaper *Granma* on January 31, 1969, was proof of his predilection for techniques that appear to be most up-to-date, without their ever having been proved profitable economically. This broadcast was doubtless a

---

7 "We'll have to see to it that this bull weighs over 1,350 kilograms (2,970 lbs.)," Castro said during the abovementioned visit. But a good producer is not a champion at a livestock show; it must not be too fat. Certain records are not at all desirable.

good popularization of the problems involved in cattle raising and animal genetics, but as it did not show the slightest interest in production costs, it caused the directors of *granjas* watching the program to continue to underestimate the importance of such a concern, which nonetheless is essential.

Ten million tons of sugar is not the Cubans' only ambitious goal. They are cautiously making a move in the direction of agricultural diversification again; this time there is less of a shortage of personnel and less of a lack of administrative personnel than in 1960–1961 when, as we have seen, such a move was a failure. Fidel still launches giant projects to dry up the lowlands along Cuba's coasts, without making economic studies of the problem a first priority. Raising the production of the rice, beans, and tubercules or *viandas* which constitute Cuba's basic foods to a satisfactory level is much more pressing. Certainly the poor are better fed than they were before the Revolution, when they were rationed by the lack of money that resulted from unemployment and low wages, but Cuba nonetheless could do better.

To announce, however, as Castro did, a cumulative improvement in agricultural production of fifteen per cent per year in geometric progression during the next twelve years does not seem like *responsible behavior*.[8] One can certainly propose higher goals than those hoped for, in the hope of getting people to work harder. But these goals must not be exaggerated, for they risk causing bitter disappointments. A goal of 700,000 tons of citrus fruit has been announced for 1975 and 4,600,000 tons in 1980, on 300,000 hectares, the greater part of which are just now being planted. But the 1968 production is around 160,000 tons, as against 98,000 in 1962.

---

[8] Since 1961, every time that the Plan is not fulfilled, the Cubans are promised the moon for the next year. I recalled above (Chapter 4, section 3) that in the issue of *Revolución* of October 1963, Che Guevara rightfully criticized "the intolerable pretension of increasing the national revenue fifteen or even twenty per cent per year," and it is a general rule that national revenue increases faster than agricultural revenue.

This would all be very well if the planting was done under the very best of conditions; but this does not always seem to be the case, due in particular to *excessive haste.* The volunteer workers (though not all of them) often demonstrate their good will, but they are not competent generally.[9] And if such quantities of citrus fruits were grown, to whom would they be sold, and at what price? Canning the juice makes citrus fruit lose much of its value, and the competition from the United States' dumping it on the market may be very difficult to meet.

On January 24, 1969, *Granma* said: "Ninety-four hectares were planted in cacao in 1968, and the goal for 1969 is to plant 1,340 hectares of it in the Victoria de Girón area . . . In the near future Matanzas will have 8,000 hectares of cacao trees . . . Individual palm shelters had to be resorted to, for the plants had become too large to stay in seed-beds; the need to transplant them was urgent. But the Angola peas that were to furnish them the necessary shade were not planted in time."

Quotations of this sort, showing the difficulties of realizing inordinate goals, could be multiplied. The directors of the *granjas* continue to worry more about fulfilling plans in terms of the number of hectares they put under cultivation than about the quality of the work and the yields per hectare. Thus *Granma* on February 14, 1969, said: "The plan for the growing of pineapples at Ciego de Avila looks forward to having 40,000 hectares in full production in 1973. The present area under cultivation is around 1,200 hectares." I saw these pineapples being planted in 1960, and pointed out at the time that there was too much space between the plants and suggested that it was a good idea to plant them in double rows close together so as to have the high density indispensable for high yields. In photographs that have appeared recently (are they really recent?) I noticed that they were still planted in single rows too far apart.

The yields per hectare were 10 tons of fruit in 1968; it was

---

9 ". . . The difficulties of the first years, caused by the lack of experience and the shortage of technicians, have again slowed down development [during the last ten years]." *Granma,* 20 enero, 1969.

then hoped that the yield would be 11 tons in 1969 and 20 to 23 tons in 1970, for "the use of better techniques of cultivation promises magnificent results." Let us wait until this doubling of the yield really comes about: I can still see in my mind's eye the semi-abandonment that I saw in 1963; it was pitiful. Cuba continues to promise sensational results "in the near future," without worrying about the many times it has had to go back on promises made in the past.

In poorer soil, on the tertiary sands east of Abidjan, African growers belonging to SALCI are currently getting 65 tons of fruit per hectare. With competition so fierce on the market for canned pineapple, even yields of 23 tons will hardly be competitive.

The Cuban effort is nonetheless very important; the rate of investment is probably around 30% of the gross product, and would seem to be beginning to bear fruit. Production is increasing, but much more slowly than promised. Milk production could increase very rapidly if the cows were much better fed than the first piebald Canadian cows of 1963; this is less costly than acclimatizing them and makes this acclimation easier.[10] But when Fidel announced: *"At the end of 1970 the production of milk is going to be four times higher than at the end of 1968"*[11] he was imitating the Chinese leaders of February 1959. These latter announced that their compatriots would be much better fed if only a third of the land that had been plowed were put under cultivation. This is not the best way to get people to take you seriously.

The milk production of a large herd of cattle has not quadrupled in two years anywhere in the world; this fact ought to make for prudence. IR-8 rice will permit rapid progress provided that it is better cared for, and its successor IR-5 should have been tried sooner. But to announce that the yield has gone in one year from fourteen to eighteen quintals per hectare,

---

[10] "Twenty per cent of good cows with a high rate of production died during acclimation," Fidel said on January 30, 1969. I suspect that most of them died of malnutrition or insufficient care.

[11] *Granma,* 31 enero, 1969.

thanks in particular to seeding by plane, as if such progress were a great success, is to neglect calling to mind the fact that this yield is not yet back to the 1959 level.

There is one crop—coffee—that has a political side to it, showing that Cuba has not given up "attacking" the South American economy at its most sensitive point. Cuba is planting millions of coffee trees[12] with all its might, *Cattura* in the plains, which represents a certain progress from the technical point of view. It is very probable, however, that its technical proficiency has not become the equal of that on avant-garde Brazilian farms, where the coffee trees are planted very close together, are kept in production only a few years, and yield up to twelve tons of dry coffee beans per hectare.

Cuba has announced a goal of 920,000 quintals of coffee for 1970, that is to say 92,000 tons (if the goal is measured in metric quintals; the statement does not specify). But in November 1967, the international coffee agreement reduced Cuba's export quota from 12,000 to 3,000 tons, for it had not taken advantage of its right to export during preceding years. No doubt Cuba hopes to find a market in the socialist countries. The U.S.S.R., however, has a political and economic interest in keeping up trade with South American coffee producers, for coffee is almost their only source of exchange currency. If consumption of coffee in the U.S.S.R. came close to that in the United States (the latter drinks *almost half* the commercial coffee in the world), there would be few difficulties. But the majority of Russians prefer tea and the amount of hard currency the Soviet Union has available is still limited.

Here again, Cuban economic policy cannot be carried out effectively if it relies on its own forces alone; this country must, willy nilly, take Soviet interests into account. From this point of view, it is easier to understand Castro's speech of August 23, 1968, on the Czechoslovakian affair. Apparently Castro took sides with the Soviet Union and approved its armed interven-

---

12 Even in the truck-garden belt around Havana where, as I have been explaining since 1960, perishable goods (vegetables, fruit, bananas, milk and fresh milk products) ought to have priority.

tion in Prague. But he did so grudgingly, and continues to keep his distance, in particular through an attack on the Novotny regime, and hence of the after-effects of Stalinism, which was even harsher than his accusations against Dubcek.

3. *Planning and management, and the rejection of cooperation*

Up until 1963, the Plans, which followed the model of the Czech Plans of the Stalin era—a model which was soon to be revised in the country where it originated—came from the top. Gutelman shows us that they were prepared, *in detail,* at the central level, where there generally was little knowledge of the situation in the field. The Center "was inclined to take its desires regarding production for objective possibilities [despite] inadequate statistics and a lack of technicians at the base." And Gutelman rightly concludes: ". . . planning becomes a matter of some discussion when it has to do with the day-to-day management of economic units . . . The final version of the 1963 goals for the province of Las Villas saw the light of day just one month before the end of the year!"

Moreover, the tasks that Castro judged to be the most important were dealt with in special plans, known in the island as the "Fidel Plans." These plans were directly dependent upon Castro, and often he entrusted them to young people with little competence. Since they had received absolute priority as regarded any and all means of production, their ill-timed requisitions disorganized the flow of supplies going to the country's main units.

It was not until the end of 1963 that the Cuban leaders recognized "the practical impossibility of managing units from the Center." After the reassembling of parcels of land on the *granjas,* a practice which the second agrarian reform encouraged, it was decided to regroup these State farms in sixty or so local groups, the *agrupaciones,* which were to be the only groups to direct the State farms and the only ones to receive financial autonomy. This is an important step forward; decisions concerning day-to-day management are thus made closer to the point where they will be carried out. Though responsibilities from this point on were more clearly outlined, Gutelman nonetheless stresses that "Such a *rigidity* in the conception that power should be given only to one level seems to inevitably bring on considerable delay in the making of decisions, as is proved by the example of the other socialist countries."

Another step forward was taken through the *drawing up of plans at the base,* which guarantees their realism and makes the prospect of their being carried out much more hopeful. But national interests must also be taken into consideration, which is apparently being done quite effectively by the mechanism that was adopted, whereby very general over-all plans are drawn up at the Center and sent out to the base as points of reference.

Gutelman's criticisms stop there, but we must go farther. For Cuba is the only socialist country that has based the most essential part of its agricultural production on the system of State farms, which in the other socialist countries are much smaller in area than those cultivated by production cooperatives. In Poland and Yugoslavia, where there are almost none of these kolkhozes, it is the private sector that is dominant.

But Cuba wants to be more socialist than the other socialist countries and accepts the Stalinist view that State property, which is also called the property of all the people, is a *superior* form of property in a socialist regime, whereas cooperative property remains an *inferior* form, and this cannot help but shock the proud Fidel.

Cuba therefore refuses to entertain the idea of a revolution parallel to that of the U.S.S.R., which this country, somewhat like the Chinese, thinks is turning bourgeois. On the State farm, everybody is a bureaucrat, and to get good results a way would have to be found to exact a really exceptional degree of devotion on the part of all those who work on it.

I continue to believe that this refusal to establish agricultural production cooperatives on the expropriated land was a vast mistake. They would naturally have groped about for some time, and it would have been necessary to help them get organized. But wages should have been proportionate to the effort each worker expended. It clearly would have been better to adopt a ground rent to be paid the State, and a normal rate of interest for the capital invested in the units. In this way, Cuba would have *trusted* its agricultural workers, given them more and more responsibilities, and they would thus little by little have taken a larger part in the management of their units: this would have been a form of *upward social mobility*.

Unless increasing trust is accorded workers, there will be no real progress toward a socialism based on freedom. But the most recent developments, described by Gutelman in the afterword we have already cited, really do not give such an impression.

4. *Regionalization, militarization, and the incorporation of the private sector*

Another great step forward is being taken at present: the regrouping of sugar plantations around the largest sugar refineries on the plains that most favor mechanization. And in order, again, to reduce shipping costs, which were excessive, and under the pressure of limited supplies of gasoline, much more intense farming is taking place on the outskirts of the large cities. I had advised a "green belt" of truck-gardens surrounding the city of Havana in the report I made after my visit of May 1960. At that time, the majority of the bananas consumed in the capital came from the province of Oriente, and traveled more than 600 miles in trucks; I have pointed out above the losses and waste that this practice gave rise to.

Since that time, the establishment of such a belt around Havana has resulted in the fact that in the year 1968 the province of Havana exported more farm products than it imported for the first time. Along with fruits and vegetables, tubercules, sweet corn, and even some 7,000 hectares of rice are being grown. This also permits the manpower of the capital to be put to better use, and allows clerks, civil servants, and workers to work in the fields without enormous expenses for transportation of manpower being incurred. The aim is to come close to self-sufficiency as regards food in each province, without tending, however, to absolute autarchy, and to concentrate crops close to where they will be consumed or processed.

Cuba is refusing more and more to use the famous so-called *material stimulants*—the lure of profit—even of a socialist sort. They have rejected piecework in principle, even though it represents the strictest application of the socialist principle: "to each according to his work." A need is felt, however, for better work discipline, which the "civilian" managers of the *granjas* has not always been able to bring about, as the visitor could easily see in 1963. It seems to us most unlikely that productivity as measured in work-days, which in 1963 often fell to around half that of 1959, has climbed back in 1969 to the same level as before liberation.

The Army, a crucible where vast efforts are being made to forge the new man, totally dedicated to his Revolution, is called upon in straits such as these. The Army has always helped in agricultural production, especially in the sugar-cane harvest, but also in the construction of schools and houses for workers, roads and canals, etc., but its role in production was not made an official policy until 1968. Recruits must henceforth devote more of their time to work in the fields and thus receive a theoretical and practical agricultural education, which is certain to contribute to the modernization of rural areas and the popularization of the latest technical developments.

Newspapers often talk about the exploits of the Che Guevara Brigade, which has a total enrollment of about 5,000 men, grouped in 36 platoons, each of which has 20 bulldozers or heavy tractors at its disposal. It has cleared tens of thousands of hectares of land, often covered with marabou, that eventually will become sugar plantations, intensive pastures, and rice paddies. It also participates in the construction of dams and irrigation canals. It seems to be thoroughly aware of errors made previously, for it carefully maintains its equipment, takes care itself of the technical education of its cadres, and works according to a list of priorities established by those in charge of the development of agriculture and cattle-raising.

It proclaims its total disinterest in material stimulants, and it is interesting to note that the whole brigade—officers and men, engineers and cooks—all receive the same salary of 160 *pesos* per month, plus food, lodging, and medical care. Gutelman stresses, however, the fact that agricultural workers on State farms earn no more than 90 to 120 *pesos;* the soldier in this brigade thus has a big advantage, even though his officer has none at all.

Battalions of civilians have been formed on this military model, for instance, the women's brigades of tractor drivers of the green belt around Havana or the province of Oriente. Government offices, nationalized companies, and so forth, furnish workers for the harvesting of cane and coffee beans and caring for the crops; they are organized on the same principles. Civil defense, finally, is working along the same lines to organize production in case of war. Cuba is already on a war footing. "*The militarization of organization,* where the interest of the group, the principle of authority, and above all the social consciousness of the group predominates, constitutes *the logical alternative to organization based on individual interest,*" Gutelman concludes.

This alternative in no way appears to us to be the only one imaginable. We always hesitate to entrust the building of socialism to military men, and many other solutions are possible.[13] The drama of Cuba is the fact that despite certain hesitant appearances of liberalization, the discussion of basic political principles is almost impossible except from within the party, and even then this is possible for only a minority of the leaders. Building a society that has rejected the profit motive is a magnificent endeavor. But the militarization of an authoritarian brand of socialism is in no way the only solution possible. It does not allow the full flowering of man, which demands that he be trusted more, that he be given more initiative and more responsibilities, and this is not very military.

---

[13] We have studied a number of others already being worked out, in *Développement et socialismes* (with Marcel Mazoyer), Le Seuil, 1969.

It is clear that Cubans must be quickly brought around to acquiring "exactitude, precision, efficiency, Cartesian reasoning, practical logic . . . that were inculcated in European workers through logic and the implacable demands of an advanced capitalist system." Certainly the Cuban military men from the revolutionary army are of a completely different caliber from our cop-adjutants and other officers of the psychological campaign in Algeria. Let us not forget, however, that the appeal for voluntary workers is justified more in terms of a political mobilization, of contact with manual labor, of a struggle against bureaucracy, than in terms of its effectiveness or its economic benefits.

If the cost of transportation were analyzed, the time lost in shifting people around, the generally very modest amount of work accomplished in the fields by urban workers, the loss of production resulting from their absence at jobs for which they are better qualified, the economic effectiveness of the whole operation would be a matter of serious doubt. The overly rigid application of certain Marxist-Leninist theories, and sometimes even the Stalinist version of them, risks prolonging the difficulties of the Cuban economy, and first and foremost those connected with its food supply.

Most farmers who owned less than 65 hectares have kept their property, and the government furnishes them credit and services, and helps them plan what to grow through the National Association of Small Farmers (ANAP); *if they request it,* the government helps them set up little production cooperatives. In Cuba no pressure such as was applied in the U.S.S.R. or in Eastern Europe—in order to force such cooperatives on the peasants—has ever been brought to bear. Moreover, these cooperatives have gained little ground since the time when Gutelman, in 1966 and 1967, stated that there were 270 of them, covering 20,000 hectares.

The Cuban government, however, is thinking up other ways of incorporating this private sector into the national production plans, without having recourse either to forced collectivization or price incentives, at least not as a prime motivation. Here again, the Cuban leaders are counting on increasing political awareness, on trying to forge the new man so as to be able to safely build a production structure that will owe nothing to the profit motive. In the farm belts around urban centers, where the principal effort to intensify farming is taking place at present, several solutions are being put before the peasants with small holdings, in the form of *private micro-plans.*

Old peasants who no longer have children at home with them can sell the State their lands in exchange for an annuity, which makes it possible for them to retire and thus permits them to abandon their land sooner, while still keeping a little plot for subsistence. Others can sell their land to the State and continue to work on it on a salary basis. Still others turn their land over to the State while retaining nominal ownership and working the land. Most of the work on these farms is done, however, by volunteer workers, with the money from the crops being given to the owner after expenses have been deducted. In every case the plan of production is fixed by the State and follows the general guideline adopted for the sector. A thousand of these micro-plans were put into effect at the end of 1968, most of them around Havana or Camaguey; however, this very flexible formula could well come to be followed more and more extensively.

5. The "New Man" of religious socialism and the role of Castro

The Soviet Union and the popular democracies are, on the contrary, once again giving profit a large role, both in order to stimulate efforts and in order to be able to measure the real economic efficiency of various enterprises more concretely. We have already shown that the logical conclusion of such a development would be more and more political liberalization, as has already happened to some extent in Yugoslavia. A somewhat analogous experiment was brutally interrupted in Czechoslovakia through the intervention of the Soviet Army and its "allies." The reduction of the prerogatives of the Party risked reducing as well the advantages of the privileged minority, that more than famous "new class" stigmatized by the heretical Yugoslavian writer Milovan Djilas. The second Prague Coup was thus aimed at supporting the privileges of all sorts—both material advantages and power—of the caste in the saddle. This is a particular form of the neo-colonialist coup, which is probably doomed to failure in the long run.

In China these privileges have been fought from the inside by the extraordinary "Revolution of Proletarian Civilization," which we call the Cultural Revolution. This movement is seeking to stamp out every trace of bourgeois ideology, and to fight bureaucratic tendencies inherent in every revolution *once it is firmly in power.* A somewhat similar fight against bureaucracy has been waged in Cuba, and the mobilization of city-dwellers for harvests and work in the fields fits within this framework. The egalitarian tendencies of the Cuban Revolution—such traits as the constant increase in free collective services (education, medical care, rent, telephones), the reduction of the role of money—are attempts to come closer to a communist society, whose utopian nature I have often pointed out.

Elsewhere I have called these attempts to forge a new citizen entirely dedicated to his Revolution *religious socialism.* Such a citizen seems to be necessary to the proper functioning of a society that refuses to use the selfish motive of individual profit as its base any longer. Certainly man is perfectible, but only slowly. If it is thought that man has gone from the age of *cavernes* to the age of *casernes*—from caves to barracks—certain aspects of his progress soon appear highly questionable. His rapid, ever-increasing mastery of Nature is not being accompanied by equal self-mastery, *by sufficient respect for other people,* whether these other people be Negroes in the United States or socialist humanists in the U.S.S.R. Socialism can no longer prove that it is more efficient economically; it can be justified henceforth only if it permits a better moral stance through a search for more solidarity. Cuba has given its humblest workers dignity, and like its immense effort to further education, this has an immense value.

With such basic premises as these, the end is no longer some sort of revealed Truth; it no longer indifferently justifies any means at all. For there is no longer *one* scientific socialism, but multiple socialist paths, all of them subject to discussion. Some paths might lead more surely to the full flowering of the individual, through service to his community, his nation, the revolution. There is no *a priori* reason whatsoever why authoritarian socialism within a framework provided by the Army should appear to be the best pattern for this development of personality. Still another path to socialism might best be followed with self-management of production units, which should, however, be corrected by giving priority to collective interests, as expressed by a National Plan.

Happily, the atmosphere of the Cuban Revolution has never permitted the Stalinist alienation, which after the massacres of Hitler was one of the greatest abominations. The artistic and literary freedom it had in the beginning, however, is no longer as certain a fact as it once was. The atmosphere around Fidel Castro is not always free of the fawning of courtiers. Dialogue with a crowd is not the best form of democracy. Not all critics enjoy the right to have their say, and finally, the fact that too few people are asking serious questions still continues to cut down economic efficiency. As for its foreign relations, Cuba has been able to escape the economic domination of the United States, but it did so only to fall within the Soviet orbit. It is no secret that Fidel Castro knows how to pull strings, how to leave himself a great deal of room to maneuver. He was not afraid to criticize revolutionary China when it wanted to make him abjure his allegiance to the U.S.S.R. and to this end applied very awkward forms of economic pressure, using the rice famine as an excuse. Fidel probably thought he was obliged to approve the occupation of Czechoslovakia. However, we have reminded the reader that in his speech of August 24, 1968, his most relentless attacks were reserved for the regime in power "before January."

By so doing, he was at the same time condemning (as could be seen by anyone who could read between the lines a bit) the Stalinist tendencies of this regime, and the recent revival of neo-Stalinism in the Soviet Union. The Cuban cane-cutter, however, being very poorly informed about European problems, is hardly in a position to understand allusions that are sometimes extremely subtle. And yet he, too, was forced to publicly proclaim his approval of the military occupation of one socialist country by another. Perhaps some Cubans remembered on this occasion their battle-cry, *Patria o Muerte,* which could well be shouted in Prague beneath the statue of Saint Wenceslas towering over the square of the same name.

It is rather characteristic of the Cuban political atmosphere that no one, to my knowledge, was able to raise his voice and publicly criticize such a position, and this despite the fact that certain aspects of the speech were clearly contradictory. Around 1959–1960, the Cuban Revolution seemed to many of the disinherited in Latin America to be their great hope. But in general it is becoming less attractive now, except for a minority of guerrillas. The support which the United States always gives the most reactionary regimes contributes on the other hand to maintaining, if not increasing, the prestige of the Cuban Revolution.

This prestige remains rather great, for Cuba is passionately searching for a new socialist path, even at the price of mistakes, which are hard, moreover, to avoid. Such a quest is of great value for the future of the Third World, and in the last analysis of humanity. But it would have an even greater value if Fidel Castro gave signs of greater humility and did not claim to know everything. In that case he would give his technicians and his economists free rein. He would be more intent on seeking out criticism of his analyses, his positions, and his acts by the people, instead of always presenting them as correct *a priori*. He would thus seek out means to make the base, "the masses," participate in momentous decisions. With this momentum behind him, he would allow various formulas of self-management to be tried out.

But in order to do this he would have to be able to run his country without being subject to more or less underhanded attacks from outside, to attempted sabotage, to an inhuman blockade. In 1959, Castro's plan was to try building a socialism that could evolve freely, and he sought an accord, a gentleman's agreement, with the United States. This latter party committed the grievous error, insofar as their rightly understood long-term interests were concerned, of rejecting such an agreement. *Errare human est, perseverare autem diabolicum.*[14] Will the United States agree some day to allow at their portals a socialist experiment that could thus travel, step by step, toward more freedom? If the United States does not, "tomorrows that do not sing" are in store for it all over Latin America, where the Alliance for Progress has largely been a total failure. Our American friends are hereby duly warned, if they still know how to listen.

---

[14] It is human to be wrong, but diabolical to persevere [in error].

Selected Bibliography

1. Works on Underdevelopment

Bairoch, Paul: *Révolution industrielle et sous-développement,* Sedes, 1963.

————: L'évolution économique du Tiers-Monde 1900–1966, Gauthiers Villars, 1967.*

Barre, R.: Le développement économique, Cahiers de l'ISEA, 1958.

Gendarme, René: *La pauvreté des nations,* Ed. Cujas, 1963.*

Lebret, L. J.: *Dynamique concrète du développement,* Ed. ouvrières, 1961.

Mende, Tibor: *Un monde possible,* Le Seuil, 1963.

Myrdal, Gunnar: *Théorie économique et pays sous-développés,* Présence Africaine, 1959.

Perroux, François: *Croissance et développement,* Cahiers de l'ISEA, 1959.

Sauvy, Alfred: *Malthus et les deux Marx,* Denoël, 1963.

2. Works on Cuba

Arnault, J.: "Cuba et le Marxisme," *La Nouvelle Critique,* Sept. 1962.

Castro, Fidel: *Cuba et la crise des Caraïbes,* Maspéro, 1963.

---

* Includes detailed bibliography.

————: *Fidel Castro parle,* Maspéro, 1963.

Debray, Régis: *Revolution in the Revolution,* Grove Press, 1968.

Draper, Theodore: *La Révolution de Castro,* Calmann, Levy, 1963.

Francos, Ania: *La fête cubaine,* Julliard, 1962.

Guevara, Ernesto: *Le socialisme et l'homme,* Maspéro, 1967.

Gutelman, Michel: *L'agriculture socialisée à Cuba,* Maspéro, 1967.

Julien, Claude: *La révolution cubaine,* Julliard, 1961.

Vilar et. al.: *Eveil aux Amériques, Cuba,* Ed. sociales, 1962.
"Cuba, révolution menacée," *Esprit,* avril, 1961.

3. Cuban Publications

Cuba socialista, a theoretical review published monthly since 1961.

Obra revolucionaria regularly publishes the speeches of Cuban leaders.

Nuestra industria.

Comercio exterior.